THE
BLACK HEART'S
TRUTH

I'd like immensely to read your autobiography.
You always rather bewildered me by your veracity,
and I fancy you may tell the truth about yourself.
But *all* of it? The black truth, which we all know of
ourselves in our hearts, or only the whity-brown
truth of the pericardium, or the nice, whitened
truth of the shirtfront? Even you wont tell the black
heart's-truth.

W. D. Howells to
Samuel L. Clemens,
14 February 1904

THE BLACK HEART'S TRUTH

THE EARLY CAREER OF W. D. HOWELLS

BY JOHN W. CROWLEY

The University of North Carolina Press
Chapel Hill and London

Library of Congress Cataloging in Publication Data

Crowley, John William, 1945–
    The black heart's truth.

    Includes index.
    1. Howells, William Dean, 1837–1920—Biography—
Youth.   2. Howells, William Dean, 1837–1920—Biography—
Psychology.   3. Howells, William Dean, 1837–1920. Modern
instance.   4. Novelists, American—19th century—
Biography.   5. Psychoanalysis and literature.   I. Title.
PS2033.C7   1985   813'.4 [B]   84-20908
ISBN 0-8078-1632-9

Set in Goudy Old Style by G&S Typesetters, Inc.
Designed by Naomi P. Slifkin

FOR GEORGE ARMS

CONTENTS

PREFACE

Howells: a poem by Allen Ginsberg. So went a gag I heard during my first year of graduate study at Indiana University in 1967–68, when the first volume of the Howells Edition was in press. Given what I knew about Howells, which is to say nothing, I was in no position to get the point either of a very in-joke or of a scholarly text of *Their Wedding Journey*. Then I read *A Modern Instance*, in a copy of William M. Gibson's splendid Riverside Edition that I am still using in my classes. And I saw in Howells one of the best minds of his generation destroyed by madness, starving hysterical naked. . . . Yes and no, as it has taken me several years to find out.

This book is an elaborately contextual study of *A Modern Instance*, which, now having read almost all of the thirty-odd other Howells novels, I still consider his best. Nevertheless, as it is commonplace to observe, *A Modern Instance* is flawed by its ending, which Howells wrote after the physical and emotional collapse that had interrupted his composition. In this collapse he came as close as he ever would in his adult life to madness. His hysteria had come earlier, in Howells' "very morbid boyhood," as he once called it; and I have found it necessary to go back forty years and then move slowly forward in order to understand how *A Modern Instance* effected Howells' breakdown in 1881 and how, in turn, the breakdown affected the novel.

My first three chapters, then, comprise a detailed interpretation of Howells' youthful neuroticism, from the 1840s to 1865, the point at which he launched his literary career. My theme is the evolution of Howells' "psychological juggle," the tactic of psychical self-defense that also became the delimiting means of his art. In the fourth and fifth chapters, I shift my attention to the first decade of Howells' work as a fiction writer, emphasizing the submerged psychological patterns and preoccupations that were to inform *A Modern Instance*, which is the focus of my sixth chapter. Here I take the aesthetic merit of the novel as given, something other critics have amply demonstrated.[1] My concern, rather, is to explain what happened in the writing of *A Modern Instance* that made it turn out to be less than the truly great work it promised to be. In a brief final chapter, I suggest that the problems in this novel, which are related to Howells' fear of the unconscious, are paradigmatic of his literary practices, at least throughout the first half of his career.

Kermit Vanderbilt proposes that "Howells may be the ideal figure to illustrate in what ways biography can illuminate the meaning of a novel and how the novel, in turn, can cast a reciprocal light on hidden recesses of the author's life and his response to his time."[2] *A Modern Instance* is the ideal text

for such an approach, which resembles what Leon Edel calls "literary psychology":[3] the attempt to break through the mask of fictive impersonality, to reverse a writer's conversion of memory into symbolic fable, and to apprehend
the animating emotions of the individual artist. Like a psychoanalyst, but
without any therapeutic intent, the literary psychologist reads with hovering
attention, alert for the psychic clues; and then, eschewing jargon except
where precision requires it, he or she tries to compose them into a pattern.

As Jay Martin observes, "Biography and psychoanalysis operate in the realm
of interpretation, where 'fictions'—probable truths—predominate." These
fictions are, on the level of microanalysis, the "reconstructions" of "particular
episodes, phases, or aspects of a life"; on the level of macroanalysis, they are
"constructions," the assemblages of "the meaning of any particular reconstruction *in relation to* many reconstructions." The literary psychologist does not
claim that "the reconstructions and constructions are identical to the subject;
that is, even the most elaborately detailed constructions are not thought of as
being the person. Rather, they 'correspond' to the person's history; they 'represent' the structure of his past; they 'imitate' the story of his development."[4]

This book is a mosaic of such reconstructions and constructions, an inter-
pretive "fiction" about the problematical workings of a neurotic writer's imagination: his black heart's-truth. My psychological assumptions are largely and
unabashedly Freudian, and I consider it especially appropriate to bring psychoanalysis to bear upon a writer whose career was nearly contemporaneous
with Freud's.

J. W. C.
Auburn, New York
April 1984

ACKNOWLEDGMENTS

Insofar as this book is a partial (in all its senses) biography, it is symbiotically related to the standard biographies of Howells by Edwin H. Cady and Kenneth S. Lynn, upon which I have often depended. I have also been guided by Cady's pioneering essay, "The Neuroticism of William Dean Howells" (1946).

I have profited from the advice, much of which I have taken, of those who troubled to read all or part of this book in typescript: my wife Susan Wolstenholme, my friends and colleagues Robert Emmet Long, Jay Martin, William Wasserstrom, Charles N. Watson, Jr., Ginette de B. Merrill, the late Roger Austen, Marcia Jacobson—and also Iris Tillman Hill, who gave me a candid editor's opinion when I most needed it. For his bracing intellectual support, I am thankful to Mas'ud Zavarzadeh.

David J. Nordloh provided the key to the Howells Center at Indiana University and allowed me to rummage the files. He and Thomas Wortham also sent me copies of essential materials.

Syracuse University, with summer grants and research leaves, provided the time and space for writing. William White Howells, the Houghton Library, the Herrick Memorial Library (Alfred University), the Rutherford B. Hayes Presidential Center, and the Massachusetts Historical Society graciously permitted my use of unpublished letters and documents in their possession; and the publishers of *American Literature*, *Journal of American Studies*, *Studies in the Literary Imagination*, and *The Old Northwest* allowed my reuse of essays that first appeared, in different form, in these journals.

No book like this one could easily have been written before now, when most of the major texts and many of the letters have been so meticulously edited. I owe a large debt to those Howellsians, at Indiana University and elsewhere, who placed so much of what I needed on my shelf, at arm's reach.

Which brings me to George Arms (who will, perhaps, forgive the pun). My dedication of this book to him only begins to say how much it is his as well as mine.

ABBREVIATIONS
AND EDITORIAL SYMBOLS

Frequently quoted sources have been identified parenthetically in the text and in the notes by use of the following abbreviations.

WRITINGS OF W. D. HOWELLS

BT — *A Boy's Town: Described for "Harper's Young People."* New York: Harper, 1890.

BT, TS — Typescript of *A Boy's Town.* The Houghton Library, Harvard University.

CA — *A Chance Acquaintance* (1873). Edited by Jonathan Thomas, David J. Nordloh, and Ronald Gottesman. Bloomington: Indiana University Press, 1971.

CP — *A Counterfeit Presentment: Comedy.* Boston: James R. Osgood, 1877.

FC — *A Foregone Conclusion.* Boston: James R. Osgood, 1875.

FR — *A Fearful Responsibility and Other Stories.* Boston: James R. Osgood, 1881.

ImI — *Imaginary Interviews.* New York: Harper, 1910.

I&E — *Impressions and Experiences.* New York: Harper, 1896. Contains "Police Report" (1882), "The Country Printer" (1893), "I Talk of Dreams" (1895).

LA — *The Lady of the Aroostook.* Boston: Houghton, Osgood, 1879.

LFA — *Literary Friends and Acquaintance: A Personal Retrospect of American Authorship* (1900). Edited by David F. Hiatt and Edwin H. Cady. Bloomington: Indiana University Press, 1968.

MI   *A Modern Instance* (1882). Edited by George N. Bennett, David J. Nordloh, and David Kleinman. Bloomington: Indiana University Press, 1977.

MLP   *My Literary Passions* (1895). In *My Literary Passions / Criticism & Fiction*. Library Edition. New York: Harper, 1911.

MYLC   *My Year in a Log Cabin*. New York: Harper, 1893.

PT   "Private Theatricals" (1875–76). Retitled *Mrs. Farrell: A Novel*. New York: Harper, 1921.

RSL   *The Rise of Silas Lapham* (1885). Edited by Walter J. Meserve and David J. Nordloh. Bloomington: Indiana University Press, 1971.

SRL   *The Son of Royal Langbrith* (1904). Edited by David Burrows, Ronald Gottesman, and David J. Nordloh. Bloomington: Indiana University Press, 1969.

TWJ   *Their Wedding Journey* (1872). Edited by John K. Reeves. Bloomington: Indiana University Press, 1968. Contains "Niagara Revisited" (1883).

UC   *The Undiscovered Country*. Boston: Houghton, Mifflin, 1880.

YMY   *Years of My Youth* (1916). In *Years of My Youth and Three Essays*. Edited by David J. Nordloh. Bloomington: Indiana University Press, 1975.

OTHER SOURCES

Cady   Edwin H. Cady. *The Road to Realism: The Early Years 1837–1885 of William Dean Howells*. Syracuse, N.Y.: Syracuse University Press, 1956.

INT   *Interviews With William Dean Howells*. Edited by Ulrich Halfmann. Arlington, Tex.: American Literary Realism, 1973.

LinL   *Life in Letters of William Dean Howells*. Edited by Mildred Howells. 2 vols. Garden City, N.Y.: Doubleday, Doran, 1928.

Lynn   Kenneth S. Lynn. *William Dean Howells: An American Life*.
            New York: Harcourt Brace Jovanovich, 1971.

MT–HL   *Mark Twain—Howells Letters: The Correspondence of Samuel L.
            Clemens and William D. Howells 1872–1910*. Edited by Henry
            Nash Smith, William M. Gibson, and Frederick Anderson. 2
            vols. Cambridge, Mass.: The Belknap Press of Harvard Uni-
            versity Press, 1960.

SE   *The Standard Edition of the Complete Psychological Works of Sig-
            mund Freud*. Edited by James Strachey. 24 vols. London: The
            Hogarth Press and the Institute of Psycho-Analysis, 1953–74.

SL   *Selected Letters of W. D. Howells*. Edited by George Arms,
            Christoph K. Lohmann et al. 6 vols. Boston: Twayne Publish-
            ers, 1979–83.

EDITORIAL SYMBOLS

↑ inserted ↓   Words or phrases inserted by Howells in a manuscript are indi-
               cated by placement within vertical arrows. No distinction is
               made between superscripts and subscripts.

\<deleted\>   Words or phrases canceled by Howells in a manuscript are indi-
               cated by placement within pointed brackets.

[added]   Editorial additions within a quoted text are indicated by place-
               ment within square brackets.

THE
BLACK HEART'S
TRUTH

CHAPTER ONE

A
VERY MORBID
BOYHOOD

A small boy, three years old, kneels on a window seat in the ladies' cabin of an Ohio River steamboat. He is watching the rain pelt the yellow river, and he imagines that each plop makes a "little man" jump up from the water. The boat lies still because a passenger is about to board: a one-legged man who is standing in a yawl, propped by a crutch under one arm and a cane in the other hand. The yawl glides alongside the steamboat, and the man begins to step on deck. But he slips somehow and vanishes soundlessly into the swirling river. There must have been a frantic search for the victim; his family, probably watching from a house ashore, must have shouted with dismay. But the small boy was to remember nothing that happened after the man had slipped down into the water (*BT*, 8–9).

Children do not "very distinctly know their dreams from their experiences," W. D. Howells wrote many years later, "and live in the world where both project the same quality of shadow" (*MLP*, 7–8). As a result, the remembered incidents of childhood have "the quality of things dreamt, not lived, and they remain of that impalpable and elusive quality in all the after years" (*YMY*, 3). Howells was never certain that his memory of the one-legged man was not the residue of something told him by his elders. He was surer of the authenticity of another memory: awaking one morning and seeing the tender, pathetic pink blossoms of a peach tree through the window beside his bed. Howells was always glad that, except for his mother's face, this vision of beauty was his very earliest memory because thereafter he would never see a peach tree in bloom "without a swelling of the heart, without some fleeting sense that 'Heaven lies about us in our infancy'" (*BT*, 7).[1]

Most of Howells' childhood recollections had a hellish cast, however. "If heaven lies about us in our infancy," he wrote and later canceled, "hell borders hard upon boyhood, and the air of its long summer days which men look back to so fondly is <often> ↑ sometimes ↓ foul as if with exhalations from the Pit" (*BT*, TS, 106).[2] His memory recalled occasions of grief and shame "with unfailing distinctness," but held "few or no records which I can allege in proof of my belief that I was then, above every other when, 'Joyful and free from blame'" (YMY, 14–15). Howells thought that his "very morbid boy-hood," as he called it (YMY, 79), had probably been gladder than it later seemed; his memory had erased the "long spaces of blissful living" between the vividly recalled "facts of unhappiness" (YMY, 14). Nevertheless, these facts clarify the complex interrelationship of Howells' neuroticism and his imaginative work.

<h1 style="text-align:center">I</h1>

In every account of his Ohio years— between his arrival in Hamilton at the age of three in 1840 and his departure from Jefferson for Europe more than twenty years later—Howells stressed the nurturing presence of his mother "in the home which she knew how to create for us" (SL, 5:313). He could not, "without an effect of exaggeration unwor-thy of her dear memory," express his sense of "her motherly perfection within the limits of her nature" (YMY, 106–7). Her chief limitations were pos-sessiveness and parochialism, which made it excruciating for her to relinquish her beloved son and to accept his desire for a life beyond the village. What might have become of Mary Dean Howells outside of her native element is suggested by Howells' touching portrait, in A Hazard of New Fortunes (1890), of Mrs. Dryfoos, hopelessly displaced in New York City, pining for the family homestead in the Midwest. But within that element, as suggested by Howells' portrait of Mrs. Saunders in The Coast of Bohemia (1893), Mary Dean Howells had the strength of her "motherly perfection": her efficient manage-ment of a large household, her "heavenly art of making each child feel itself the most important, while she was partial to none" (BT, 21), and her "great warmth of mind which supplied any defect of culture" (SL, 5:312). Whatever her defects, Mary Dean Howells was far from uncultured. She often recited the poetry and sang the lyrics she had learned in her youth at seminary school; she passed a sharp editorial eye over everything her husband and son wrote, making "constant objection to poorly finisht work."[3] Together with her husband she formed, as Howells said, "our church and our academy" (SL, 5:313).

Quiet and sweet-tempered as she was, Mary Dean Howells had no patience with "complainers" and no indulgence for "the luxury of grumbling or fault-finding." In her view, bad tempers were "not altogether the children's fault, but if they failed to control them, that was something for them to be heartily ashamed of."[4] She also possessed "little humor of her own," although she ex-pressed "a childlike happiness in the humor of us others" (YMY, 86). In her slender sense of humor and her stocky figure, she presented the greatest contrast to her husband. William Cooper Howells, who was slim and slightly stoop-shouldered, loved a joke "almost as much as he loved a truth" and "despised austerity as something owlish" (*BT*, 14).

This dear "father-man," as one of his children called him, was a "friend and companion to his sons" (*INT*, 25), and he set them an example for his philosophy that "people are more apt to be true if you trust them than if you doubt them" (*BT*, 15). A family friend described William Cooper Howells as "a man of the Franklin mold, having but little of the 'Poor Richard' side, however, and much of gentle scholarship, earnest conviction, and poetic insight, with a devout mysticism."[5] Whereas his own father Joseph, a religious fanatic, had "fervently hoped to reach a heaven beyond this world by means of prayers and hymns and revivals and conversions," William Cooper Howells no less religiously "lived for a heaven on earth in his beloved and loving home; a heaven of poetry and humor, and good-will and right thinking" (*YMY*, 84). His poetry was expressed both in utopian dreams for humankind and in a "passion for nature as tender and genuine and as deeply moralized as that of the English poets, by whom it had been nourished" (*MYLC*, 2). His humor was expressed in a ready wit and a jaundiced view of "outward shows and semblances" (*BT*, 5). He particularly relished the follies of sectarian wrangling, but William Cooper also respected earnest belief. His good will was expressed in a remarkable toleration of every shade of opinion; he was willing "to meet any one in debate of moral, religious, or political questions, and the wildest-haired Comeouter, the most ruthless sceptic, the most credulous spiritualist, found him ready to take them seriously, even when it was hard not to take them in joke" (*I&E*, 23). In these debates, William Cooper Howells never compromised his own idea of right thinking: adherence to the more earthbound doctrines of Emanuel Swedenborg.

William Cooper's speculative flights were ballasted by his inventive temperament. His son Joseph described him as "intensely practical as well as idealistic."[6] His common sense was nowhere more evident than in his religious beliefs. As Edwin H. Cady says, "It seems clear that at bottom Swedenborgianism was ethical rather than mystical for William Cooper. It had its emotional side, its 'metaphysical pathos' for him; but the deepest issues were those of conduct" (pp. 18–19).

The religious instruction in the Howells home may have lacked the formality of Sunday school lessons, but it was abundant and pervasive. At the heart of what the children were taught was Swedenborg's conception of life as a psychomachia, that "in every thought and in every deed they were choosing their portion with the devils or the angels, and that God himself could not save them against themselves" (*BT*, 14). As William Cooper Howells once explained to a skeptic, Swedenborgians "believed in a hell, which each cast himself into if he loved the evil rather than the good, and that no mercy could keep him out of without destroying him, for a man's love was his very self" (*BT*, 12).

Young Will Howells, overhearing this explanation, felt his "blood run cold," and he resolved to save himself from hell by always loving the good. Posted on strict watch against the slightest of childish transgressions, the boy believed that teasing was fiendish, that angry and vengeful feelings summoned evil spirits to his side, that "wicked words were of the quality of wicked deeds, and that when they came out of our mouths they depraved us, unless we took them back" (*YMY*, 21). Even innocent words could imperil his soul. After his mother had jokingly warned him that "he who talks to himself has the devil for a listener," Will never "dared whisper above his breath when he was alone, though his father and mother had both taught him that there was no devil but his own evil will" (*BT*, 199).

The boy became exceedingly conscientious. When a girl at school mislaid a pencil she thought she had lent to him, Will developed the "morbid belief" that he had stolen it. Frantic with "the mere dread of guilt," he neither ate nor slept until he had replaced the pencil; and only when the girl said she had found the missing one in her desk, was he saved from the "despair of a self-convicted criminal." Despite his father's efforts to temper Will's punishing conscience, the boy was "always in an anguish to restore things to their owners, like the good boys in the story-books." When he found a bag of raisins in the graveyard and ingenuously showed it to his friends, they promptly devoured the raisins, leaving Will—although he had not eaten one—to suffer "pangs of the keenest remorse" for his complicity in this "sin" (*BT*, 198–99).

Small wonder that Will and Joe made a secret pact against lying after reading "The Trippings of Tom Pepper" (an unfortunate boy caught in the web of his own deceit). And if Will ever strayed, his elder brother, a veritable Sid Sawyer of rectitude, was there to put him on the straight-and-narrow again. Joe's uprightness, unselfishness, and truthfulness—he would not lie even about going swimming—were a daily reproach to Will; and he rebelled sometimes against his brother's vigilance, calling him every kind of hard name. But he "would not call him a fool, because then he would be in danger of hell-fire" (*BT*, 185).

One "lurid day," when the boys were fishing with no success, a younger brother persisted in throwing stones at Will's line until his patience snapped and he shoved his tormentor into the river. "It was shallow enough, but his offence was the same as if it had been fathomless." All the way home, Will begged Joe not to reveal his crime. But "that just spirit could not spare him," and Will "duly suffered," as must anyone "who abandons himself to an evil temper, which is truly an outburst from hell, a fire of pure hate" (*BT*, TS, 351–52).

During his Hamilton years, Will Howells lived in continual fear. When he was not stabbing himself with morbid conscience, he was peopling the nooks and corners of his cheerful home with "shapes of doom and horror" (*BT*, 18). He also adopted the ceremonials of superstition, such as sidestepping the cracks between the paving stones and touching every tree or post along the sidewalk. Howells had a special terror of ghosts. Once, when he was spending the night with some neighborhood boys, he became so frightened by their spectral tales that he had to be escorted home. Even in broad daylight, Will had to screw up his courage in order to run past Aaron Potter's tombstone-cutting shop. A painting of Death on a Pale Horse harrowed him "to the bottom of his soul by its ghastliness" (*BT*, 216).

Death entered early into his consciousness when he saw the corpse of a Negro baby with red copper coins over its eyelids and witnessed the interment of a schoolmate. Inspired perhaps by reading Poe's "Premature Burial," Will once fell into a "trance" in which he envisioned the preparations for his own funeral. Amid the lamentations, he was unable to move or speak, and he was saved only at the last moment by someone's putting a mirror to his lips and noticing a blur of mist on it. Later, when he began to write sketches, he would imagine a character's dying and then become afraid that *he* was that character and was going to die (*BT*, 204). He questioned his parents about another fantasy, of someone's dying right in the center aisle of the Methodist church, where his mother sometimes took him before she converted to Swedenborgianism. Wouldn't such a death be advantageous? Wouldn't that person's chances of going straight to heaven be "so uncommonly good that he need have very little anxiety about it"? The boy noticed that his parents exchanged grave glances after receiving this "revelation of his darkling mind" (*BT*, 202–3). His most horrifying fantasy was the presentiment that came to him at the age of nine or ten when the moonlight washed his room "in a very strange and phantasmal way"; he was possessed by a perverse fear that he was going to die when he was sixteen (*BT*, 204).

At times he feared that he would not last even that long. At the age of twelve, in the summer of 1849, Will contracted a mild case of cholera. The "brooding horror of the pestilence sank deep into the boy's morbid soul," and throughout his illness he lay in the Valley of the Shadow of Death despite his mother's attempts to coax him out of his irrational fears (*BT*, 242–43). As the side effect of a prolonged malarial fever a few years earlier, he had had a very distressing "sort of continuous dream," of gliding down the schoolhouse stairs without touching his feet to the steps (*BT*, 235; *I&E*, 119). During this or another siege of lightheadedness, Will suffered almost indescribably from a recurrent fantasy: he "shrank in horror from the inevitable oncoming of a vast, impalpable something that seemed to be rolling toward me to surround and swallow me up in enormous airy billows. I used to flee to my parents for refuge from this airy nothing, and vainly try to tell them what it was like." [7]

This waking horror invaded his dreams as well. Howells confessed in the *Atlantic*'s anonymous "Contributors' Club" in 1880 that he had seldom dreamed pleasantly and that he tended to have recurrent nightmares, "one form prevailing for a term of years, to be succeeded by another form which seemed to drive out the earlier from possession of the brain." The earliest form was "the apparition of a tall, white-clothed figure encountered suddenly at the turning of long corridors, the glimpse of whose shadowy shape at a distance thrilled me with ghostly terror." This dream was eventually supplanted by one in which "shapes of armed men, who, sometimes heralded by martial noises, sometimes approaching with awful, silent tread, passed in procession to the house where I was concealed, prone upon the floor or crouched cowering in corners, in the frenzied endeavor to keep out of the range of sight of the windows through which the death shot was to strike me." [8]

Hamilton's harmless village idiot regularly stalked the boy in his dreams. Will once passed the man, of whom he was unaccountably terrified, on a covered bridge; and he later dreamed, or thought he dreamed, that the plank footpath had been taken up and that he was obliged to cross the bridge by balancing on its girders, his brain reeling from the sight of the swirling river beneath. Another nightmare was inspired by his discovery in a cornfield during spring thaw of "knots and bundles of snakes writhen and twisted together, in the torpor of their long winter sleep" (*BT*, 200); his dreams were to be "infested by like images of these loathsome reptiles" (*I&E*, 124).

The boy's worst nightmare—"nothing in my experience has been more dreadful to me"—was dreamed at or before the age of ten, and it remained more vivid in his memory "than anything that happened at the time." He had been reading Poe, and his dream recalls the alarm bells' "tale of terror" in "The Bells": "it involved simply an action of the fire-company in the little town where I lived. They were working the brakes of the old fire-engine, which would seldom respond to their efforts, and as their hands rose and fell they set up the heart-shaking and soul-desolating cry of 'Arms Poe, arms Poe, arms Poe!'" Soon thereafter Howells had another "threatening and awful" dream, of a clown rising through the air and floating over the rooftop in a sitting posture, snapping his fingers, and vaguely smiling, while the antennae on his forehead nodded elastically (*I&E*, 106–7). [9]

During the later years in Hamilton, William Cooper Howells often received free tickets in exchange for advertising in his newspaper, and young Will began to frequent the theater. His brother recalled how Will, who was "an imaginative, sensitive boy, whose head was always full of strange fancies," would see a play or read all evening and then "would often lie awake for hours, unable to set his mind at rest." [10] During those hours of wakefulness, Will would often fantasy that the statue of the Commendatore in *Don Giovanni* had come to life; and his pursuit of "the wicked hero" set a pattern for another recurrent dream, in which he was "chased by a marble statue with an uplifted arm" (*I&E*, 107).

The melodramas he saw left the boy burning to have a black mustache and "to end bloodily, murderously, as became a villain." His father had no inkling of "the riot of emotions behind the child's shy silence, or how continually he was employed in dealing death to all the good people in the pieces he saw or imagined." The violent fantasies coexisted with equally hidden erotic ones, aroused by two lovely child actresses from Cincinnati, "for whose sake he somehow perpetrated these wicked deeds." So bold in his mind, Will shrank from the girls in reality; when he passed them once in the street and they seemed about to speak to him, he "ran so that they could not" (*BT*, 181–82).

Howells recalled that he had been aware of girls as early as the day when his wearing his first suit had put him "beyond the shameful period of skirts" and had commended him to the little girl "who used to look for him, as he passed" (*BT*, 6). "She is still a phantasmal presence on the thither side of a paling fence; and I know <I> ↑ my boy ↓ used to be plagued about her, but that is all I know; and a thick darkness dwells on the whole of that time, shot here and there with a few rays of consciousness that have no shape <or form> of association" (*BT*, TS, 14). Later, when girls were said to have their beaux, Will did not understand what was meant, being unable to "disentangle the idea of bows from the idea of arrows" (*BT*, 58).

He was in love himself with a girl who once caught her hand on a meat hook in the village market, and on whose account he secretly suffered. He had a vision of her hanging from the meat hook, although "this was probably one of those grisly fancies that were always haunting him, and no fact at all" (*BT*, 58). Howells identified her as "Julia" in a canceled passage of *A Boy's Town* (*BT*, TS, 88), probably the same Julia Van Hook whose death in 1908 stirred him to remember her as, "after Mary Ellen McAdams, my first love" (*LinL*, 2:251). In his boyhood, "Julia" had "long seemed to him the most beautiful name for a girl; he said it to himself with flushes from his ridiculous little heart" (*BT*, 58). But she had never spoken to him, and he had always been "petrified" when he looked at her, wanting to run away (*LinL*, 2:251). When he heard at the age of ten that she had married, he realized that she must have been considerably older than he. At about the same age, he established a "boy-and-girl acquaintance" with Anna Harrison, the granddaughter of President William Henry Harrison, and he used to walk a mile and a half to the farm where she lived, carrying a book under his arm. Still too shy for any but literary passions, Will, as Anna recalled, "seemed to regard these visits as favorable opportunities to wander off by himself and read."[11]

Joe recollected that in early boyhood his brother had "preferred a book to any sport that could be devised," although he later "manifested some interest in swimming and skating."[12] But a friend remembered that even at the swimming hole, while the others dove in, Will would prop himself against a cottonwood tree and "'gaze dreamily out over the water for hours at a time.'"[13] Howells himself admitted that long before he had left Hamilton, "the world within," the fantasy world that was inspired by his voracious reading, had "claimed him more and more." He had ceased to be "that eager comrade he had once been" and had come to see "much of the outer world through a veil of fancies quivering like an autumn haze between him and its realities, softening their harsh outlines, and giving them a fairy coloring" (BT, 240). He was living, in fact, a double life: "the Boy's Town life and the Cloud Dweller's life." Of the latter he was "secretly proud," although he never would have exposed this private self to his friends (BT, 184).

Will Howells knew over a hundred boys in Hamilton, but he had no intimates among his schoolmates. His only chum was a boy who also stood apart: the hooky-playing, Huck Finnlike pariah John Rorick, with whom close association was regarded by parents and boys alike "'as distinctly and deliciously perilous.'"[14] Howells soothed against Rorick's "soft, caressing ignorance" the ache of his own "fantastic spirit," and he reposed his "intensity of purpose in that lax and easy aimlessness." Their comradeship was not only "more innocent" than any other friendship the boy had; it was "wholly innocent": "they loved each other, and that was all" (BT, 192). But this alliance of the Cloud Dweller and the "kindly earth-spirit" was broken as soon as Will became uncomfortably aware of his friend's disrepute, especially of his lack of conventional ambitions. Embarrassed for Rorick, and also for himself, Will blunderingly tried to elevate his friend's standards by enticing him to attend school. Rorick could stand it only half a day; he must have suffered "a wound" from the shame he sensed in young Howells. Afterward they never met again "upon the old ground of perfect trust and affection" (BT, 193).

Will was left alone. Neither a Huck Finn nor a Boy's Town boy, he hardly seemed a boy at all. The journeymen in his father's printshop dubbed him "The Old Man" for a "habitual gravity" that was relieved only by sudden "bursts of wild hilarity" (YMY, 16; BT, 238). Will turned more and more to reading; and the "love of literature, and the hope of doing something in it" became his life "to the exclusion of all other interests, or it was at least the great reality, and all other things were as shadows" (MLP, 91). But he did not expect his reading to win the respect of boys "who were more valiant in fight or in play" (MLP, 12).

One of these was Joe, who usually did the fighting for his brother, younger by four and a half years. Joe was as aggressive as Will was passive, as hardheaded as Will was fanciful; Joe was "a calm light of common-sense, of justice, of truth," while Will was "a fantastic flicker of gaudy purposes" (BT, 185). Even as a child, Joe was full of money-making schemes, and his thrifty practicality endeared him to his mother. Joe sometimes vented his "grotesque" sense of humor at the expense of Mary Dean Howells' "implicit faith in everything he said," but she in turn "would not suffer joking from any but him" (YMY, 86). "My eldest brother and she understood each other best," Howells remarked (YMY, 20).

On occasion Joe trained his satirical wit on Will, who "shuddered at his brother's burlesque of the high romantic vein" of his fledgling verses (BT, 184). Joe never quite understood "why poetry in literature should be so all in all" with Will; his own literary taste was decidedly earthier (YMY, 85). No doubt Joe was envious of his brother's erudition and the attention it gained him, and Will was not above responding in kind. He deleted from A Boy's Town this cutting recollection: "We had Campbell's Poems at home, and my elder brother knew Hohenlinden by heart; he supposed that he was the only boy who had ever heard of that poem, and he was astonished and mortified beyond measure to find that it was familiarly known even to the boy who lived next door" (BT, TS, 67).

II

With four boys in the Hamilton household—a fifth was to be born in Columbus in 1852—there was "often the strife which is always openly or covertly between brothers"; and the friction between Will and Joe increased as the older boy was transformed from "the whimsical tease and guardian angel of our childhood to the anxious taskmaster of our later boyhood requiring the same devotion in our common work that his conscience exacted of himself." Will believed that he was working as hard as Joe in the printshop, and he "hotly resented" any suggestion to the contrary (YMY, 84–85). Less consciously, perhaps, Will envied Joe his greater share of their mother's devotion, which had been spread thinner with every new baby. Starting with Victoria in 1838, the year after Will's birth, Mary Dean Howells gave birth regularly, every two years, through 1846.

Howells recalled, in an early memory of his mother, coming home with her from a visit upriver to her family and romping in the purple blossoms of the tall June grass. "The mother threw herself on her knees in it, and tossed and frolicked with her little ones like a girl" (BT, 19). The sweet intimacy of that time was recaptured on those occasions when Will's physical ailments or his homesickness earned him favored treatment. With her evenhanded policy toward child-rearing, Mary Dean Howells "would have felt such a preference wicked" under any other circumstances (YMY, 25).[15] But there was "rich compensation" for any suffering child in the "affectionate petting" his mother gave when sickness removed him from the "rough little world" of boys and restored him to her care again. "Then she makes everything in the house yield to him. . . . She is so good and kind and loving that he cannot help having some sense of it all, and feeling how much better she is than anything on earth. . . . [I]n his weakness, his helplessness, he becomes a gentle and innocent child again; and heaven descends to him out of his mother's heart" (*BT*, 236).

If illness was the way to his mother's heart, Will found another to his father's. One of his earliest memories was of tracing an engraving of a bull from a book and then boasting to his father that he had drawn it freehand, a claim that Joe loudly contested. William Cooper Howells sided with Will "though he must have known he was lying," thus causing him "a far worse conscience" than if he had whipped him (*BT*, 15). But Will quickly learned that his surest hold on his father's favor was his own artistic achievements, whether tracing pictures or, later, writing poems. When the boy began to show a liking for literature, William Cooper was eager to encourage him. Howells fondly recalled the kindling of one of his first literary passions by his father's tales of Cervantes, whom he came to love "with a sort of personal affection, as if he were still living and he could somehow return my love" (*MLP*, 19). The boy was displacing some of his love for his father upon Cervantes, and the identification was strengthened by William Cooper's giving Will his own copy of *Don Quixote*, which the boy read nearly to tatters. Later William Cooper also gave him a Spanish grammar and prodded him to learn the rules of that language before he had much command of the rules of English.

The father was even prouder than his son of what the boy could learn on his own; he was convinced—mistakenly, Howells later thought—that he "could do everything without help" (*YMY*, 82). There came a time, early in their companionship, when his father took him aside to say that he regarded him "as different from other boys" of his age; and Will had "a very great and sweet happiness without alloy of vanity, from his serious and considered words" (*YMY*, 83). When Will began to write, often composing his pieces from the type font as he composed them in his mind, William Cooper could not have been more pleased. Indeed, Howells' first published poem, in 1852, was one that his father had surreptitiously submitted on his behalf. Ten years later William Cooper confided to a friend that "Will is so much a continuation and development of my own aspirations and efforts that he seems almost myself" (quoted in Cady, 45).

Howells' earliest memory of his father (from his fourth year) concerned nestling with him under his blue broadcloth cloak: "To get under its border, and hold by his father's hand in the warmth and dark it made around him was something that the boy thought a great privilege, and that brought him a sense of mystery and security at once that nothing else could ever give." William Cooper once brought him an axe he badly wanted, concealed under the same cloak: "his father said, 'Feel, feel!' and he found his treasure"—although "his abiding association with it in after-life was a feeling of weariness and disgust" (BT, 5). Howells explained this reaction by saying that he must have been "laughed at" for his axe and his failure to keep the family in fire-wood with it. But there were deeper reasons. Feeling the axe under his father's cloak involved both identification and fear: the boy's love for his father and craving for his approval coexisted with equally intense, but repressed, feelings of aggression and fear of reprisal and abandonment.

Howells never forgot "with any detail of the time and place" another inci-dent of his boyhood. His father, as he often did, failed to come home on time for supper. While the family waited impatiently for him, Will "came out with the shocking wish that he was dead." Called instantly to account by his mother, Will waited in dread until his father arrived and his mother, as she felt bound to do, told on him. For an outburst of "reckless fury" Will had once endured a "circumstantial whipping" from his father; for this far greater of-fense, miraculously, there was to be no physical punishment: William Cooper's "explanation and forgiveness were the sole event" (YMY, 21).[16]

A related incident occurred during Howells' trip with his father upriver to Pittsburgh, aboard one of his uncle's steamboats. Although the journey was a wondrous experience for the boy, his first sight (at the age of nine or ten) of the "splendor of the world" beyond Hamilton, it was also fraught with anxi-ety. With his "insatiable interest in every aspect of nature and human nature," William Cooper would disembark at each landing to chat with bystanders and sample the wares of the wharf peddlers, while Will "waited for him on board in an anguish of fear lest he should be left behind." Of course steam-boats never departed on time, and Captain Dean would never have aban-doned his brother-in-law. But the boy's anxiety mounted to a frenzy one day when, awaking from a daydream, he imagined that the boat had changed course and was heading downstream. "It was in this crisis that I saw my father descending the gang-plank, and while I was urging his return in mute agony, a boat came up outside of us to wait for her chance of landing. I looked and read on her wheel-house the name *New England*, and then I abandoned hope. By what fell necromancy I had been spirited from my uncle's boat to another I could not guess, but I had no doubt that the thing had happened, and I was flying down from the hurricane roof to leap aboard that boat from the lower-most deck when I met my uncle coming as quietly up the gangway as if nothing had happened" (YMY, 26–28).

Nothing had. The *New England* turned out to be another boat—his uncle's was the *New England No. 2*—and the illusion of going downstream had re-sulted from an "obsession" that bothered Howells throughout his life: "when the place where one is disorients itself and west is east and north is south" (YMY, 28).[17]

After this crisis, William Cooper Howells promised a reform in his dilatory habits to appease Will's unreason, but he could not relieve his son's deeper anxieties. In a dream from this time, Will imagined that his father, who was away from home, came into the room where he was sleeping and stood by the bed. "He wished to greet me, after our separation, and he reasoned that if he did so, I should wake, and he turned and left the room without touching me. This process in his mind, which I knew as clearly and accurately as if it had apparently gone on in my own, was apparently confined to his mind as absolutely as anything could be that was not spoken or in any wise uttered." Howells added shrewdly: "Of course it was of my agency, like any other part of the dream, and it was something like the operation of the novelist's intention through the mind of his characters" (*I&E*, 112).

The boy really missed his absent father, and his dream is partly an undistorted fulfillment of a wish for his return. That it also expresses some hidden, negative wishes is suggested by the extreme self-consciousness of the dreamer, a sign that censorship is operating. The mental process attributed to the father, which Howells himself recognized as his "own agency," seems to be a displaced rationalization, a substitution for the dreamer's own rationalization of the desires that his father should *not* touch him (for fear that he might touch him harmfully) and that his father should disappear.

In 1900, Sigmund Freud asserted that "anxiety-dreams are dreams with a sexual content."[18] The terrors of Howells' childhood dreams and fantasies point to underlying psychosexual conflicts. After recalling the one about snakes, for instance, Howells continued without transition: "I suppose that every one has had dreams of finding his way through unnamable filth, and of feeding upon hideous carnage; these are clearly the punishment of gluttony, and are the fumes of a rebellious stomach" (*I&E*, 124–25). More likely, they were the fumes of the brimstone in Swedenborg's excremental hell, which Howells learned to associate with sexual thoughts of any kind. The most terrifying of his childhood visions, the "Arms-Poe" dream, seems to reflect anxiety about childish masturbation—hence the fire company's working of the engine brakes ("which would seldom respond to their efforts"), the rising and falling of their hands, and their rhythmic chant. In a similar vein is the erection dream of the "vaguely smiling" clown who is gradually elevated (in a sitting posture) over the rooftop, with his fingers snapping and his antennae elastically nodding. The fantasies of gliding down stairs and of vertiginously crossing the bridge over the river also seem concerned with fear of sexual arousal. Fear of the punishing father, as well as of the engulfing mother, may be seen in Howells' fear of the impalpable airy billow and more clearly in his later dreads of the tall, white-clothed figure, of the armed men who threaten to shoot through the house windows, and of the erect statue of the Commendatore, who unstiffens in order to punish "the wicked hero."[19]

Many of the psychosexual currents of Howells' boyhood are present in the early memory with which I began: the drowning of the one-legged man who was trying to board the steamboat *Boston* (*BT*, TS, 20).[20] The boy is kneeling in the ladies' cabin, that is, in the company of his beloved mother in a place from which his father would have been excluded. He is watching the rain make "little men" jump up from the river's surface: at his mother's side, the boy is absorbed in a literally procreative fantasy. The passenger, who is carrying the crutch and cane symbolic of the missing limb that would have allowed an unmaimed man to mount the steamboat successfully, suddenly falls into the water, sinking beneath the surface in counterpoint to the little men rising from it. Howells explicitly relates the two images by saying that the drowning "had exactly the value in the child's mind that the jumping up of the little men had, neither more nor less" (*BT*, 9). It is as if the child, like some omnipotent and wrathful god, has caused this death by the force of his imagination; as he gives life to the little men, he takes life from the big man.[21]

Although there is no way to prove it, this early memory may have been screening repressed feelings from Howells' crisis aboard the steamboat in 1846 or 1847, which, as we have seen, also involved the idea of a man's "missing the boat." In both cases, the steamboats were piloted by one of the Dean uncles, and their names—*Boston* and *New England No. 2*—were as closely related. Indeed, just as New England contains Boston, so the memory of the *New England* incident may be seen to "contain" the "screen memory" of the *Boston* one.

Aboard the *New England No. 2*, young Howells felt truly anxious for his father on the numerous occasions when he seemed to be risking abandonment. But he also, likely, felt anxious for himself and angry at his father for causing him to worry about his own abandonment. He may well have suppressed the thought, "I hope he *does* miss the boat; it would serve him right!"—a thought only slightly removed from the one he had let slip on that other occasion of impatient waiting for William Cooper, when he wished his father dead. At the moment of crisis, when this wish seemed to be coming true, as if by the same magic that seemed to have spirited him from one steamboat to another, the boy was paralyzed by conflict. His agony was "mute" because his desire to warn his father was neutralized by his repressed desire *not* to warn him. The "obsession" of sudden reversal in direction symbolized this psychical loss of bearings, in which what was fantasy seemed to be reversing itself into an opposite reality. The south of the unconscious angry wish seemed to be turning into the north of its fulfillment.

Throughout the Pittsburgh trip, the tensions between father and son were apparent beneath the surface of their mutual devotion. When William Cooper exhorted Will to notice this or that feature of the passing landscape, the boy mutely resisted. His father later reported "that he never could get anything from me but a brief 'Yes, indeed,' in response" (*YMY*, 28). When he and his father later toured the glass factories and rolling mills of Pittsburgh, William

Cooper was brimming with excitement over the mechanical wonders; but the boy, who "feigned an interest in the processes out of regard for him," could hardly wait to escape the city and its "abhorred foundries" (YMY, 30–31).

III

As Will approached adolescence, his differences with his father centered more explicitly on William Cooper's treatment of Mary Dean Howells, whose unhappiness seemed to rise as her husband's fortunes fell. Howells began to blame his father for incompetence as a provider and to take his mother's side in the unspoken family strife.

The Howellses' life in Hamilton during the 1840s had been relatively stable. If William Cooper wrote off some of the subscription payments due him, if he needed to work his sons very hard in order to make ends meet, and if his wife was often careworn and homesick, at least the Howellses were no poorer than their neighbors—Howells later idealized life in Hamilton for its freedom from economic extremes—and the emotional life of their home was rich. But bad times came suddenly in 1848, when William Cooper's abolitionist principles impelled him to attack his own Whig party for its nomination of Zachary Taylor. The more he editorialized for Free Soil politics, the more he lost of his readership; and he was driven out of business after the presidential election.

Mary Dean Howells, as always, stood by her husband "anxiously, fearfully, bravely, with absolute trust in his goodness and righteousness" (YMY, 20). But his reverses jeopardized their hard-earned independence and threatened to lower them a rung or two on the social ladder, possibly to the level of hired hands. For months their future remained uncertain. William Cooper did odd jobs in Hamilton; the boys were sent to work for other printers. In early 1849, William Cooper bought on credit a Whig newspaper in Dayton, but it failed after a year or more of back-breaking effort. Then, with his three brothers, he hatched a scheme for a family settlement, a kind of utopian commune, to be supported by a paper mill. The idea was doomed from the start by the Howells brothers' ignorance of the business they intended to enter. Furthermore, at the site they eventually chose, aptly named Eureka Mills, the housing and manufacturing facilities were completely inadequate. The large family was to live in a deteriorating log cabin.

Howells remembered the year in the log cabin, which began in October 1850, as an idyll for the children and their father but a nightmare for their mother. Glad to be rid of his newspaper chores, invigorated by the natural surroundings, and hopeful for the future, William Cooper felt at home in Eureka. The neighboring farmers often congregated around the Howellses' fireplace on rainy days, their coats dripping on the rough plank floor, their stoga boots stinking of manure, and their expectorations sizzling on the coals. Mary Dean Howells had no more in common with these crude men than with their equally rough-hewn wives, who sometimes came calling. Her "housewifely instincts" were perpetually offended by a life that was, if poetic to the others, "not far from barbaric" to her (MYLC, 15). Worked harder than ever, cramped and oppressed by the log-cabin life, she found her homesickness mounting from time to time to "an insupportable crisis" when she would leave for a while and visit her parents upriver—though perhaps not so often as it seemed to her anxious son (YMY, 25).

The older children lived with a "sense of my father's adversity" and a "knowledge of our mother's unhappiness from it" (YMY, 34–35). Joe, especially, "knew all the anxiety of the time" and shared it fully with his mother (BT, 237). But Will was no less affected. Many years later when he was writing *New Leaf Mills* (1913), his oft-postponed novel about his life at Eureka, Howells was capable of rendering a balanced judgment on his parents. "Father was what God made him, and he was on the whole the best man I have known," he wrote to Joe in 1911, "but of course he was trying. . . . Mother was splendid, too; how my child's heart used to cling to her, and how her heart clung to each of us! Of course she could not do justice to father's limitations; I suppose a woman is always bewildered when a man comes short of the perfection which would be the logic of him in her mind" (SL, 5:356–57).

In the years after 1848, young Howells had identified himself strongly with his mother's resentment of his father's imperfections. The strength of Will's bond to Mary Dean Howells was evinced by several childhood episodes of homesickness, in which his sense of loss was so severe that it must be considered neurotic. In the summer of 1849, after the family had moved to Dayton, Will was taken back to Hamilton by his uncle Joseph, an apothecary and physician, to learn the drug business in his store. The boy was miserable, feeling that "all the world was one hopeless blackness" around him (MLP, 20). After a tearful night, he told his uncle that he could not stand it and was going home.

Two years later, after the family had moved to Eureka Mills, Will was dispatched again, this time to a printing office in Xenia.[22] As before "a terrible homesickness fell instantly upon me—a homesickness that already, in the mere prospect of absence, pierced my heart and filled my throat, and blinded me with tears" (MYLC, 50). Joe, who had accompanied him to Xenia, tried to reason with Will; and his father then stayed with him a week, hoping to nurse him past his fears. Nothing helped but returning to his mother, who welcomed him "as from a year's absence" (MYLC, 53). Finally, in November 1851, Will was sent to work for another printer, in Dayton, where his favorite uncle Israel boarded him. The first days were torture, but Will managed to choke his sobs at mealtime by gulping water. After dinner he would leave the table in a burst of tears, and every night he would run outside to cry alone in the dark behind the house. Once again he was rescued by Joe and taken home, and once again he was rewarded for his homesickness by his mother. "Doubtless she knew that it would have been better for me to have conquered myself; but my defeat was dearer to her than any triumph could have been." As she had done during his childhood illness, she pampered her ailing prodigal son, treating him as "company," giving him the "best place at the table, the tenderest bit of steak, the richest cup of her golden coffee" (*MYLC*, 56).

Such seductive attention could only have intensified Will's psychosexual conflicts at a time in his development when they were strong enough already. For Will was fourteen years old when this last incident occurred, and he was embroiled in the sexual awakening of puberty. In the summer of 1849, at the age of twelve, Will had seen his first female nude in the sprawling diorama of Dubuffe's "Adam and Eve." Many decades later Howells was still uneasy with his recollection of this painting: "If that was the way our first parents looked before the Fall, and the Bible said it was, there was nothing to be urged against it; but many kind people must have suffered secret misgivings at a sight from which a boy might well shrink ashamed, with a feeling that the taste of Eden was improved by the Fall" (*YMY*, 35).

What the Bible said to young Howells was strongly influenced by what Swedenborg had said it said. Swedenborg preached a theory of correspondences, by which (in Emerson's formula) particular natural facts correspond to particular spiritual facts, and Nature is a symbol of Spirit. Accordingly, William Cooper Howells conceived of "all tangible and visible creation as an adumbration of spiritual reality," and he accepted revelation as the mask of "interior meanings."[23] Every good and evil deed has a symbolic value, says Swedenborg, who places great emphasis on sexual deeds. The sixth commandment, he teaches, forbids more than lascivious acts and obscene thoughts and words. "In the spiritual sense, to commit adultery means to adulterate the goods of the Word, and to falsify its truths"; symbolically, "the falsification of truth is fornication, and the perversion of good is adulteration." Thus, whereas marriage signifies the "conjugial love" of heaven, adultery signifies eternal damnation: "Adultery is hell; and hell in general is called adultery."[24] All infernal spirits, according to Swedenborg, take the form of their own evils; and the hell of adulterers lies under their buttocks, where they wallow in their own excrement. From an early age, Will Howells imbibed such ideas, what Cady calls the "aura of dirty disgust with which Swedenborg surrounded selfish, lustful sex" (p. 33).

Swedenborg's excremental vision of hell contributed to Howells' formation of a powerful super-ego, which was brought into activity and given direction by the strength of his forbidden erotic wishes. Howells' conscience was so strict, in fact, and his self-chastisement so severe, that he developed a decidedly sado-masochistic streak in his character, which was evident in another incident of his thirteenth year.

In Dayton, some time between the summer of 1849 and the spring of 1850, a seamstress named Ann Stepmeyer took refuge with the Howellses.[25] The unfortunate young woman had been seduced by a prominent man who left her alone to bear "the blame for their sin." When her "shame" became physically obvious, young Howells waged a campaign of persecution against her "in the cause of social purity." At table he refused either to take any dish she had handled or to hand her one; he refused to speak to her and even to look at her if he could avoid it; he left a room whenever she entered it. As if he were one of the Puritan elders sitting in judgment upon Hester Prynne in the romance Hawthorne was writing the same year, Howells expressed "by every cruelty short of words" his sense of being "society incarnate in the attitude society takes toward such as she." The situation came to a crisis when the bewildered seamstress cast herself upon Mary Dean Howells' mercy, and she quickly put her son "to bitter shame" for his hardheartedness. Howells recalled: "It could not be explained to me how tragical her case was; I must have been thought too young for the explanation; but I doubt if any boy of twelve is too young for the right knowledge of such things; he already has the wrong" (YMY, 36–37).

Howells was sexually informed in some fashion, then, before the age of twelve, although his parents were apparently unaware of what he knew or too embarrassed to ask. A few years later William Cooper Howells conveyed to his son a copy of Chaucer from the state library, along with the librarian's "question as to whether he thought he ought to put an unexpurgated edition in the hands of a boy, and his own answer that he did not believe it would hurt me." This was, Howells shrewdly realized, "a kind of appeal to me to make the event justify him" (MLP, 83). Howells explained that his father's liberality of mind may have induced him to believe that "no harm could come to me from the literary filth which I sometimes took into my mind, since it was in the nature of sewage to purify itself" (YMY, 24). No harm did come so long as the boy remained naive. Although indecent literature "leaves the mind foul with filthy images and base thoughts," he later reflected, the boyish reader, "unless he is exceptionally depraved beforehand, is saved from these through his ignorance." But young Howells began to realize what sorts of lives his literary heroes had actually led—"how they were drunkards, and swindlers, and unchaste, and untrue"—and try as he undoubtedly did, he could not suppress altogether the titillating effects of "literary filth" (MLP, 43).

He admitted later: "I am not ready to say that the harm from it is positive, but you do get smeared with it, and the filthy thought lives with the filthy rhyme in the ear, even when it does not corrupt the heart or make it seem a light thing for the reader's tongue and pen to sin in kind" (MLP, 83–84).

Even with Chaucer, he would not pretend that he had been "insensible to the grossness of the poet's time, which I found often enough in the poet's verse" (*MLP*, 82); and he implicitly faulted his father for having put such a temptation before him.

For his brother Johnny, when he reached adolescence, Howells tried to fill the censorial role he felt William Cooper had shirked. "I can't tell you how sick at heart and stomach it made me—the other day, to look over some bad poems of Byron that I admired at sixteen," he wrote in a confidential letter to Johnny in 1863. "If such things don't spoil you, they'll make you ashamed and remorseful, some day" (*SL*, 1:152).[26] Later, when he had become an influential critic, Howells generalized this family duty to his readers at large, prophesying that in a more civilized future, when the "beast-man will be so far subdued and tamed in us that the memory of him in literature shall be left to perish," then the "lewd and ribald" passages in the great poets shall have been omitted from all editions for general readers. "The literary histories might keep record of them, but it is loathsome to think of those heaps of ordure, accumulated from generation to generation, and carefully passed down from age to age as something precious and vital, and not justly regarded as the moral offal which they are" (*MLP*, 43–44). In a better day, the "noxious and noisome channels" of filth, which sometimes make literary history seem "little better than an open sewer," will have ceased to flow (*MLP*, 83).

Howells' excremental imagery in such passages suggests that his view of human sexuality had been deeply affected by Swedenborg's vision of the hell of adultery. His boyhood reading had stimulated fantasies for which Howells had felt obliged to punish himself as mercilessly as he had punished the unfortunate seamstress. The self-torture of Howells' adolescence reached a climax in his collapse into "nervous prostration" (*YMY*, 81) at the age of seventeen.

CHAPTER TWO
THE BLACKNESS OF INSANITY

Looking back on the time of his breakdown, shrouded in what he felt he "must almost call the blackness of insanity," Howells believed in 1868 that he "must always be a different man from that [he] could have been but for that dreadful year" (SL, 1:296).[1] When he came to write about it frankly some sixty years afterward, Howells still thought that the episode was "necessary to a full realization of [his] life" (SL, 6:77). It is also necessary to a full realization of his work, for like any writer, but especially one beset by neurotic obsessions, Howells used imaginative acts as a means of emotional self-defense. Learning to "deal with my own state of mind as another would deal with it" became the protective mechanism that Howells called his "psychological juggle" (YMY, 81).

I

The Eureka experiment ended in late 1851, when William Cooper Howells was hired as the legislative reporter of the *Ohio State Journal* and the family moved to Columbus. In early 1852, he bought a share in the *Ashtabula Sentinel*; and the next year, completing a gradual migration from the southwestern to the northeastern corner of Ohio, the Howellses transferred themselves and the newspaper to their final home in Jefferson.

A town of some seven hundred residents, many of whom were transplanted New Englanders, Jefferson was known as a hub of abolitionist activity. Howells fondly recalled it in 1895 as "the center of a most extraordinary amount of reading and thinking. Outside of Massachusetts, I do not believe that an equal average of intelligence could have been found, among all sorts and conditions of men, who were there of an almost perfect social equality."[2] But Jefferson, after all, was not a Concord or a Cambridge; and while he lived there, Howells frequently bemoaned the oppressive atmosphere of what he once called "this not-to-be-sufficiently-detested village" (SL, 1:11). He came to associate Jefferson with the threat of imprisonment, both in the small-town narrowness that cramped his larger ambitions and in the neurotic hell of his life there.

It was in Jefferson that Howells began his intensive and compulsive study, first of Spanish and then, more or less simultaneously, of Latin, Greek, French, and German. He recalled how he used to rush home after a full day of setting type in the printshop to closet himself in his cubbyhole den under the stairs, "which I did not finally leave until the family were in bed" (MLP, 68). During these hours of self-enforced solitude, the youth would drill himself in languages or labor over his imitations of his favorite writers or dream of becoming the writer he himself longed to be, no less famous than his literary idols. Later Howells regarded much of this endeavor as "mere purblind groping, wilful and wandering" (MLP, 69); and he also wished that he had spent less time in his study or "that world of books which it opened into," rather that he had seen "more of the actual world, and had learned to know my brethren in it better" (MLP, 63). But this was the Tolstoyan convert speaking; the literary votary had had other ideas. "There was a hope to fulfil, an aim to achieve," Howells explained, "and I could no more have left off trying for what I hoped and aimed at than I could have left off living, though I did not know very distinctly what either was" (MLP, 69).

"Trying to burn my candle at both ends," Howells believed, was the cause of his breakdown in the summer of 1854, little more than a year after his family's arrival in Jefferson (MLP, 68). At first, he began to suffer from insomnia and sick headaches; then his "nerves gave way in all manner of hypochondriacal fears," which eventually "resolved themselves into one, incessant, inexorable" (MLP, 71): the fear that he had contracted rabies.

> By some chance there was talk with our village doctor about hydrophobia, and the capricious way the poison of a dog's bite may work. "Works round in your system," he said, "for seven years or more, and then it breaks out and kills you." The words he let heedlessly fall fell into a mind prepared by ill-health for their deadly potency, and when the summer heat came I was helpless under it. Somehow I knew what the symptoms of the malady were, and I began to force it upon myself by watching for them. The splash of water anywhere was a sound I had to set my teeth against, lest the dreaded spasms should seize me; my fancy turned the scent of the forest fires burning round the village into the subjective odor of smoke which stifles the victim. I had no release from my obsession, except in the dreamless sleep which I fell into exhausted at night, or that little instant of waking in the morning, when I had not yet had time to gather my terrors about me, or to begin the frenzied stress of my effort to experience the thing I dreaded. (YMY, 79–80)

Howells understood that it was not the fear of hydrophobia that he was suffering, "but the fear of the fear." Still he was "helpless in the nervous prostration which science, or our poor village medicine, was yet many years from knowing or imagining" (YMY, 81).

Howells believed that his terror of hydrophobia had originally been caused by his hearing as a child "of that poor man who had died of it in the town where we then lived" (YMY, 79). This incident, as Edwin H. Cady has discovered, concerned a Hamilton neighbor named Bowers, whose death in the summer of 1841 prompted William Cooper Howells to publish a lurid four-column description, which someone must have read to four-year-old Will, of the victim's mortal agonies. "The neighbor's fear of water, sensation of smothering and smelling smoke, his spasms, fits, and delusions, his calling in Joseph Howells [Will's grandfather] for religious comfort, and making his peace with God before death were chronicled in vivid detail" (pp. 23–24). That the unfortunate Bowers, bitten by his own dog some two months earlier, had shown no ill effects for weeks and then had died suddenly led the editor to speculate ominously that "it is far from being certain that a dog will not communicate hydrophobia by biting at any time when he is enraged though he may never have been bitten" (quoted in Cady, 24).

It was the law in Hamilton during rabies season that all dogs be muzzled, and Howells remembered one small red dog that had been shot on account of his reporting it to the sheriff (BT, 138). If his father was right, even this seemingly harmless creature had been capable of inflicting a dreadful fate upon any boy foolish enough to go near it. Logically, even Tip, the gregarious family pet, was potentially an angel of death; and at about the same time as the Bowers incident, very likely in the same summer, Howells suffered one of his worst childhood traumas when he found himself with the dog in the woodshed, "where, one dreadful afternoon, when he had somehow been left alone in the house, he took it into his head that the family dog Tip was going mad" (BT, 15). Thereafter, as his brother remarked, "One of Will's most striking characteristics as a boy, was his mortal fear of dogs and hydrophobia. Once a dog snapped at him as he passed along the street, and though the bite was a very slight one it cost him years of anxiety."[3]

In his diary, on 10 March 1852, Will noted the disappearance of the second Tip, a frisky Newfoundland pup: "Mother thinks he has got the hydraphobia [sic]."[4] This conjecture seemed groundless to Howells in 1915, as he reviewed the old diary; but he recalled ruefully that, "as if to avenge Tip's fate," whatever it was, others of his kind had begun "an active persecution of the Diarist."[5] As Will had complained in another entry: "I do think, that wherever we live, my path is beset with perils, i.e. dogs. There are five, yes six separate, particular, and individual dogs that feel themselves called on to make me 'stir my stumps' every time I go up to work. It is working me up into a fit of desperation! I believe the next time they come at me, I'll, I'll————run!"

(p. 12). Although, as the boy rejoiced, an old Irishman was going to shoot his little pet, "so that that will be one less dog on my way" (p. 13), Will had occasion to test his new strategy. In summer, along the riverbank, another dog took after him and a cousin, "whereupon some tall running was 'did'" (p. 19).

II

Animal phobias are commonplace in normal childhoods, but Howells' fear was so persistent and intense that it must be regarded as a neurotic symptom. Indeed, as Howells' own account of his breakdown suggests, there was an underlying linkage between this childhood phobia and his "nervous prostration" at the age of seventeen. This linkage is strongly implied, for example, by one of his stories, published in the *Ashtabula Sentinel* in May 1854, when he was just on the verge of his collapse.[6]

"How I Lost a Wife" is an ostensibly comic tale in which the narrator, an elderly bachelor, tells how his youthful dreams were dashed and his entire life blighted by the malice of a Newfoundland dog. The point of the story is to justify the narrator's loathing of "the whole canine race"; and it opens with a diatribe that could have been copied from Howells' diary: "I am 'down' on dogs! I have the greatest possible antipathy to dogs of all breeds. — Your 'noble Newfoundland' . . . your faithful St. Bernard; your wiry-haired, active, rat-destroying Scotch terrier; your long legged, consumptive looking greyhound; your pug-tailed, pug-nosed, and very pugnacious bull-dog; your sickly looking and snarling poodle—all, individually and collectively, I abhor." Later, the narrator urges the formation of a "Dog-Exterminating Association."

The narrator hates dogs, as he goes on to explain, because a dog caused him to lose a beautiful maiden named Mary, whom he had hoped to wed. One summer day when he was courting her, the narrator decided to take a morning bath in a stream. Still rapt by a dream in which he had beheld Mary as an angel in Paradise, he shed his clothes on the riverbank and plunged in. Meanwhile, Ponto, a favorite of Mary and her girl friends, was stealing his pants. Even more distressing to the young man than his dread of embarrassment were the taunting antics of the dog. "Taking my fine cassimeres in his jaws, he would run towards me, as if in obedience to my call, but before he got half way to where I stood [stark naked], he would halt suddenly, snuff the earth, bark, and dart back again like lightning, carrying my pants in his jaws, tossing them high up in the air again, and catching them, shake them in a manner that appeared as if he really enjoyed the sport. —"

Covering himself as best he could in his hat, boots, and fashionably narrow coat (which "served only to hide a very small portion of my nudity"), the narrator hoped to catch the attention of his friend Charley and to be rescued before Mary could see him. Alas, Mary and her companions appeared first;

the narrator clambered up a tree to hide; the limb on which he was leaning snapped off, dropping him in the midst of the girls; Mary gazed for only a moment and then fled, shrieking like a locomotive whistle. To Charley it was all "a capital joke," but the narrator felt too mortified ever to face Mary again. Afterward, she married someone else, had several babies, and lived happily ever after. The narrator has pined his life away in vain remembrances of her "classic form" and "brilliantly black" eyes, fantasies which even now cause his "rather aged blood . . . to course more rapidly and warmly." But every "enchanting illusion" of Mary is soon dispelled by the "horrid image" of the detestable dog. "Don't you think my antipathy to the brutes is justly founded?" he asks at the end.

Even if we accept the preposterous *donnée* of the story, the answer to this question must be "no." The narrator's reaction to the whole affair and his subsequent hatred of dogs seem unaccountably strong; and it is the motivation for this emotional excess that claims attention to this otherwise forgettable piece of juvenilia. Like one of Poe's perfervid madmen, buttonholing the reader to argue the good sense of his irrational crimes, the narrator of "How I Lost a Wife" arouses distrust and points to darker motives than he consciously admits.[7] It seems that young Howells was projecting his own hysteria upon this narrator's, giving shape to the menacing shadows that were about to engulf him.

It does not take much effort to translate "How I Lost a Wife" into a psychosexual allegory; the symbolism is so plain as almost to obviate analysis. Its nakedness, in fact, suggests the power of Howells' unconscious fantasies at this time. Writing a "funny" story about his own phobia was the act of a vulnerable young man whistling in the dark. The narrator is Howells' adolescent self, displaced into the future; maiden Mary is his idealized, desexualized, but sexually alluring mother (also Mary); Ponto is his cruelly playful and interdicting father. Charley, who is Mary's brother, seems to represent brother Joe. The plot is a humiliating Oedipal drama of repressed desire for the mother, fear and loathing for the father. The snatched pants and the broken limb are images of castration: a decapitating capital joke at the narrator's expense. Having acted too cockily—as in wearing a narrow-tailed coat "in the height of fashion"—he is figuratively cut down to size. "How I Lost a Wife" implies that the breakdown that followed quickly upon its publication was rooted, like Howells' phobia, in Oedipal anxiety. This hypothesis is supported by a variety of evidence.

First, there is a passage in *Years of My Youth* in which Howells confesses an inability to remember "when fear first came into my life," but cites the "awe" inspired by the Bowers case as a "belated substitute for far earlier acquaintance with it." Howells recognizes here the substitutive nature of his phobia: that it was symbolic of primal fears obscured by childhood amnesia. He begins the same paragraph: "the experience of the specialized boy that I was cannot be distinctly recovered and cannot be given in any order of time; the events are like dreams in their achronic simultaneity" (*YMY*, 19). Often in his autobiographies, Howells stresses the phantasmal aura of childhood recollections; and the entire sequence of remembrances in this section of *Years of My Youth* follows the unconscious logic of dreams or free associations. The unconscious significance of the hydrophobia incident and its roots in "forgotten" primal fears may be glimpsed in the associative context of Howells' telling of it.

The "awe" of the Bowers case, Howells continues, "was not lessened by hearing my father tell my mother of the victim's saying: 'I have made my peace with God; you may call in the doctors.' I doubt if she relished the involuntary satire as he did; his humor, which made life easy for him, could not always have been a comfort to her" (*YMY*, 19). The awe inspired by hydrophobia, then, is associated with the awe—or, more precisely, the fear—aroused in Howells by his boyish perception of subtle conflicts between his parents, conflicts in which William Cooper was on the attack (using humor as a weapon) and in which Mary Dean was on the defensive. Howells offers next a clearer example of how his father's humor could discomfit his mother.

This "tragical effect" of William Cooper's "playfulness" is an occasion when Will, as a toddler, was incited by his father to play a practical joke on his mother: "my father held out to me behind his back a rose which I understood I was to throw at my mother and startle her." Unfortunately, when the rose struck her head, his mother mistook it for a bat. She whirled about, saw her son "offering to run away," and made him "suffer for her fright." She could not forgive Will at once; and the boy, whose love of her was "as passionate as the temper I had from her," ached with remorse (*YMY*, 20). Thinly concealed in this account is the boy's fear of his mother's explosive temper, which had impelled her to reject him angrily.

By the narrative logic of his own account, therefore, Howells' awe of hydrophobia is related to fear of his parents' conflicts, which in turn is related to fear of his mother's temper, which in turn is related to fear of her rejecting him. Howells' phobia, it seems, represented a dread of irretrievably losing his mother's love. This linkage of the phobia to fear of abandonment is also implied by Howells' account of the woodshed incident. Significantly, the boy "took it into his head" that Tip was rabid on a dreadful afternoon "when he had somehow been left alone in the house" (*BT*, 15). Similarly, when he later was bitten by a dog, his "terror was the greater because I happened to find myself alone in the house when I ran home" (*YMY*, 79).

But the rose-throwing incident had a happy ending: Howells goes on to recall how his mother later "stole up-stairs" to console the boy in his bed (*YMY*, 20). As if to reassure himself, Howells dwells fondly on his mother's devotion for half of the next paragraph, then modulates into memories of punishments received from his parents. This subject leads to an admonitory paragraph imploring parents never to strike their children. Then follows Howells' recollection of the day he wished his father dead.

The narrative placement of this incident, nearly adjacent to the "tragical" incident of the rose throwing, seems to imply an underlying connection between them. Again, this linkage is revealed by the unconscious logic of the associative chain. The positive face of Howells' fear of abandonment was his Oedipal desire for his mother. Recollection of his intimacy with her leads to thoughts of punishment by her and by his father, which leads to a self-protectively generalized statement on the evils of corporal punishment, and finally culminates in a memory of compensatory aggression toward his father.[8] Thus a second associative chain leads to another fear that was symbolized by Howells' phobia: dread of his father's wrath.

The linking of the phobia to Oedipal anxiety is further supported by Freud's studies of childhood neurosis, as in the cases of little Hans and the "wolf man."[9] Like Howells, Freud's patients exhibited a boyhood terror of animals: Hans of being bitten by a horse, the "wolf man" of being devoured by a wolf. "There can be no doubt," Freud generalized, "that the instinctual impulse which was repressed in both phobias was a hostile one against the father. One might say that that impulse had been repressed by the process of being transformed into its opposite. Instead of aggressiveness on the part of the subject towards his father, there appeared aggressiveness (in the shape of revenge) on the part of his father towards the subject."[10] But Freud also found that such phobias, simultaneously and to varying degrees, mask two other buried impulses: a tenderly passive attitude toward the father (a wish for incestuous homosexual union) and a tenderly active desire for the mother (a wish for incestuous heterosexual union). In the case of Hans, it was Oedipal anxiety that led the boy to renounce, by repressing it, his active desire for the mother. In the case of the "wolf man," who was more homosexual than Hans, it was also Oedipal anxiety that motivated the boy's repression of his passive wish to be loved sexually by the father.

Howells seems to have fallen between these extremes of a "positive" and an "inverted" Oedipus complex, but evidently closer to the first. More like Hans than the "wolf man," Howells showed an active heterosexual curiosity in childhood and became a heterosexual adult. Also like Hans, Howells was capable of expressing affection openly for his father, despite his ambivalence toward him. But like the "wolf man's," Howells' childhood psychosexuality sometimes took a "passive" form—most apparently in his male friendships.

In 1855, the year after the breakdown, Howells developed a "special comradeship" that resembled his close boyhood attachment to John Rorick (YMY, 88). Jim Williams, a compositor in his father's printshop, was a few years older than Will, but they met "in an equality of ambition and purpose"

(*I&E*, 31). They shared an enthusiasm for songs and literature, especially Cervantes and Shakespeare, whom they read to each other during long excursions in the woods. Although Will did not show his own poems to Jim, he otherwise kept from him "few of my vagaries in that region of hopes and fears where youth chiefly has its being" (*YMY*, 89). They grew close enough for Jim once to be "momentarily estranged from me, jealous in that world where we had our intimacy" (*YMY*, 88). Decades later Howells could still recall Jim's "strange" face—"very regular, very fine, and smooth as a girl's, with quaint blue eyes" (*I&E*, 31)—and his "challenging, somewhat mocking smile" (*YMY*, 90).

When Jim departed in 1856, Will replaced him with Harvey Green, with whom he felt "a warmth of affection such as I did not know for J. W., though he had so much greater charm for me, and in the communion of our minds I was so much more intimate with him" (*YMY*, 106).[11] Will also befriended a man of nearly three times his age, an eccentric English organ builder named Goodrich. A "rarely intelligent creature, and an artist in every fibre," he used to stretch his "long, tremulous hands" on the organ keys, throw back his "noble head," and lift his "sensitive face" in the rapture of his music (*MLP*, 73).[12] He also found rapture in reading Dickens; and, as with Jim Williams, Howells' friendship with Goodrich became inseparable from literary passion: "though I knew Dickens long before I knew his lover, I can scarcely think of one without thinking of the other" (*MLP*, 78).

It is very unlikely that there was overt homosexuality in any of these relationships; they are best described, in the nineteenth-century term, as "romantic friendships."[13] In his imaginary attachments to his literary idols, however, Howells gave freer rein to erotic impulses. As he asserted in *My Literary Passions* (1895), the title of which figures a sexual trope that dominates the book, the young writer must "form himself from time to time upon the different authors he is in love with," and his adoration will be "truly a passion passing the love of women" (*MLP*, 16). Howells recalled, for example, that to his younger self the paper and ink of a particular book published in Paris had been redolent of "a certain odor which was sweeter to me than the perfumes of Araby"; the look of its type "took me more than the glance of a girl, and I had a fever of longing to know the heart of the book, which was like a lover's passion" (*MLP*, 105).

In literature as in life, Howells remarked, "kissing goes by favor," and one "cannot quite account for one's passions in either" (*MLP*, 82). In adolescence his affection for any one of his beloved authors had tended to be brief, "not to say, fickle" (*MLP*, 102). But his most enduring passions took the form of spellbound submission to a powerful seducer. Reading book after book of Macaulay's essays was "like a long debauch" from which he emerged "with regret that it should ever end" (*MLP*, 87). Here was an author whom he could "dream of and dote upon," to whom he could offer his intimacy "in many an impassioned revery." But when the youth's "frenzy" for Macaulay had abated, he felt the "charm of quite different minds, as fully as if his had never enslaved me" (MLP, 88). After next giving his heart to Thackeray, Howells was "effectively his alone, as I have been the helpless and, as it were, hypnotized devotee of three or four others of the very great" (MLP, 102).

One of these was Tennyson, with whom he dwelt "in that sort of charmed intimacy . . . in which I could not presume nor he repel, and which I had enjoyed in turn with Cervantes and Shakespeare, without a snub from them." Howells "never ceased to adore Tennyson, though the rapture of the new convert could not last," and it faded "like the flush of any other passion" (MLP, 119). He found a deeper intimacy with another poet, Heine, whose "peculiar genius" provided a liberating domination; "for if he chained me to himself he freed me from all other bondage" (MLP, 128). When a friend pointed out that Heine had derived some of his literary tricks from Sterne, Howells was galled, "as if he had shown that some mistress of my soul had studied her graces from another girl, and that it was not all her own hair that she wore." Long after he had ceased to idolize him, Howells still felt a tenderness for Heine that was "not a reasoned love" (MLP, 141–42).

In My Literary Passions, such erotic fantasies seem to jar against Howells' denunciations of "literary filth" (see Chapter 1); but his passion and disgust may be seen to fit together as the Janus faces of a homosexual desire through which, as Freud said, every boy must pass in his psychosexual development. The more a boy identifies himself with the mother (as love object of the father), the stronger is the "feminine" element in his adult gender identity.

As Alfred Habegger observes, Howells was "painfully double, both male and female"—a person who "lived on the boundary between woman's sphere and man's world" and who could not easily decide, either as a child or an adult, "whether he wanted to be a good boy at home or a bad boy with his peers." One of the major themes of A Boy's Town was "my boy's" divided self: his contradictory allegiances to the savage boy world and the civilized home world, to what Habegger sees as the masculine and feminine spheres of nineteenth-century American culture. Howells' choice of a literary life, "which promised to be at one and the same time a pleasant feminine pursuit and a public career," partly served as "an escape from both the threat of feminization and the pressures of normal masculinity." [14]

III

When Howells' childhood psychosexual conflicts were intensified by the onset of puberty, he suffered a series of neurotic attacks climaxed by his breakdown in 1854. In the early Freudian

nosology, Howells' was a case of "anxiety hysteria," the commonest of childhood neuroses and the one associated with phobias. Freud would likely have
concurred with Howells' own suggestion of a linkage between his phobia and
his adolescent breakdown.[15] This connection will become clearer as I trace
another strand of his childhood psychosexuality: his fear of death, specifically
his terror of dying at the age of sixteen.

Howells was obsessed by death throughout early childhood, and at the age
of nine or ten, he had a presentiment that he would die at sixteen. "The perverse fear sank deep into his soul, and became an increasing torture till he
passed his sixteenth birthday and entered upon the year in which he had appointed himself to die." The agony then became too great for him to bear
alone, and "with shame he confessed his doom to his father." William Cooper
Howells, with his usual tact and wisdom, readily found a psychic remedy, telling his son, "'You are in your seventeenth year now. It is too late for you to die
at sixteen.'" (BT, 204).[16] And, according to Howells, "all the long-gathering
load of misery dropped from the boy's soul, and he was free once more."

So ends the typed version of the episode in the draft of A Boy's Town.
But before publication, Howells amended the passage (in longhand) as follows: ". . . and he <was free once more> lived till his seventeenth birthday
and <long> beyond it without <the least difficulty> ↑ further ↓ trouble"
(BT, TS, 385). Of course, he was prevaricating, and his revisions show
Howells trying to shade the untruth closer to the facts he was not prepared to
divulge in 1890. Then he added a final sentence in which he hinted at a psychological explanation of the breakdown he was concealing: "If he had
known that he would be in his seventeenth year as soon as he was sixteen, he
might have arranged his presentiment differently" (BT, 204).

Implicit here is the idea that the death fantasy, like the animal phobia, had
expressed young Howells' unconscious desire for punishment. Through the
fantasy, Howells turned upon himself Oedipal aggression toward the father,
thereby exacting upon himself the retribution he "deserved" for this aggression and for his rivalrous desire for the mother. Since he did not really want to
die, the boy compromised with his super-ego by deferring the execution of
sentence. In the fantasy, as in his animal phobia, the executioner was deper-
sonalized and made exterior to himself.

Like every neurotic symptom, Howells' phobia and his death fantasy were
partly adaptive. The symptom, as Freud explained, is "erected like a frontier
fortification against the anxiety." By establishing a dynamic equilibrium of
conflicting psychic forces, a phobia "is designed to avert a hysterical attack."[17] Howells used his phobia and his death fantasy to forestall the kind of
breakdown that finally overcame him in 1854, in which his defenses collapsed and his repressed wishes were converted into organic symptoms. Anxiety hysteria, that is, became hysteria.

Why the breakdown occurred just when it did must remain something of a mystery, but the timing had something to do, undoubtedly, with the expiration of Howells' self-imposed death warrant on his seventeenth birthday in March 1854. Although he claimed he had received a psychical pardon from his father the year before and had been freed from his anxiety, it seems unlikely that William Cooper's verbal sleight of hand had really dispelled the power of the death fantasy.[18] It had been too integral a part of Howells' defenses. Indeed, if he *had* known that he would be in his seventeenth year as soon as he was sixteen, he might have, almost certainly would have, arranged his presentiment differently.

Possibly, he did the next best thing: unconsciously, he clung to the old fantasy, waiting out the fatal year when he was sixteen (1853–54) to see what would happen, while seeking a means to make sure that something *would* happen to turn his father's pardon into merely a reprieve. This means was provided by the village doctor's remark about hydrophobia's working round in the system for "seven years or more" and then breaking out in a fatal attack. The remark fitted Howells' unconscious purposes by providing him a way to honor the spirit, if not the letter, of his original contract with his punishing super-ego, to die for his Oedipal sins at sixteen.[19] Howells unconsciously willed himself to die from hydrophobia when it became clear, after he had ceased to be sixteen on his seventeenth birthday, that no outside agency was going to enforce the sentence. He faithfully developed all the symptoms he "somehow" knew about, and waited for the end. All the while, he felt "so horribly afraid of dying" that, like Mark Twain's Emmeline Grangerford, he "could have composed an epitaph which would have moved others to tears for my untimely fate" (*MLP*, 115).

Hydrophobia not only suited Howells' timing, but its symptoms provided a perfect vehicle for his repressed desires. Freud discovered that every hysterical symptom reveals symbolically its hidden psychosexual origin. For Howells, "the subjective odor of smoke" expressed figuratively his unacknowledged sexual burning, and the "dreaded spasms" that he feared would come at the last (but never did) represented the wish for erotic release he was repressing. Simultaneously, the symptoms gave substance to Howells' sense of guilt by replicating the atmosphere of Swedenborg's hell for sexual sinners.

At the age of seventeen, Howells was burning with more than the repressed desires of childhood; he was suffering as well the usual torments of adolescent sexuality. Sometime before 1855, there had come to him "the radiant revelation of girlhood, and I had dwelt in the incredible paradise where we paired or were paired off each with some girl of his fancy or fancied fancy" (*YMY*, 90).

Howells never identified the earliest object of his adolescent fancy, but his pairing with her apparently came to a bad end. Sounding like the voice of experience, perhaps the same experience that had inspired "How I Lost a Wife," he later counseled his brother Johnny that young men should expect to fall in love and to be jilted at "about seventeen years of age." This was all to the good, Howells rationalized: "When you are much older, you will understand that the first object of one's affections is fearfully overrated, and is apt to be the most commonplace little creature in the world." Then he added, probably referring to himself, "I once knew a young man in Jefferson, who was thrown very high and had a very hard fall. It affected his mind for several years, and he thought that most if not all of his feelings were blighted. But he outlived the occurrence, and is now happily married, and extremely glad to have escaped the danger and the lady whom he once courted" (SL, 1:151).

At the time, however, Will had lacked perspective, and he had been hurt. How badly is implied in a letter to his female cousin Dune Dean in September 1857, in which he alluded bitterly to a "perfidious schoolmarm" who had recently married (SL, 1:12).[20] Later, in Columbus, Howells was pleased to discover that he was considered attractive by the sophisticated young women of the city, but his fitful romances in Jefferson must have caused him considerable frustration.

IV

The problems in Howells' life at seventeen were not exclusively psychosexual. As he said of his adolescent devotion to Tennyson: "It was a time of melancholy from ill-health, and of anxiety for the future in which I must make my own place in the world. . . . [A]nd I had many forebodings, which my adored poet helped me to transfigure to the substance of literature, or enabled me for the time to forget" (MLP, 122). Literature had been Howells' calling since childhood, and reading and writing were what pulled him through his adolescent crises and pointed him toward his adult career. Literature became both the means and the end of his psychic recovery.

Howells had learned as a child how to use books to mitigate emotional stress. When he was leaving Hamilton in 1849, "the parting was an anguish of bitter tears," relieved only by the exciting prospect of a journey by canal boat. But during the trip, which must after all have brought him more grief than joy, the boy kept his nose in a book, "aware of the landscape only from time to time when he lifted his eyes from the story he was reading" (BT, 239–40). Later he clung to Don Quixote as a rock of security during his first bout of homesickness (MLP, 20–21). In Ashtabula in 1852, young Howells studied in a room in which a former inmate of the house had supposedly hanged himself. "I do not know to this day whether it was true or not," he later reflected. "The doubt did not prevent him from dangling at the door-post, in my consciousness, and many a time I shunned the sight of this problematical suicide by keeping my eyes fastened on the book before me. It was a very simple device, but perfectly effective" (*MLP*, 51).

The device worked again in 1854. Howells tried several ways to ease the grip of his hypochondriacal fears, including therapeutic tramps in the woods and a kind of talking cure administered by his father. But nothing helped any better than reading novels "where the strong plot befriended me and formed a partial refuge" (*YMY*, 80). Dickens was particularly potent medicine: "I devoured his books one after another as fast as I could read them. I plunged from the heart of one to another, so as to leave myself no chance for the horrors that beset me" (*MLP*, 71). Later, immersing himself in Tennyson had an equally tonic effect; Howells never read any other poet "so closely and continuously, or read myself so much into and out of his verse" (*MLP*, 117).

Even when he was not under unusual stress, Howells sometimes used reading simply to escape, as he said, "to take my mind away from unhappy or harassing thoughts" (*MLP*, 113). But the compulsive reading he did in 1854 and 1855 was something more complex: a desperate act of self-preservation. Howells used the "strong" plots to supply vicarious defenses by which he might ward off, or at least endure, the debilitating anxiety of his real life. Dickens and Tennyson truly "befriended" him by becoming his psychological allies.

This process of borrowing strength from literature was part of a survival tactic, which Howells described in *Years of My Youth*: "In self-defense I learnt to practise a psychological juggle; I came to deal with my own state of mind as another would deal with it, and to combat my fears as if they were alien" (*YMY*, 81). He worked this juggle at first through reading, by identifying himself with the characters of other writers and learning to understand his own state of mind by simultaneously observing and "living" theirs. Later he practiced the juggle by writing himself, in the senses both of making up his own poems and stories and of projecting his most dangerous conflicts into them. Thus, although writing was a means of psychical self-defense for Howells, it also involved great emotional risks. There was always the possibility that his unconscious impulses would break through, as they had in 1854, and trigger a collapse. What Howells needed to keep "alien" might then become overwhelmingly familiar—almost in the spiritistic sense, in that Howells' writing might serve as the medium to his own "familiars," the suppressed phantasms that were threatening to possess his being.

As Howells and other nineteenth-century Americans used the word, "juggle" meant "to practice artifice or imposture" and, more specifically, "to play tricks by slight [sic] of hand; to amuse and make sport by tricks, which make a false show of extraordinary powers."[21] The psychological juggle, in effect, was a kind of self-trickery—a sleight of mind, a false show of extraordinary will power—and its efficacy depended upon Howells' preserving a safe emotional distance between his conscious thoughts and his unconscious impulses.

What might happen if he did not is suggested by the serial novel he wrote in the late fall of 1854. "The Independent Candidate: A Story of To Day," Howells' first extended work of fiction, was a botch. "My material gave out; incidents failed me; the characters wavered and threatened to perish on my hands," he recalled. "Somehow I managed to bring the wretched thing to a close, and to live it slowly into the past" (MLP, 67).

Howells had extemporized the novel at the typecase, setting it up as he thought it out. The first three weekly installments came easily enough, but inspiration flagged for the fourth, and he was forced to skip a week. He never regained his composure. The novel limped through several more installments while Howells frantically tried to put it and himself out of misery. "Every week I resolved that that story should be finished in the next week's paper; every week it refused to be finished" (INT, 42). Finally, making only a feeble pretense of tying up the loose ends, he just stopped.[22] This "really terrible" experience filled Howells with "shame and anguish." He compared it to "some dreadful dream one has of finding one's self in battle without the courage needed to carry one creditably through the action, or on the stage unprepared by study of the part which one is to appear in" (MLP, 67). He was so demoralized that he made up his mind that he "could not invent" (INT, 42), and he did not publish another story for nearly four years.

Why did Howells suffer so deeply over a failure that was not really so disastrous as he later made it sound? After all, "The Independent Candidate" had its points: flashes of wit, a few sharply drawn characters, some well-wrought descriptive passages, not far in style from his mature work.[23] A more resilient youth might well have shrugged the experience with a laugh; but like the narrator of "How I Lost a Wife," Howells was in no state of mind to enjoy a capital joke at his own expense. Writing the serial novel was a test of his psychic strength; Howells wished to discover just how badly he had been damaged by his breakdown and his temporary slackening of literary activity.

He was also practicing his psychological juggle, as becomes clear toward the end, in his making one major character a victim of hereditary insanity. One of the best things in the novel, in fact, is this portrait of George Berson, cracking under pressure and dissolving into madness. Into Berson, Howells was projecting one of the fears that must have tormented him the previous summer: that he would go insane.[24]

Howells' identification with Berson probably caused most of his problems with "The Independent Candidate." By bringing this character to life, Howells risked reviving his own psychic distress; for he could animate George Berson only by shortening the protective narrative distance he had maintained toward the other characters. By attempting too soon after his breakdown to make fiction from his own experience, Howells lost his imaginative grip. Writing the novel became a nightmare because it released unconscious fears that felt too threateningly close to be treated "as if they were alien." Howells' difficulties with "The Independent Candidate" foreshadowed his profounder problems in writing A Modern Instance. In both novels, Howells immersed himself so far into the destructive element that his psychological juggle failed to protect him.

Despite his discouragement after "The Independent Candidate," Howells never seriously considered forsaking his literary ambitions. His vocation was strengthened, in fact, by his brief dalliance, in May 1855, with an alternative career. Howells came to an agreement with his father that he would leave the printshop and study law with Senator Benjamin Franklin Wade, who kept a summer office in Jefferson. The idea was not only for the young man to fit himself for a new profession, but to earn some money in the process through "a season of pettifogging before justices of the peace, which I looked forward to with no small shrinking of my shy spirit" (MLP, 93). Although it had been mainly his own idea to study law, Howells proved to be no more committed than the erstwhile law student Bartley Hubbard. From the start Howells was half-consciously seeking a reason to change his mind; and he quickly found one: a passage in Blackstone, in which the jurist confessed "his own original preference for literature, and his perception that the law was 'a jealous mistress,' who would suffer no rival in his [sic] affections." Within a month Will concluded that he must give up either law or literature, and his "whole being turned from the 'jealous mistress' to the high-minded muses" (MLP, 93–94).

What is surprising is not that Howells' literary passions prevailed but that he had flirted with law in the first place. The whole incident makes sense, however, in light of Erik H. Erikson's notions of adolescent development. Although Howells' breakdown had its psychosexual and defensive aspects, it may also be regarded, in Erikson's term, as part of an "identity crisis": a psychic attack that "occurs in that period of the life cycle when each youth must forge for himself some central perspective and direction, some working unity, out of the effective remnants of his childhood and the hopes of his anticipated adulthood; he must detect some meaningful resemblance between what he has come to see in himself and what his sharpened awareness tells him others judge and expect him to be." [25]

Howells had come to see in himself the makings of a writer, but his confidence had been shaken by the fiasco of "The Independent Candidate." He was prepared to think, in early 1855, that his future lay in another direction, and he was encouraged in this belief by his sense of his neighbors' opinions. What the people of Jefferson expected him to be is implicit in his account of their reaction to his leaving Wade's office—or, more precisely, in his fantasy of their reaction. Because the village was so egalitarian, Howells "could have suffered no slight in the general esteem for giving up a profession and going back to a trade [i.e., printing]; if I was despised at all it was because I had thrown away the chance of material advancement; I dare say some people thought I was a fool to do that" (*MLP*, 95).

Howells afterward felt himself to be a fool, especially in the presence of Senator Wade, who came in his mind to represent the village at large. Will shrank from telling Wade his true motives: "Probably he would not have understood my forsaking the law, and I evaded the explanation he once sought of me when we met in the street, dreading the contempt which I might well have fancied in him" (*YMY*, 94). The contempt, if it existed, would have arisen from Wade's opinion that Howells "had chosen a path in life, which if it did not lead to the Poor House was at least no way to the White House" (*MLP*, 94).[26]

As Erikson suggests, the adolescent's conflict between "devotion" (commitment to a possible true identity) and "repudiation" (rejection of false identities) is resolved by a quasi-religious experience. The adolescent adopts an "ideology." As Erikson defines it, "ideology" is at the most "a militant system with uniformed members and uniform goals; at the least it is a 'way of life' . . . a world-view which is consonant with existing theory, available knowledge, and common sense, and yet is significantly more: an utopian outlook, a cosmic mood, or a doctrinal logic, all shared as self-evident beyond any need for demonstration" (p. 41). "Ideology" resembles a code of religious beliefs, and the adolescent embraces it with the zeal of a convert.

Howells' youthful "ideology" consisted, as Lewis P. Simpson puts it, of "idealizing the vocation of the American man of letters, feeling a sacerdotal obligation to represent the literary life as a transcendent, redeeming spiritual order." He imbibed this ideal from what Simpson calls the New England clerisy, a group of Bostonian writers and intellectuals who had brought to fruition during the early nineteenth century "a functional association between 'liberal Christianity' and the humanistic ethos."[27] Once converted to its "ideology," which he made over into his own "theology of realism,"[28] Howells rose quickly through the orders of the New England clerisy: novice (literary autodidact), deacon (initiate during his 1860 pilgrimage to Boston), priest (James T. Fields's assistant on the *Atlantic*), and bishop (editor of the *Atlantic*).

In 1855, such a career still lay beyond the most feverish dreams of a young man whose literary ambitions were "so strong that my veins might well have run ink rather than blood" (*LFA*, 8). More immediate was Howells' struggle to take his first step from his father's printshop into the literary world. Although he had published a few sketches, translations, and poems in the *Sentinel* and other Ohio newspapers, he longed to expand his range and enlarge his reputation. But his first attempt to publish a book was a failure; J. P. Jewett and Company, the Cleveland publisher, showed no interest in his proposed translation of *Lazarillo de Tormes* in the fall of 1855. Then in December, William Cooper Howells was appointed clerk of the Ohio legislature; and when he went to Columbus for the session of 1856, he left Will and Joe in charge of the *Sentinel*, a full-time responsibility. Will must have wondered if he would ever escape the printshop. Joe himself had tried to do so in 1851, but after a few months as a cub pilot for his Dean uncles, he had returned home for good. Will's chance had seemingly passed in the summer of 1855, when, after he had quit the law office, he had been forced to decline an admiring neighbor's offer to put him through Harvard. Even the local academy was beyond his reach. Will might have been spared from the printshop for the law, since that would have earned him enough to hire a replacement. But his labor, "which was worth as much as a journeyman compositor's, could not have been otherwise spared; much less could my father have afforded the expense of my schooling; and I cannot recall that I thought it an unjust hardship when it was decided after due family counsel that I could not be sent to an academy in a neighboring village" (*YMY*, 97–98).[29]

Unjust or not, Howells still felt the hardship. But deeper than his regret of lost opportunities was his guilt for feeling regret. Although he tried to fight it in himself, he could not suppress a book-bred sense of his superiority. "My convictions were all democratic, but at heart I am afraid I was a snob, and was unworthy of the honest work which I ought to have felt it an honor to do; this, whatever we falsely pretend to the contrary, is the frame of every one who aspires beyond the work of his hands" (*MLP*, 95–96).

Howells was discovering that a literary vocation would require him to strive "away from his home and the things of it." Rebellion and its concomitant guilt were the price of adult identity. Any ambitious youth, Howells generalized, "will be many times ridiculous and sometimes contemptible, he will be mean and selfish upon occasion; but he can scarcely otherwise be a man; the great matter for him is to keep some place in his soul where he shall be ashamed" (*YMY*, 110). When a chance to rise up from Jefferson finally came in the fall of 1856, Howells seized it, but he was also seized by a hidden shame that betrayed itself in continuing psychic attacks. Long after he left the village behind, Howells had not escaped it entirely. For Jefferson, too, Howells kept some place in his soul.

CHAPTER THREE
UP FROM
JEFFERSON

When William Cooper Howells returned to Columbus in the fall of 1856, he was accompanied by his son Will and his daughter Victoria. Since the departure of Jim Williams, Will had "grown more and more into intellectual companionship" with his sister, who alone of the family had penetrated his "ungracious reserves" about his literary aspirations. Sharing a "discontent with the village limit" of their lives, they had fantasied an expansion into a "great world of wealth, of fashion, of haughtily and dazzlingly, blindingly brilliant society, which we did not inconveniently consider we were altogether unfit for" (YMY, 106–7). Columbus could never have matched such expectations, but it possessed infinitely more dazzle and sophistication than Jefferson, and it offered Will at least a foothold in the "great world."[1]

At the same time he was serving as legislative secretary, William Cooper Howells planned to gather material for the newsletters he had been commissioned to write for the *Cincinnati Gazette*. In fact, most of the articles that appeared during the winter of 1856–57 were written by his nineteen-year-old son whose youth and inexperience were masked by his precociously urbane style. Ironically, the letters from Columbus by this refugee from the village were signed "Jeffersonian." The editor of the *Gazette* was so delighted with the results of the Howellses' collaboration that he offered Will the job of city editor, and the youth went off on his own to Cincinnati.

Within two months, however, he was back in Jefferson, having quit his editor's desk for the familiar printshop. What had sent him running home, he later admitted, "might have been the necessity of my morbid nerves to save themselves from abhorrent contacts" (YMY, 122). With a longing for "the cleanly respectabilities," Howells had not been able to abide the seamy realities that were a city editor's stock in trade. Everything would have been fine if his work could have been limited to "the reporting of sermons, with intervals of sketching the graduation ceremonies of young ladies' seminaries" (YMY, 123). But his job often took him to the police station, where he was horrified once by the obscene ravings of a drunken woman, and it forced upon him some distasteful compromises, as when he complied in suppressing an exposé of the sexual indiscretions of a locally prominent man.

Howells began to see corruption everywhere he looked. Where he usually ate lunch, he was scandalized by the presence of shopgirls and female clerks: "I was so altogether ignorant of life, that I thought shame of them to be boldly showing themselves in such a public place as a restaurant. I wonder what they would have thought, poor, blameless dears, of the misgivings in the soul of the censorious youth as he sat stealing glances of injurious conjecture at them" (*YMY*, 123). The censorious youth of twenty, like the boy of twelve who had persecuted Ann Stepmeyer, was projecting upon women his own guilty sexual disgust.

I

Howells had not fully recovered from his first breakdown, and he was about to suffer another, milder one. Throughout his brief stay in Cincinnati, he had been plagued by his "old malady of homesickness" (*MLP*, 125); and in the summer of 1857, he took ill with "rheumatic fever"—an attack, as he told Harvey Green, that "racked my joints till I was almost crazy. . . . [M]y right arm was so full of pain and so stiff that I could not handle my knife and fork deftly, let alone a pen" (*SL*, 1:15). By October the pain had ceased, but Will was still feeling depressed, having fed his melancholy all summer with a steady diet of Heine. He was more than ready to accept an invitation from the *Gazette* to resume his old position as legislative correspondent.

In January 1858, soon after he had resettled in Columbus, Howells awoke one morning to find the room going round him like a wheel: "It was the beginning of a vertigo which lasted for six months, and which I began to fight with various devices and must yield to at last. I tried medicine and exercise, but it was useless, and my father came to take my letters off my hands while I gave myself some ineffectual respites" (*MLP*, 133). Under medical advice, Howells resigned his post and returned to Jefferson. He set off in early May on a therapeutic river cruise aboard his uncle's steamboat, and he recuperated the rest of the summer at home, again taking a cure of long walks and reading.

This time, he immersed himself in Longfellow and De Quincey, in whom he found "a deep sympathy with certain morbid moods and experiences so like my own" (*MLP*, 131). The most effective remedy, however, was Theodore Mügge's novel *Afraja*: "There was a supreme moment when he [the protagonist] was sailing through the fiords, and finding himself apparently locked in by their mountain walls without sign or hope of escape, but somehow always escaping by some unimagined channel, and keeping on. The lesson for

him was one of trust and courage; and I, who seemed to be then shut in upon a mountain-walled fiord without inlet or outlet, took the lesson home and promised myself not to lose heart again" (*MLP*, 135–36).[2]

Like William James in his nervous collapse of 1870, Howells willed himself to recover. By the fall of 1858, he felt sound enough to accept a position on the *Ohio State Journal* that was virtually identical to the one he had abandoned in Cincinnati. Howells hoped that "in the smaller city the duties would not be so odious or so onerous." At least his new chief shared Howells' "preference of decency." Henry D. Cooke scolded his young assistant soon after his arrival for a "too graphic paragraph" he had written about a murderously jealous husband. "'Never, *never* write anything you would be ashamed to read to a woman,'" Cooke admonished him; and Howells later made the advice the watchword for his fiction (*YMY*, 125–26).

For now Howells regarded himself as a poet-journalist, and he was equally happy in either role. In retrospect he considered this time in Columbus, when he was "finding opportunity and recognition," as "the heydey of life for me . . . for then I was in the blossom of my youth, and what I had not I could hope for without unreason, for I had so much of that which I had most desired" (*MLP*, 146). First, he had a challenging job that stimulated his imagination and brought him into contact with other young men who shared his quasi-collegiate boardinghouse life and his literary idealism.

Second, Howells had the kind of social success he had always dreamed of. He was introduced into exclusive Columbus circles by no less than the governor's daughter, who twitted him affectionately for his shyness on and off the dance floor. Another woman who had known him in Columbus recalled that Howells had been "exceedingly self-depreciatory in his youth," lacking "that confidence in himself which his friends thought his ability warranted." In fact, his "ready wit and brilliant conversational powers made him a welcome visitor everywhere."[3] Howells was especially welcome in the homes of two older women, Mrs. Francis Carter and Mrs. Samuel Smith, who prized him as an addition to their Ohioan salons. "I like women best, who are older than myself," he told Vic (*SL*, 1:31); and he later cherished his memories of Columbus "because they seem so full of honor and worship for the girlhood and womanhood which consecrate it in my remembrance" (*YMY*, 157).

Finally, Howells had increasing confirmation that he was becoming a successful writer. During 1859, his poems were appearing not only in local newspapers but in the *Saturday Press*, the organ of the New York literary avant-garde that included Henry Clapp (the self-proclaimed "King of Bohemia"), E. C. Stedman, T. B. Aldrich, William Winter, and Walt Whitman. After he had visited New York in 1860, Howells was to develop a strong distaste for the *Saturday Press*, whose literary airs were to become indistinguishable in his mind from the beery fumes of Pfaff's cellar bar, where Clapp and his court had made him feel completely out of place. But from the distance of Columbus, appearing in the *Saturday Press* had seemed second in importance only to appearing in the *Atlantic Monthly*; and even this recognition came to Howells in July 1859, when James Russell Lowell accepted "Andenken." During the rest of the year, while he and J. J. Piatt were preparing their *Poems of Two Friends* for publication, each issue of the *Atlantic* brought fresh disappointment to Howells when he failed to find himself in it. What he did not know was that Lowell had put "Andenken" aside until he could verify that it was not a translation of Heine—so close was Howells' poetry to being a plagiarism of his current idol's. The poem finally appeared in January 1860, and it was followed by four others the same year.

Howells' anxiety over "Andenken" was compounded by two other worries in 1859. One was the deteriorating financial condition of the *Ohio State Journal*, which finally led to his losing his job in May 1860. The other was the recurrence of his neurotic symptoms.

The year had begun calmly enough. "I dream almost every night something about home," Will wrote to Vic soon after his arrival in Columbus. "But so long as I continue to improve in health, I shall not be homesick" (*SL*, 1:20). In February 1859, however, he reported that he had been "more or less depressed all day" (*SL*, 1:24), and in his journal he wrote in April that he had had "a regular turn of 'hippo,' being nervous I think from drinking coffee at supper" (*SL*, 1:31). Although his letters home that spring were full of high-spirited news of his party going, flirtations, and busyness at the *Journal*, Howells was gradually losing control. He wrote to Joe on 14 August: "For two months, my familiar devil, Hypochondria, had tormented me, so that I sometimes thought that death would be a relief. Yesterday, I could bear it no longer, and went [to] Dr. Smith, telling him my trouble, and receiving for answer that there was nothing the matter with me" (*SL*, 1:40). Dr. Samuel Smith, married to one of Howells' older woman friends, was to see him "through the many maladies, real and unreal," of his late adolescence: "it was as if he became another father to me" (*YMY*, 144).

II

No one could replace Howells' mother. He wrote to her in August that he was out of bed and feeling better and expecting to return to work. Then he added: "With convalescence comes intolerable gnawing and longing for home. I sit in my lonesome room all day, and read, and look warily at the tree-tops and chimneys. The Prospect is charming but I think I would be more pleasantly occupied in lounging on the settee in our little 'oak(paper) chamber,' reading choice scraps of Dickens to you and Vic."[4] Despite these nostalgic sentiments, Howells chose *not* to recuperate in Jefferson, and he battled his familiar devil by himself.

The underlying cause of his "hippo" was Howells' acute ambivalence about separating himself from his family. Throughout 1859, as his letters to Jefferson reveal, Howells felt a pull between the old claims of the family and the new claims of his adult independence, a pull between homesickness and rebellion. Quite typical was his letter to Mary Dean Howells on 24 May 1859, in which he began by denying his neglect of the family and ended by justifying it:

> I would have written promptly in reply to all your letters, but I was keeping a journal for Vic, and tho't that would suffice for the whole family. You mustn't think me neglectful, mother? It is of you I think most, whoever I write to. Last night I took a walk with Comly, and told him how I knew you were sitting upon our little front porch, and counting up the days until I should be with you. I tell you, it seems a long time since I saw you, and I can hardly wait, now, that the time of meeting again is so near. . . .
>
> I have heard nothing from Sam yet, though he promised to write to me from Hamilton. I can't imagine what is the reason. —When he was here, he told me that some of you, Joe particularly, thought I ought to send money home occasionally, help pay for the house, etc. Now, mother, I had better have left off this explanation until I saw you, but the suspicion that you tho't me perhaps neglectful of my duty, has been rankling ever since Sam told me this. I have never failed to send you money whenever you asked for it; and I have certainly wanted to do everything for you. But you know what a slender salary mine is; and I have to meet many expenses here that you don't know of. I live more frugally than any other young fellow of my acquaintance, and I aim to economise all the time, but it is a continual struggle with me to save anything. I must dress well—I can't go about the city streets looking as shabbily as Joe does at home. . . . Clothes cost more here than in the country. (*SL*, 1:38–39)

How shrewdly Howells appealed to his mother: assuring her of his constant devotion in thought and word, comparing his family loyalty invidiously to that of his brother Sam, playing to her dread of shabbiness and her pride in him, reminding her of his superior knowledge of city ways. Howells intended no duplicity in this letter, and his own needs were real enough. Nonetheless he was unconsciously manipulative in a way that suggests his underlying conflicts about home and mother.

Will could not resist a jab at his brothers Sam and Joe with whom relations had always been touchy; but so far as he felt justified in resenting their insinuations, Will could ignore them.[5] He could not so easily dismiss the subtler recriminations of Vic, with whom he had once shared his dreams. Will kept a journal just for her, so that she might taste his freedom vicariously. But clearly she expected more from him. With unwitting cruelty he reminded her of the days when they had "comforted each other in our hard task of making bricks without straw for those Jefferson Egyptians," and he resolved some day "to rescue my kindred out of the bondage" (SL, 1:21). Vic must have taken this figure of speech more literally than Will had ever intended, for he was compelled a month later to dampen the hopes he had raised, giving Vic elaborate reasons—of the same sort he had rejected himself—why she should see the "silver lining" in her Jefferson cloud (SL, 1:24–25). Painfully conscious of the depth of Vic's misery in Jefferson, and yet helpless (and, finally, unwilling) to rescue her, Howells guiltily counseled her to resignation.

In a letter to Vic in March 1859, he combined protestations of his devotion with hints of his resentment of the need to make them, and even to write:

> You don't know how much I am denying myself for your sake. This is one of the divinest days. . . .
>
> You can guess how much I long to be out every moment—but you can't rightly estimate the sacrifice after all.
>
> I know well enough what you and the other dear "grils" are doing this morning—and of you "my eyes make pictures when they're shut." I am so glad to think I have such sisters to love; and every day's separation endears you to me more and more. I see no other girls whom I think half so good and wise as you. . . .
>
> I have been to so many places, and had so many adventures, socially speaking. . . . Mrs Carter took me to Mr J. W. Andrews, where I attended the pleasantest sort of a party, and spent the whole evening in talking with Miss Lallie Swain. She is so intelligent and sprightly. . . . Do you remember her? I think you used to go to school together, but I don't recollect. (SL, 1:28)

Feigning to miss life in Jefferson, Howells was revealing just the opposite. Insisting that he preferred Vic's country innocence to the allure of city girls, he could not help giving Vic reason to disbelieve him and to envy Lallie Swain's advantages.

In all these letters home, the pattern was essentially the same: Howells tried to honor his family commitments at the same time he asserted, in various ways, his independence from the family. As his sense of independence grew stronger, his expressions of caring sounded more and more insincere and his burden of guilt mounted. Guilt arose both from not feeling all the tenderness and regret he "should" have felt and from feeling anger, turned upon himself, for having to pretend otherwise.

Repressed anger and guilt, then, underlay Howells' hypochondriacal relapses. It is no coincidence that his attack in the summer of 1859 followed upon a visit to Jefferson—a visit on which he brought along his Columbus friend James Comly as if to present his family with a symbol of his new attachments and to remind himself reassuringly of his life without the old ones. Independence meant loneliness as well as guilt. At a time of rapid change, when he needed the emotional support his family could have provided, Howells did not turn to them as before, both because he needed to reduce his dependence on them and because they could not fully understand problems of his that were increasingly different from theirs.

In *Years of My Youth*, Howells generalized that the period of finding one's way into manhood "is a space of blind struggle, relieved by moments of rest and shot with gleams of light, when the youth, if he is fortunate, gathers some inspiration for a worthier future" (YMY, 153). Howells was a fortunate youth, and the inspiration for a worthier future sustained him as he removed himself by increasingly larger steps from the psychological sphere of his family. In 1860, he took the first of these steps when, as a traveling correspondent to the *Cincinnati Gazette*, he made his pilgrimage to the literary shrines of New England.

So much has been written about Howells' famous journey to the East—his ordination by Lowell and Holmes into the "apostolic succession" of the New England clerisy; his subsequent visits to Fields, Hawthorne, Thoreau, and Emerson; his encounter with Whitman in New York—that there is need to discuss only one aspect that has generally passed notice: namely, that Howells brought his psychic infirmities with him. Just a few weeks before his departure, Howells told his family, "As the summer approaches, I begin to feel touches of hypochondria, but I hope not to go crazy" (SL, 1:55). He had been under constant pressure that spring from the insecurity of his job and from the labor of rushing out his campaign biography of Abraham Lincoln. He was also still tormented by the anxiety of separation. Anticipating his visit to Jefferson on his way east, Will confided to Joe: "It seems to me that I am growing away from whatever was gentle and good in the influences of my life. Sometimes I shudder to think how nearly beyond them I am; and I believe if I can be with you all a few weeks, I shall renew and better myself. I *do* nothing bad, I hope, but my habit of thought is harsh and skeptical, and I am the victim of an *ennui* which I cannot escape" (SL, 1:56).

The ennui was succeeded by an attack of vertigo when Howells reached Niagara Falls in July. The cataract itself dumbfounded him, and he was equally impressed by the death-defying feats of the French acrobat Blondin. Before watching him cross above Niagara on a rope, Howells had wondered perversely if he "might have the fortune to see him drop in."[6] Several times in his travel letters, he mentioned that the falls evoked a mad impulse to jump.

He was alluding to a shocking experience he chose to conceal from his readers in 1860. In 1893, however, he told of having seen the decomposed body of a man who had jumped or fallen from the Table Rock on the Canadian side of the falls: "He was a very green and yellow melancholy of a man, as to his face, and in his workman's blue overalls he had a trick of swimming upwards to the eye of the aesthetic spectator, so that one had to push back with a hard clutch on the turf to keep from plunging over to meet him." In the same confessional essay, Howells divulged another detail he had suppressed in 1860. One day he had crossed the rapids by stepping stones to climb Terrapin Tower on the brink of the American falls. "What is so amusing now to think of, though not so amusing then, is that all the while I was clambering about those heights and brinks, I was suffering from an inveterate vertigo, which made plain ground rather difficult for me at times. At odd moments it became necessary for me to lay hold of something and stay the reeling world; and the recurrence of these exigencies finally decided me against venturing into the Cave of the Winds." [7]

It was with the corpse's face, his own suicidal impulses, and his vertigo attacks fresh in his mind that Howells arrived in Boston in 1860. Without his father or Dr. Smith to counsel him, he turned to the most avuncular of his new Brahmin friends, Dr. Oliver Wendell Holmes. They spoke of "the intimations of immortality, of the experiences of morbid youth, and of all those messages from the tremulous nerves which we take for prophecies." Howells was not ashamed to lay before Holmes's "tolerant wisdom" the psychic effects of his own "broken health and troubled spirit"; and he long remembered the exquisite tact with which Holmes recognized them "as things common to all, however peculiar in each, which left them mine for whatever obscure vanity I might have in them, and yet gave me the companionship of the whole race in their experience" (LFA, 42).

Perhaps Holmes's reassurance that nervous problems were "common to all" gave Howells courage once more to attempt a novel from experiences that were peculiarly his. Certainly he followed Holmes's literary example in the story he began in the fall of 1860. "Geoffrey: A Study of American Life"—or "Geoffrey Winter," as it has become known—resembled Holmes's *Elsie Venner* in its concern with morbid psychology. [8] As he was writing it, Howells found the novel to be "so frightfully analytical" that he sometimes thought it bore "the same relation to a romance, that an accurate print of the human heart would bear to the picture of a soul-illuminated face" (SL, 1:66).

III

The plot of "Geoffrey Winter" is easily summarized; for, as Howells suggested, more of the novel is given to psychological analysis than to narrative action. After an absence of seven years, which he has spent among sophisticated city friends, Geoffrey returns to his native Dulldale. He had fled the village in despair because he had failed to win the hand of his cousin Clara—here the story recalls "How I Lost a Wife"—and he is returning because he cannot resist seeing her again, now that she is a widow. But Geoffrey conceals his true motives from himself. "For was it not as much his unconscious desire that she should regret him, as it was his wish to behold her again, that had brought him to Dulldale?" (p. 12).[9]

At first, Clara seems as unattainable as before, but the sudden death of her mother, during the time of Geoffrey's visit, makes her vulnerable in her grief to his gentle goodness. They marry, for all the wrong reasons. Geoffrey, whose earlier desire has been strangled by bitter regret, feels only compassion and romantic nostalgia. "He loved no one else," he tells himself, "and she was dearer to him than all others, being, as she was, so lonely and helpless. At least they could be happy together? He reasoned briefly to the great error of his mistaken life, and as often happens with hesitating, undecided men, mistook his conclusion for a wise decision, simply because he had been able to reach it" (p. 48). Clara, who lacks "fine individual perceptions" (p. 62), projects upon Geoffrey an ideal of husbandly virtue he does not possess, and she loves him with a dangerous intensity.

As the years pass, the hollowness of the Winters' marriage grows painfully apparent to them. "These mistakes were in truth sad ones. Clara had learned too late for him that she had never loved any other, and Geoffrey in his yearning after a dead ideal had only allied himself to a woman who constantly reminded him of what she was no more. There was no butterfly in the chrysalis which he had gathered to his heart" (p. 97). Although Clara senses their "irreconcilable difference" (p. 63), she cherishes a vain hope that she can rekindle her husband's love. But Geoffrey's "natural introspective tendency" secludes him more and more; and when Clara does not "alienate him with affectations of indifference," she wearies him with "repentance and protestations of sorrow" (pp. 97–98). For relief, he dabbles in journalism and politics but finds no lasting satisfactions.

The only light in the Winters' bleak existence is the presence of Jane Grove, an impoverished waif they have taken in. Jane possesses the intellectual acuity and ironic sensibility that Clara lacks, and Geoffrey takes pleasure in tutoring the girl and in sharing with her a taste for literary subtleties that are lost upon Clara. Indeed, as Jane realizes, she and Geoffrey are much alike: "she felt the occult alliance of pain, and renunciation that bound them" (p. 128). This bond seems certain to draw them closer, perhaps into a love affair. But, as Howells hastens to assure us, this is an American novel about "people of a new civilization, purer and nobler than the old"; and their relationship, for all its erotic possibilities, is "quite innocent and commonplace" (p. 79).

Rather than fall in love with Geoffrey, whom she continues to admire as a manly paragon, Jane dreams of a storybook prince who, she hopes, will whisk her away to a life of idyllic domesticity. Repeating Clara's error, Jane projects her fantasy upon a man unworthy of it: Frank Walters, who is rich, clever, jaded, idle, and "selfish almost to egotheism" (p. 178). Bored by city life, Walters descends upon the Winters for a visit and decides, quite cynically, to divert himself by falling "'a little in love'" with Jane (p. 170). Before he jilts her, the affair provides Walters with a sadistic *frisson*: "He saw that she loved him truly and inscrutably, as women seem always to love—as much for what was bad and mean in him, as for what was good and great; and that her passion was a sorrow and not a joy. He saw all this with that strange and cruel delight in the ability to give pain to patient love, and yet be loved, which is the last excess and most exquisite sense of power" (pp. 179–80).

Jane, however, has always been prepared for her fate. Her harsh childhood has instilled in her a "habit of disappointment and pain" that darkens her every joy. She yields to the spell of her romantic dreams, but with a guilty awareness that they are "evil and wanton" and with a "dim fear" that future disaster will be the "recompense of the present dreamful delight" (p. 118/119). Unlike Geoffrey's or Clara's, Jane's romanticism is held in check. As a result she is more firmly grounded in reality than they are, and her adversity leads to spiritual growth. "Through passion she arrived not at greater power than she had possessed before, but at positive sense of it" (p. 203).

Clara too achieves limited growth at the end. Stricken by heart disease, she lies near death, "recalling the unthoughtful days of girlhood, and the doubts and confirmations of the doubts that revealed her to herself an unloved wife, bitterly remembering the slow waste of hours, that passed in lonesomeness and made the desert of her married years " (p. a-212). It suddenly occurs to her that after her death Geoffrey will probably marry Jane; and Clara rebels jealously against this injustice, determining to lay her fears of his treachery before her husband. But as she is about to speak, she feels overwhelmed by her love for him and his own faithful devotion (if not love) for her; the harsh words die in her heart as she dies in silence.

Clara's fears prove to be groundless; Geoffrey is incapable of marrying Jane because he has blinded himself to the subtle affinities between them. In fact, he vehemently denies it when Walters suggests, "'Perhaps you're something alike?'" (p. 163). From the start he has felt a superstitious dread of Jane— "one of those reasonless aversions which sometimes surprise us at the first encounter with certain faces" (p. 23). He once tells Walters that Jane "'is in fact so good I don't altogether like her'" (p. 162). Although he has softened slightly toward her, Geoffrey still harbors his aversion at the conclusion of the novel, which like so many endings in Howells' maturer work is left deliberately open.

Howells does not follow his characters beyond the time of Clara's death, but he speculates on their futures. Jane will "go forth into the world, and seek amid its new unfriendliness, the home which she has lost" (p. 224). It is possible, but most unlikely, that she and Geoffrey will achieve intimacy. In "Geoffrey Winter," as in his later novels, Howells employs a Swedenborgian theory of character formation: "Doubtless, men do not radically change in anything, and the seeming transformations of their lives are but the development of the principles that existed in the uncreate atoms of their being before the beginning" (p. 222/223). Thus Geoffrey is largely helpless to overcome his prejudice toward Jane. "The unreasonable aversion with which she first inspired Geoffrey, returns oftener and oftener to his brooding melancholy, and must grow with the growth of whatever else is mean and pitiful in him. . . . Shall we not then, make this antipathy to the only being who could truly have been his wife, a part of his remorseful memory of Clara, and in his weakness, cherish an error in regret for error?" (pp. 225–26). On this note of love thwarted by psychological barriers, Howells closes the novel.

"Geoffrey Winter," like many first novels, has interest for its adumbration of later artistic developments and for its autobiographical implications. But the novel is by no means without aesthetic merits of its own. Howells' drawing of the major characters is skillful and psychologically penetrating; and his rendering of small-town life, though lacking sufficient density, is nonetheless satirically effective. In the scene after Clara's mother's death, for example, Howells captures the morbid curiosity of the villagers who swarm through the house, assessing the worldly goods and even the person of the deceased. Upon seeing Mrs. Winters laid out, one neighbor declares "that it was the prettiest sight she ever saw; though she had once been known to award the distinction of supreme loveliness to a baby's corpse" (p. 30). There are also some memorable minor characters: the vulturine Miss Moore, chief of the Dulldale gossips; Mrs. Grove, the tragically brutalized victim of a "rude and clownish" husband (pp. 71–72); Mr. Rounce, the well-traveled printer with a stock of yarns and a rough-hewn integrity that resembles Kinney's in *A Modern Instance*.

Indeed in setting, theme, and character, "Geoffrey Winter" closely foreshadows *A Modern Instance*. Equity, Maine, is a more richly imagined Dulldale; the Hubbards' disastrous marriage is a variation on the Winters': in *A Modern Instance*, the neurotic and passionate woman (Marcia/Clara) marries the spoiled and selfish man (Bartley/Frank) instead of the melancholy and passive one (Ben/Geoffrey). This last pairing is especially suggestive, since Winter's character is fleshed out in some ways that Halleck's is not. Geoffrey serves as a gloss on Ben, especially in his psychological peculiarities. Both men are Hawthornean types of the self-absorbed idealist, literary descendants of Arthur Dimmesdale. Ben turns at the last to the ministry in order to avoid what he must regard as an unholy marriage to Marcia; Geoffrey, whose mar-

riage suggests what Ben's would have been, "might have fared well" as a "minister of religion" (p. 102).

Howells pleads at one point that Geoffrey's nature is "so wholly intro-
verted, that the attempt to bring his real character in contact with the world
would be a useless violence" (p. 40). But he manages to give some salient
details of Geoffrey's inner life. Geoffrey is superstitiously obsessive: "All of us,
I think, have known enough of this to recognize the morbid impulse which
would drive him from his bed at night to change the position of a book, and
so avert the unknown fearful consequences of suffering it to remain as he had
laid it down. He had outgrown much of this vagary, but often still the 'weird
seizures' came" (p. 35). Geoffrey is idealistic to the point of living in abstrac-
tions. His "yearning after the unattainable" (p. 101), his loving an ideal of a
woman more than any real woman, leads to his indifference toward Clara. He
is no less idealistic in his public activities: he "dealt somewhat abstractly with
political principles, and dreamed of a political career in which he would have
risen above party into individual honesty, and usefulness to a great cause"
(p. a-95).

Geoffrey, as a consequence of his solipsism, has difficulty differentiating his
inner world from the world outside. "He was like most sensitive people, and
could not well distinguish between the effect of a wrong done in thought and
a wrong done in act, and he always made eager amends in kindness for the
tacit injustice which had not been committed" (p. 70). Geoffrey is loath to
share the things he cherishes for fear of losing them. For example, he regrets
having initiated Jane and Clara's young daughter into a delight for nature:
"They were quick to learn, and yet it was with a subtle regret that he imparted
the secrets of this delight. He felt in making them known like one who shares
the acquaintance of his oldest and dearest friend with others. Was it for this
reason that he ceased to go with these [sic]—vexed in his fine selfishness that
any one should have these things as well as he?" (pp. 114–15).

Geoffrey's sweet kindness—"he had the gentleness of a woman" (p. 63)—is
more a matter of his social conditioning (what Howells was to call "implanted
goodness" in A Modern Instance) than willful virtue. Geoffrey's goodness is
"no part of his consciousness" and belongs "to that inheritance of goodness
bequeathed him by his mother" (p. 64). Although Howells insists on Winter's
essential decency and morality, he reveals him to be less than fully admirable.
There is something wintery about Geoffrey Winter. Like Hawthorne's villains
of rarefied intellectuality, he has lost saving contact with the magnetic chain
of humanity.

In psychoanalytic terms, Geoffrey is a narcissist, one whose love is directed
toward the *image* of himself and, thus, one who is not able to love another
person as "other," but only as a self-reflection. Geoffrey also suffers from what
Freud called the "narcissistic neurosis" of melancholia, of which he exhibits

most of the distinguishing features, including a tendency to convert unconscious revilings of the lost "other" into self-reproaches.[10] In Geoffrey's case,
the loss of Clara years before has rendered him incapable of loving anyone
else; instead he yearns "after the unattainable" (that is, identifies himself with
an image of what she should have been), and at the same time punishes Clara
for her abandonment of him by punishing this image of the unattainable
within himself. This self-punishment, insofar as it makes him an unloving
husband, accomplishes an indirect vengeance upon Clara. As Freud remarks:
"The self-tormenting in melancholia, which is without doubt enjoyable, signifies . . . a satisfaction of trends of sadism and hate"; melancholiacs usually
succeed, "by the circuitous path of self-punishment, in taking revenge on the
original object and in tormenting their loved one through their illness, having resorted to it in order to avoid the need to express their hostility to him
openly" (SE, 14:251).

Geoffrey's melancholia also explains his "unreasonable aversion" to Jane
Grove, whom, like Clara, he narcissistically identifies with himself. So far as
Jane is like him, he must punish what he unconsciously sees of himself in her,
all the while denying that he sees anything. His reviling Jane is another form
of Geoffrey's self-hatred. As Howells observes at the end, the inexorable logic
of Geoffrey's neurosis condemns him to a life of bitter isolation. The complex of
melancholia, as Freud says, "behaves like an open wound, drawing to itself
cathectic energies . . . from all directions, and emptying the ego until it is
totally impoverished" (SE, 14:253). In other words, the melancholiac com-
mits suicide of the ego—either, as Geoffrey does, by attrition, or, if his need
for punishment is strong enough, by a single act of self-destruction.

Geoffrey's melancholia, it seems clear, reflected Howells' own depression,
including intimations of suicide, during the year or more previous to his writing the novel. There was something of his father in the character of Geoffrey
Winter but more of himself. The negative side of Geoffrey was a projection of
Howells' worst self-image in 1860: a gnarly and narcissistic intellectual, out of
touch with the "real" world and incapable of love. Howells' sense of being a
selfish deserter of his family found fuller expression in his portrait of Frank
Walters, who prefigures the absconder Bartley Hubbard. Melancholia stems
from an unconscious loss of a loved one; for Howells this was his mother, by
whom he had unconsciously felt abandoned since early childhood and whom
he was abandoning now. There were obvious similarities between Clara
Winter and Mary Dean Howells: both women were trapped in a parochial
village life; both lacked intellectual sophistication and a sense of irony; both
were embittered by their husbands' failures to live up to their idealized expectations of them. If Clara represented Howells' tragic view of his mother, Jane
represented his more hopeful view of Vic: a woman who might endure loss
and still prosper spiritually.

IV

Howells understood that his melancholia, like Geoffrey's, was exacerbated by village life. The novel expressed Howells' fear that if he were ever to return to Jefferson, his life would become as barren as Geoffrey's. To escape was a matter of psychological survival, and "Geoffrey Winter" was part of that escape insofar as Howells used the writing of the novel to work through some of his emotional conflicts.

As "Geoffrey Winter" implies, Howells was preparing himself psychologically for a break with Jefferson/Dulldale; and during the winter of 1860–61, he was alert to any opportunities. Two dramatically different ones immediately presented themselves: marriage and war. For a time Howells chose neither; and when he finally did escape, it was by a different route altogether: his consular appointment to Venice. Once he was settled in Europe, well beyond his family's reach, he chose marriage at last, although his not choosing war haunted him for years.

Marriage first became a possibility with Howells' meeting of Elinor Mead during the winter of 1860–61.[11] Elinor was the well-bred daughter of well-placed Yankee parents. Her father, honorifically known as Squire Mead, was the first citizen of Brattleboro, Vermont. Her mother, Mary Noyes Mead, held a commensurately high social position, although some neighbors must have buzzed when they read of the exploits of her brother John Humphrey Noyes, the professional utopian and guru of the notorious Oneida Community. Elinor, her father's favorite, was one of nine children, and she grew up to be a cultivated young woman with a wide literary range and discriminating taste.

Dark-haired, light in coloring, very slight in build, Elinor had a squarish face and deeply set blue eyes that made her appear slightly forbidding in photographs. In fact, she was high strung, with a quick tongue and a nervously haughty manner that irritated some people. But not Will Howells, who was attracted by her keen intelligence and puritanical force of character. Her appeal, that is, was predominantly cerebral; she was more of a Jane Grove than a Clara Winter. As Kenneth S. Lynn remarks: "Instead of intimidating the sexually inexperienced Will Howells, this petite and wraithlike creature, just two months younger than Will, made him feel strong and protective; like the girl whom Mark Twain would marry, she did not pose an overwhelming threat to an uneasy suitor" (p. 103).

Elinor had a gayer side, however, which showed to advantage during the Columbus parties she attended with her Ohioan relatives. At one dance, also attended by J. Q. A. Ward, Elinor sketched on her fan a caricature of the young sculptor that delighted the victim and his friends, including Will Howells. By March 1861, their involvement had become so intense that

Howells joked about it uneasily to his sister Vic: "I presume, you have heard from father . . . of a violent flirtation which has been going on here this winter. Father is very curious about it, but masks his anxiety under a pretence that you girls would like to know" (SL, 1:76).

As the family began to realize how seriously Will was in love, his relationship with Elinor became a further complication in an already tangled emotional life. The more he and Elinor looked toward a possible future together, the more guilty Will felt about leaving his past behind. In the same letter to Vic in which he alluded to his flirtation, Howells dropped a more revealing hint of his feelings. "I am sure, when I think of the good, unselfish life you live, devoting yourself to poor little Henry," he told Vic, "I am quite ashamed of myself, and want to do something better than achieve reputation, and be admired of young ladies who read the 'Atlantic'" (SL, 1:76). Howells was alluding to an anecdote circulating in the capital about how Elinor Mead had been snobbishly amazed to find the *Atlantic* in her cousin's home, and how Laura Platt had retorted, "There are several contributors to the *Atlantic* in Columbus" (LinL, 1:24). That Will Howells was one of them surely impressed the young lady from Brattleboro. What right had he, Howells was asking himself, to be so carefree while Vic was so unhappy? How paltry his ambitions and even his love for Elinor appeared next to his sister's sacrificing devotion to her unfortunate brother. But Howells knew that punishing himself was merely a sop to his conscience. "I take myself quite sharply to task," he continued to Vic, "and go on being just as 'languid and base' as before" (SL, 1:76).

When Elinor departed for Vermont in the spring, she and Will may have had a tentative understanding; if so, the details are unknown. A break in their correspondence after August 1861 suggests that they subsequently had a falling out. From Howells' accelerated efforts to secure a diplomatic post, it might be inferred that he was seeking a way to put some healing distance between himself and Elinor.

Another concern must have been the imminence of the Civil War; for Columbus was stirring with war preparations, and Howells was facing the possibility that military service would disrupt his career. However, he never came closer to direct involvement in the war than reporting on the Ohio volunteers who were assembling day after day in Goodale Park.

Years later he remembered the "tidal wave of youth" that descended upon Columbus "in the wild hilarity of their young vision": "With interlinked arms they ranged up and down, and pushed the willing citizens from the pavement, and shouted the day and shouted the night away, with no care but the fear that in the out-pour of their death-daring they might not be gathered into the ranks filling up the quota of regiments assigned to Ohio. The time had a sublimity which no other time can know . . . and the spectacle had a mystery and an awe which I cannot hope to impart" (YMY, 200–201). But Howells had resisted the temptation to enlist, despite the offer of a lieutenancy. "Besides the natural curiosity and willingness to see military service, the fact that all kinds of business and especially literature, will be dull for the next year, formed an inducement to enter upon the adventure," he wrote to his mother. "I have not yet wholly relinquished the idea, but from my natural tendency to have spells and to get over them, I presume I shall recover from this" (SL, 1:79).[12]

It is telling that the prospect of a slump in the literature "business" should have weighed heavily in Howells' deliberations over enlistment. As Daniel Aaron observes, "Howells's almost unseemly haste at this time to escape his military obligations, his self-solicitude, and his irritation with a war that threatened to derange 'all my literary plans' are hardly endearing."[13] All through the summer and fall of 1861, while the eager volunteers were marching to battle, Howells was negotiating for a lucrative but undemanding consular appointment as political payment for his campaign biography of Lincoln. After rejecting a post at Rome because it paid too little, Howells finally accepted assignment to Venice, where he waited out the war.

In light of Howells' emotional vulnerability in 1861, it is probably true, as Edwin H. Cady says, that "military service was psychologically out of the question" for him (p. 89). Nevertheless he felt that in leaving America he had perhaps placed personal ambition above national obligation. As Howells wrote in 1881, "Every loyal American who went abroad during the first years of our great war felt bound to make himself some excuse for turning his back on his country in the hour of her trouble" (FR, 3). Guilt about his nonparticipation is evident in all of Howells' fiction that touches, however obliquely, on the Civil War.[14]

V

One of Mary Dean Howells' daughters recalled "'how in the far back days, when our young people would grow rebellious over our narrow surroundings, mother, while always sympathizing with our longings for a wider sphere, would often quote to us, "From our own selves our joys must flow," and thus make us feel that happiness, after all, lay within.'"[15] In 1861, her son Will had yet to discover inner happiness, but he knew it was not to be found within the confines of Jefferson, or even Columbus. When he left Ohio—for good, as it turned out—it was a wrenching separation for both mother and son, with each struggling to reconcile the other to their finally incompatible desires.

With fitting irony, their last letters, before his ship sailed, crossed in the mail. For his part the son patiently reiterated all the arguments for his European sojourn: the dearth of job opportunities at home, his need for pleasure and recuperation, the folly of forsaking a "chance of livelihood and self-improvement" that "hundreds" would envy him. Yet he felt the pang of leaving his mother "so far for so long—no, I cannot write of it without tears" (*SL*, 1:88–89). His mother as well was choked by feelings "too much for my control"; and in her last appeal she touchingly voiced her deepest fears at the same time she unconsciously manipulated his: "But my dearest Willie I can only lend you for a while, in a few, very few, years you will have achieved fame and a name that will reach beyond your highest ambitions. Then dear Willie if our lives are spared you will return to us again, all unchanged. We want you to come back unchanged, come just as you went, for we could never love you more than we do and want you to come the same dear boy that you always were and you will find full warm hearts only too happy to receive [you]. But I must quit for, dear Willie, I do not want to make you feel sad for you must be cheerful and the time will pass pleasantly."[16] She could not help but make him sad with her impossible wish that he should return to her "all unchanged," and with her covert threat that she would not love him so well if he became something other than her "dear boy."

The need for change was what had impelled Howells to leave home. Still, during his first months in Venice, he was often disgruntled and homesick. He suffered in March 1862 an illness that reminded him of "a fever that I had in Hamilton when I was a very little child, and used to doze upon the old settee, and mother would come and kiss me, and ask me if I had slept." But now was the "sad time," he told his father, when those who had been so eager "to fly away from the nest, (God forgive us)" could not "fly back again with our poor broken plumes" (*SL*, 1:110). In April he reported to Vic a recurrent dream of returning to America that succinctly expressed his self-division: "in my dream I said to myself—looking round on the low houses nestling in the beloved trees on either side of the wide streets—'Well this at last, is no dream, and I'm at home and awake.' But a pang of regret for Venice went through my heart, for I thought I had left it too soon, and before I knew perfectly all the glorious and beautiful things that are in it. So comfort mother, dear, and beg her to spare me a little while longer" (*SL*, 1:113).[17]

As warm weather approached, Howells felt "hints of hypochondria" that he was determined to suppress. "Now's the time, if ever, to encounter the dragon and overcome it," he wrote to his father. "I think I shall manage to struggle through the hot season, and then I'll feel better again" (*SL*, 1:116). But Howells fell into "a low fever of some sort," through which he was nursed by an Italian friend (*YMY*, 230).

Other worries besides his health were crowding upon Howells in 1862. Foremost was his relationship to Elinor Mead, who had surprised him with an encouraging letter in January; within a month they had reconciled and were making plans to marry the following year. Afraid that it might upset his mother, if not the others, Howells tried to break the news gently by telling Vic first. But this was a tactical error, and a want of tact, which understandably annoyed his parents. They had already received an unflattering impression of Elinor from Mrs. Carter in Columbus, and Will hastened to repair the damage, apologizing to his father and refuting Mrs. Carter. Elinor was "not violently intellectual, by any means," he insisted. "She has artistic genius, and a great deal of taste, and she admires my poetry immensely. I think she's good looking, and rather suppose she was picked out for me from the beginning of the world" (SL, 1:119–20).

Mary Dean Howells, evidently, was not so sure. When she failed to respond to his announcement, Will read her silence as disapproval; and he made a special plea that is notable, like some of his earlier letters, for its rhetorical ingenuity. After hinting broadly about his anxiousness—"I've been expecting a letter every day now, for a week"—Howells meandered toward his real concern by way of reports on his health and some unexceptionably pious sentiments about the suffering mothers of the war dead—subjects calculated to soften his mother. Then he came to the point: "I haven't heard from home since I got father and Vic's letters, referring to a matter on which I had expected you to say a word or two at any rate, by way of condolence or rejoicing. But I'm sure you'll like E.G.M. when you see her, and till then I suppose a suspension of opinion is all I can ask for. I suppose that if I come home next summer, as I now intend to do, I shall get married. But if you don't like that part of the subject, I'll only talk of the return home." [18] This letter prodded Mary Dean Howells to grant her blessing, although she still hesitated for nearly a month. But Will's plan of marrying at home proved to be impracticable, and the wedding took place instead at the American embassy in Paris on Christmas Eve 1862.

Afterward Elinor did her best to help Will smooth things over at home, but she was sometimes at a loss for words for these parents she had never met—especially when Will was standing over her shoulder and putting words in her mouth. "It is with timid strokes that I begin a letter now-a-days," she began, half jokingly, in one letter to William Cooper Howells; "for every one of them has to be submitted to the critical inspection of Mr. Howells before it leaves the house, and it's as often to go into il fuoco [the fire] afterwards as to the Post-office." The letter rambled on, as if Elinor were groping for something more to say; and then Mr. Howells intervened, adding in his own hand, "Here Elinor got hopelessly tangled up, but I think she may be unwound to the general effect that she's your affectionate daughter." [19]

Comparable strain was evident from the side of the affectionate parents. Out of pique and disappointment that her son had broken his promise to return, Mary Dean Howells stopped writing to him early in 1863; and when he pressed her to explain, she wondered if she would *ever* see him again. This plaint provoked a firm response: "And now, mother, in regard to my absence: I know how it grieves you; and why you should feel it peculiarly, for I remember how hard it used to be for me to leave home, and you doubtless remember that, too, and contrast it with my present willingness to be away." But he could not just quit his post and return without a suitable position, especially when he had "new cares and responsibilities" before him. (He was alluding to Elinor's pregnancy.) As soon as he had carved himself out a place, he promised, he would leave Europe, and "a long visit home" would be his first priority (SL, 1:154). But Mary Dean Howells kept pressuring him, with increasing leverage, as the months and years passed.

Meanwhile Howells contended with professional setbacks. His primary purpose for being in Europe, after all, was to advance his literary career, but he was frustrated by an apparent lack of progress. There were petty irritations to endure, such as the complicated logistics of getting his manuscripts into circulation. Because of high postal fees and low funds, Howells was sending bundles of poems to his father in Jefferson, to be distributed by him to various editors. The arrangement invited confusion and delay, and Howells disliked passing his work under his father's editorial hand. And then his work was not being accepted. After the publication of "Louis Lebeau's Conversion" in November 1862, the *Atlantic* rejected everything Howells submitted, and he could not find an English publisher willing to issue either "Geoffrey Winter" or a volume of poems. "Upon literary topics you were particularly depressing, and quite made poetry a burden to me," Howells wrote to his father early in 1863. "I suppose it will really be better to versify for Elinor—whom I find a most indulgent public,—at present, and put aside all thoughts of celebrity" (SL, 1:138).

Howells began to doubt if he was a poet at all. He told his father that he was fitting himself "for something in the nature of a professor of modern languages, in case I should find on my return to America the intellectual life of the country yearning more decidedly for professors of modern languages than for journalists, or even poets" (SL, 1:142). By the end of the year Howells perceived despairingly that he was losing the race: "Since I commenced writing many others have outrun me in popularity, and sometimes I've felt bitter and despondent at what I thought their unmerited good fortune" (SL, 1:169). But Howells always had another kind of good fortune: the knack of being closest to the door when opportunity knocked.

By chance, in the spring of 1862, he had met in Venice a Bostonian tourist named Charles Hale, who happened to be the publisher of the Boston *Advertiser*. Howells made a deal with Hale to write a series of Venetian travel letters. At the time the arrangement had interested Howells primarily as a way to supplement his income, but it turned out to be a decisive step in his career. These "Letters from Venice," which began to appear in January 1863, earned Howells some of the popularity he coveted with the Eastern audience. Writing them encouraged him to think of himself less and less as a poet, to slough his youthful romanticism, and ultimately to transform himself into a prose writer and a realist. He had only to discover, as he soon did, his true *métier* (fiction) and his true *donnée* (contemporary America) in order to attain his artistic maturity. By the beginning of 1864, Howells was writing prose more seriously and professionally than he ever had; and he was putting his scholarly preparation to use in a long and well-researched paper, "Modern Italian Comedy," which he submitted to the *North American Review*. The acceptance of this essay by editors James Russell Lowell and Charles Eliot Norton was "the turning point" of Howells' life, as he later said.[20]

It came at a time when his emotional stamina had been pressed to the limit again. As he told his sister Aurelia, he had "overworked" himself on "Modern Italian Comedy": "I've been sick, and am so nervous that it's torture to write" (*LinL*, 1:82). As before, overwork was a signal of his heightened anxiety; and Howells was too psychically weak to withstand the next blow: the sudden death from diphtheria, in April 1864, of his favorite brother Johnny at the age of eighteen. For several weeks he lived in a stupor of depression that was deepened by other family problems.

Almost from the time of his arrival in Venice, Howells had been intermittently alarmed by the war news from home, and especially by the possibility that his brothers Joe and Sam might be drafted. He was concerned not only for their safety but for his own future; for if Joe were drafted, his parents would expect him to come home to run the *Sentinel*. In August 1864, when his parents were pressing this familial obligation upon him, Howells tried to escape it by quoting in his self-defense the "turning point" letter from Lowell that had praised his Italian essays and given him hope after all of a career in Boston letters (*SL*, 1:196–98). As Lynn remarks, "A less guilt-ridden son, a son less attached to his mother, might have written a more forthright letter. But instead of frankly saying no and assuming moral responsibility for his decision, Howells began by saying that of course he would fill in for Joe; then carefully built up a case against his doing so; and ended by asking his parents to decide whether his return was 'desirable'" (p. 121).

Since Jefferson was primarily his mother's sphere, Howells' "old morbid horror of going back to live in a place where I have been so wretched" (*SL*, 1:197) reflected his wish to be less attached to her. Escape from the village could be accomplished only by severing this emotional bond; and Howells' true break with the Ohio past came not with his establishment in Boston in 1866, but with his mother's death two years later.

Not surprisingly, it was an occasion for remorse as well as grief. Howells felt guilty, first, for having failed to be at her side in her last days. Although she had been languishing throughout the summer of 1868, Mary Dean Howells had, as her son later recalled, "continually sent me word, 'Tell Willy that I'm not sick—only just miserable'" (SL, 2:225). Deep in editorial work and reluctant to make a tiring and expensive journey, Howells had not heard his mother's summons until too late. When he finally did heed an urgent dispatch, telling him to take the next westbound train, Howells arrived several hours after she had died.

A deeper guilt arose from his sense of having been liberated by this sad event. Certainly Howells' grief for his mother was real. But so was the undercurrent of relief that broke through, for example, in the letter he wrote to his father just two months afterward, a letter he was "a little too nervous" to finish in one sitting: "Dear father, I know where this snow fell as well as in Boston streets [i.e., on his mother's grave], and there is no aspect of the day that does [not] recall that solemn place to my mind. If the impression of our loss is less constantly with me than at first, its recurrences, it seems to me are even more painful, and I have somehow lost the power to idealize or spiritualize the fact. Believe me I do not forget you or those at home. In whatever enjoyment I have, I feel as if I committed a wrong against you; but I know you do not think so" (SL, 1:309–10).

The slip of the pen in the first sentence—the omission of the crucial word, "not"—expressed a concealed desire *not* to recall his mother, a desire that Howells more or less admits in the conditional clause that follows and then rationalizes in the rest of the letter, in his protestation that he has *not* forgotten those at home but that he is punishing himself anyhow to atone for a wrong he has [not] committed. Howells felt guilty that his consciousness of his mother's death did not always seem so real as he felt it should. As he told his friend and patron Charles Eliot Norton, "At times, her death, and all I know of it, seems the most insubstantial dream, and at times the only fact in a world of vagaries" (LinL, 1:136).

In fact, Mary Dean Howells became the stuff of recurrent dreams, in which she appeared "in such characteristic ways,—as for instance we all being in a place together where there was some person of distinction whose attention she wished to draw to me, she said to him, 'My son,' and then when he simply bowed, and went on talking with another, she wore such a grieved and hurt expression that it woke me out of my sleep." In a variation, which Howells reported in the same letter, "it seemed to me we were at home, and I was paying less regard than she thought I should to one of the family, and she insisted with her tender jealousy on my noticing that one, whom she praised" (SL, 1:311).

Howells' ambivalence is figured in the male characters of these dreams: he is both "my son," whom the mother (with "tender jealousy") recognizes and would have recognized by others, and also the "person of distinction," the

Atlantic editor who ignores her claims on his attention and implicitly rejects her valuation of his place as her son. In the second dream the center of consciousness has shifted from "my son" to the "person of distinction" who neglects to recognize "one of the family," that is, his familial alter ego ("my son") and/or "my son's" mother. The psychic resonance of his mother's death persisted in Howells' dreams for many years.[21]

If his mother continued to claim him in sleep, her hold over his waking life was apparently broken after 1868. Her death did not cause any recurrence of Howells' neurotic symptoms. In fact, after 1868 Howells enjoyed a sustained psychic stability that would last, with some occasional teetering, until 1881.

CHAPTER FOUR

NATIVE

DECENCY

In the months before he left Venice in July 1865, Howells recast his *Advertiser* essays for book publication and readied himself for reimmersion into American life. He had found much to admire and to enjoy in Europe but, unlike Henry James, little to engage his imagination deeply. Like Marcellus Cockerel, the self-styled "roaring Yankee" in James's "The Point of View" (1882), Howells had rid himself of the "superstition . . . that there is no salvation but through Europe." Cockerel crows, "I sha'n't trouble Europe again; I shall see America for the rest of my days." [1] Even while he was living in Europe, Howells had sometimes seen only America, as when the "bucolic associations" aroused by Virgil's tomb in Naples had made him think "of a spring-house on some far-away Ohio farm," or when the "rare and saddening beauty of evanescence" at Petrarch's house in Arquà had awakened his "memory of all beautiful scenery, so that I embroidered the landscape with the silver threads of western streams, and bordered it with Ohio hills." [2] Like Mark Twain, who in *The Innocents Abroad* (1869) takes the measure of Lake Como by his beloved Lake Tahoe, Howells had clung always to a native standard, even when the allurements of Europe had tempted him to abandon it.

In *Venetian Life* (1866) he wrote that "the charm of the place sweetens your temper, but corrupts you"—by inducing a morally indolent tolerance for customs and conditions that would naturally offend an American sensibility. "One's conscience, more or less uncomfortably vigilant elsewhere, drowses here." But Howells' conscience could not be lulled into ignoring European poverty, squalor, social injustice, and (most of all) sexual licentiousness. In the most cultivated of Italians, he found that polished manners served to cloak undisciplined passions. By contrast, he believed, the education of the American gentleman disciplined the impulses and left "the good manner to grow naturally out of habits of self-command and consequent habitual self-respect." [3] Europeans lacked such self-respect because, as Howells wrote to his sister in 1862, "The pleasure which we have innocently in America, from our unrestrained and unconventional social intercourse, is guilty in Europe— brilliant men and women know something of it; but they are also guilty men and women" (SL, 1:115).

In *The Lady of the Aroostook* (1879), Howells' own reaction was reflected in Lydia Blood's puritanical revulsion from the sexually guilty men and women she encounters in Europe: "'that married woman who lets a man be in love with her, and that old woman who can't live with her husband because he's too good and kind, and that girl who swears and doesn't know who her father is, and that impudent painter, and that officer who thinks he has the right to insult women if he finds them alone!'" (*LA*, 282–83). In this ostensibly "international" novel, Howells shrunk the image of Europe, as Olov W. Fryckstedt says, so that "it merely represents moral corruption as contrasted with American innocence."[4]

In a review of *The Lady of the Aroostook*, T. W. Higginson perceived: "Mr. James writes 'international episodes;' Mr. Howells writes interoceanic episodes; his best scenes imply a dialogue between the Atlantic and Pacific slopes."[5] Like any writer alert to the literary potential of his own experience, Howells capitalized on his years abroad in such early works as *Venetian Life*, *Italian Journeys*, *No Love Lost*, *A Foregone Conclusion*, *A Fearful Responsibility*, and *The Lady of the Aroostook*. But even his most international tales were interoceanic episodes at heart. Long before he debated James about the proper sphere of the American writer, Howells had made his commitment to native decency and native subject matter. As he later argued in his review of James's *Hawthorne*, with its famous litany of American cultural deficiencies: "After leaving out all those novelistic 'properties,' as sovereigns, courts, aristocracy, gentry, castles, cottages, cathedrals, abbeys, universities, museums, political class, Epsoms, and Ascots, by the absence of which Mr. James suggests our poverty to the English conception, we have the whole of human life remaining, and a social structure presenting the only fresh and novel opportunities left to fiction, opportunities manifold and inexhaustible."[6]

I

During his years abroad, Howells had realized that America's social structure was being transformed by the Civil War. In 1862, he told his father: "I fancy things must be greatly changed since I left home. Couldn't you give me some idea of how people actually talk and feel—what they hope and fear? It would be very interesting to me, for I dread this war has wrought many sad changes not apparent on the surface" (*SL*, 1:125). Howells also dreaded that he had become too removed from American life ever to grasp the nuances of change. But like Owen Elmore, the guilty expatriate in *A Fearful Responsibility* (1881), Howells found, paradoxically, that those who had experienced the war more directly than he were no less likely to be out of touch with the new America.

In the novel Lily Mayhew, recently arrived in Venice from the home front, brings news of alterations in American life that she has blithely accepted but that Elmore can scarcely believe. "'Camps, prisoners, barracks, mutilation, widowhood, death, sudden gains, social upheavals,—it is the old, hideous story of war come true of our day and country. It's terrible!'" (FR, 29). Later, Elmore is impressed by the "'indomitable hopefulness'" of Hoskins's romantic bas-relief titled "Westward the Star of Empire," or "American Enterprise." Despite his having lost part of one foot in battle, the sculptor remains as "'serenely undisturbed by the facts of the war as if secession had taken place in another planet.'" To Elmore, there is something sublime, something Greek in Hoskins's "'treatment of such a work at such a time.'" His "'repose of feeling'" is like "'the calm beauty which makes you forget the anguish of the Laocoön'" (FR, 108–9).

Lily and Hoskins have lived so close to war that they do not recognize the changes it has wrought; only a detached observer like Elmore (or Howells) can truly perceive its significance. By reaching this conclusion, which was partly a rationalization, Howells managed to exorcize his guilt about not having participated in the Civil War and to banish his fear of having become too alienated from American life. In his fiction he stressed what he saw to be the opportunity of nonparticipation: the challenge of interpreting not the war itself, but rather its profound effects on American culture. His theory of literary realism would be informed by this idea.

Consider, for example, this scene from The Rise of Silas Lapham (1885). Over cigars and wine the men at Bromfield Corey's dinner party are swapping stories. Corey muses that the "'abundance—the superabundance—of heroism'" evident during the war seems to have vanished from American life and may not materialize again until a new conflict calls it forth. "'Till it comes,'" the Reverend Mr. Sewell replies, "'we must content ourselves with the everyday generosities and sacrifices. They make up in quantity what they lack in quality, perhaps.'" "'They're not so picturesque,'" Corey complains, "'You can paint a man dying for his country, but you can't express on canvas a man fulfilling the duties of a good citizen.'" The latter is what Charles Bellingham labels "'the commonplace'"—that "'light, impalpable, aërial essence which they've never got into their confounded books yet'" (RSL, 200–202).

As if to show what *does* get into the "confounded books," Howells juxtaposes this conversation to Silas Lapham's account of his wartime friendship with Jim Millon, who died from a sharpshooter's bullet meant for Lapham. Throughout the dinner party and especially in this scene, Lapham has felt out of place; but as he warms to the telling of his story, the others listen with a profoundly flattering interest. As he finishes, Lapham becomes aware of a fuzziness in his mind and looks about, as if for something to clear his thoughts. Bellingham obligingly offers him a bottle of mineral water, but Lapham grabs the Madeira, thereby reminding the reader that alcohol has been the catalyst of his tale. Howells deflates the story by linking it to Lapham's drunkenness, which has become painfully obvious to Corey and his guests.

The purpose of Howells' undercutting becomes clear later in the novel when Lapham risks even his marriage to continue his faithful support of Millon's wife and daughter. "'I want to live for poor Molly and Zerrilla,'" Millon had cried the day of his death (*RSL*, 203); but it was Lapham, the guilty survivor, who gave meaning to these sentiments by his loyalty to his friend's family. Howells contrasts the romantic heroics of Millon to the commonplace heroism of Lapham. Whereas Lapham, through Millon, has painted "a man dying for his country," Howells, through Lapham, has portrayed "a man fulfilling the duties of a good citizen." Whereas it is Lapham's romantic tale that makes an impression at Corey's dinner, it is Lapham's steadfast deeds that should make an impression on us. One goal of Howells' realism was to suggest that "dying for one's country" is neither the only nor the best measure of heroism. This was the challenge of having survived the Civil War: to recognize that it might require as much courage to live as to die.

Howells' commitment to literary realism in the 1870s involved, no doubt, his conscious moral and aesthetic choices. But realism also seems to have satisfied his less conscious psychological needs. By focusing on the native decency of the average American, he could blink the sort of indecencies he had observed in Europe. Writing of the commonplace center also permitted Howells to minimize his apprehension of his own psychic fringes.

The essence of Howellsian realism was the revelation of character through the dramatic method—an approach that was incipient in his earliest fiction ("The Independent Candidate," "Geoffrey Winter"), and that was refined by his discovery of European realists, particularly George Eliot and Ivan Turgenev. After rereading *Italian Journeys* in 1875, Charles Dudley Warner admonished Howells: "The time has come for you to make an *opus*—not only a study on a large canvas but a picture. Write a long novel, one that we can dive into with confidence, and not feel that we are to strike bottom in the first plunge" (*SL*, 2:103–4n). Although he would later, under the aegis of Tolstoy, attempt to fill a large canvas, Howells at this time rejected Warner's advice. "But isn't the real dramatic encounter always between two persons only?" he replied. "Or three or four at most? If the effects are in *me*, I can get them into six numbers of The Atlantic, and if they aren't, I couldn't get 'em into twenty. Besides, I can only forgive myself for writing novels at all on the ground that the poor girl urged in extenuation of her unlegalized addition to the census: it was such a very *little* baby!" (*SL*, 2:103). In this witticism, the tone of which is curiously defensive, there is a key to Howells' ambivalence toward writing fiction. Unconsciously, for most of his career, he engaged in writing a novel as if it were the imaginative equivalent of bearing a bastard— something as reprehensible as Ann Stepmeyer's unlegalized addition to the census had seemed to the adolescent Howells. Like that "poor girl," he felt a need to be exonerated for his guilty activities.

When Howells talked about the way his novels were actually written, he often stressed that he was in strict control of them, at the same time admitting that he was not. In 1864, he wrote to E. C. Stedman that he had changed his mind about "the subjective German poetry and its kindred English and American schools" that once had charmed him. He had come, he said, "to dislike personality and consciousness, and to hate any work in which I find present anything of the author besides his genius" (*SL*, 1:177). Twenty-eight years later, in an interview, Howells asserted that he had "long ago learned to distrust and utterly to disbelieve in the idea of losing one's self in one's work." For the sake of efficiency as well as good art, the writer must "retain his self-possession, his self-control, and be constantly in the position of an outsider studying carefully his effects." Howells admitted that "every character created by an author comes from his own individuality," that to have felt hatred is to know "what it would be to murder," and that the same "may be said of every passion" (*INT*, 22–23).[7] The trick, therefore, was to draw a character from the inside but to remain outside as well.

In other words, Howells' psychological juggle corresponded to the dramatic method, which he described as "standing aside from the whole affair, and letting the characters work the plot out" (*MLP*, 170). Taking the position of "an outsider studying carefully his effects" was the narrative equivalent for Howells of dealing with his own state of mind "as another would deal with it" and of combatting his fears "as if they were alien." But the psychological juggler, unlike his circus counterpart, did not allow the right hand to know what the left hand was doing: as a writer Howells was given to splitting off conscious control from unconscious inspiration and allowing his characters to arise as mysterious strangers from his own unacknowledged depths.

In a letter to Norton in 1874, Howells said of *A Foregone Conclusion*: "If I had been perfectly my own master—it's a little droll, but true, that even in such a matter one isn't—the story would have ended with Don Ippolito's rejection. But I suppose that it is well to work for others in some measure" (*SL*, 2:78n). These "others" have usually been identified as Howells' publisher or his readers, who purportedly pressured him to adulterate the ending of the novel. But the "others" may have been Howells' own characters, and what was "a little droll" may have been the way they had subverted his mastery.[8] Earlier in 1874, to an inquiry about his intentions in creating Colonel Ellison in *A Chance Acquaintance*, Howells had replied: "I am not so good authority on such a point as you seem to imagine; for my experience is that one's characters take themselves into their own hands to a great extent, and refuse allegiance to their author in quite a surprising way" (*SL*, 2:53). The allegiance of such characters was to Howells' own repressed self, which had not been integrated into his identity as author. The presence of this unconscious material tended to disrupt the conscious design of Howells' fiction and to result in uncalculated narrative ambiguities, especially when what he was repressing in himself tallied with the cultural repressions of Victorian America.

II

Take *Their Wedding Journey* (1872), the first of his published books to contain fully rounded characters. Ostensibly, *Their Wedding Journey* is an idyll of the ordinary, a charming and entertaining slice of the "poor Real Life" that Howells was at pains to demonstrate was a proper and sufficient condition for American fiction (*TWJ*, 42). Certainly this was the unanimous opinion of contemporary reviewers, such as Henry Adams, who had presented a copy of the novel to his own bride. He rhapsodized that this "lovers' book" deserved "to be among the first of the gifts which follow or precede the marriage offer." Nowhere, he added, will our descendants find "so faithful and so pleasing a picture of our American existence, and no writer is likely to rival Mr. Howells in this idealization of the commonplace."[9]

This prophecy of the young Adams has been fulfilled in an unexpected way that would have delighted the acidulous author of *The Education*. Recent readers of *Their Wedding Journey* have been detecting a "dark side" to this "pleasing" book, and seeing it as an all too faithful picture of the *horrors* of nineteenth-century American existence. Marion W. Cumpiano writes: "On the journey, deaths and catastrophes of all sorts occur frequently or are recounted. Danger lurks unexpected at all times or looms ominous. War, savagery, and evil are shown to be the heritage of the modern American; poverty, illness, pain, and death surround or assail him. The most beautiful setting appears to have had the most bloody history; the happiest marriage conceals the bitterest anguish."[10]

Howells himself would not likely have recognized his novel in this description of it, and yet this "dark side" is clearly present. On the surface the novel does offer an idealized and pleasing picture, but through the cracks of the narrative, it also affords glimpses of an American netherworld, which consists of those subtle contradictions in Victorian American culture that struck a responsive chord with Howells' own unconscious conflicts. As Kenneth Seib argues, the Marches may be seen as "a symbol of post–Civil War America on the road to self-discovery." What they discover is "not harmony but a profound disunity, not national identity but irreconcilable diversity, not a smiling satisfaction but a terrifying uneasiness."[11] This uneasiness derives partly from Howells' own psychic disunity. As Gary A. Hunt observes, *Their Wedding Journey* is "permeated by a tone of sexual panic and frustration" that is evident both in Howells' suggestive symbolism and in his characterizations of Basil and Isabel March. [12]

The predominating symbol at the center of the novel is Niagara. In 1860, standing at the foot of the American falls, Howells had felt in "the real presence of the Cataract . . . such repression that it was a divine rapture to remain dumb." [13] Of course, Howells was not using "repression" in its psychoanalytic sense, but he was anticipating Freud's later meaning. The anarchic energy of Niagara had spoken to, had called forth Howells' unconscious self, which had to remain dumb, had to be sublimated into divine rapture, lest it sweep him over the edge of sanity.

In *Their Wedding Journey*, Isabel tells Basil that the falls have grown "'stranger and dreadfuller'" to her, have begun "'to pervade me and possess me in a very uncomfortable way'":

> "I'm tossed upon rapids, and flung from cataract brinks, and dizzied in whirlpools; I'm no longer yours, Basil; I'm most unhappily married to Niagara. Fly with me, save me from my awful lord!"
> She lightly burlesqued the woes of a *prima donna*, with clasped hands and uplifted eyes.
> "That'll do very well," Basil commented, "and it implies a reality that can't be quite definitely spoken." (*TWJ*, 103)

Despite her self-mockery, Isabel's exclamations voice a dread for which she cannot account. By making Isabel burlesque her fears, Howells attempts to make light of them and to divert our attention (and his own) from their source in the repressed "reality that can't be quite definitely spoken." What is figured in the writhing and heaving of the lord Niagara is the Marches' sexuality, which they have suppressed in conformity with the approved, and sexually differentiated, codes of genteel Victorian morality.

The operation of these codes is epitomized in the Marches' eating habits, that is, in their attitudes toward "appetite." Basil is shown to have the stronger appetite; at least he gratifies it more shamelessly than Isabel, whose fastidiousness about food is meant to signify a refined self-denial, a moral and spiritual superiority to her grosser husband. Throughout the novel food and sex are symbolically related. As the Marches wait for their train in the opening chapter, Basil shows signs of restlessness to which Isabel gives "a subtle interpretation": "'I don't want anything to eat, Basil, but I think I know the weaknesses of men'" (*TWJ*, 10). The narrator interjects:

> I suppose it is always a little shocking and grievous to a wife when she recognizes a rival in butchers'-meat and the vegetables of the season. With her slender relishes for pastry and confectionery, and her dainty habits of lunching, she cannot reconcile with the ideal her husband's

capacity for breakfasting, dining, supping, and hot meals at all hours of the day and night. . . . But Isabel would have had only herself to blame if she had not perceived this trait of Basil's before marriage. She recurred now . . . to memorable instances of his appetite in their European travels during their first engagement. "Yes, he ate terribly at Susa. . . . At Rome, I thought I must break with him on account of the wild-boar; and at Heidelberg, the sausage and the ham!—how could he, in my presence? But I took him with all his faults—and was glad to get him," she added, ending her meditation with a little burst of candor; and she did not even think of Basil's appetite when he reappeared. (*TWJ*, 10–11)

Isabel's toleration of Basil is a calculated tradeoff: she suffers his brute appetite in exchange for enjoying the social advantages of having "gotten" a husband. For American ladies in the nineteenth century, the same principle applied to the marriage bed as to the dining table.

By contrast, as Basil points out to Isabel, the immigrant lovers they encounter in the Rochester *hofbrau* find nothing odd in mixing tender German love songs with beer, sausage, bread, ham, and "odorous crumbs of Limburger cheese": "'they did not disdain the matter-of-fact corporeity in which their sentiment was enshrined; they fed it heartily and abundantly with the banquet whose relics we see here'" (*TWJ*, 69–70). Such corporeity is as disgusting to Isabel as the public lovemaking of the bridal couples she is determined not to resemble. The things of the flesh are to be endured, their pleasure to be sublimated into duty. Thus, after a sensuous and idyllic afternoon in Quebec, Isabel finds it necessary to justify her own hunger: "'If there were not dinner after such experiences as these . . . I don't know what would become of one. But dinner unites the idea of pleasure and duty, and brings you gently back to earth. You *must* eat, don't you see, and there's nothing disgraceful about what you're obliged to do; and so—it's all right'" (*TWJ*, 163). Even Isabel, it is clear, takes pleasure in food; but she relies upon the decorous trappings of the dining table to civilize her appetite, to spiritualize passions into sentiments. The purpose of the genteel code of social intercourse is to protect respectable types like the Marches from the dizzying whirlpools and plunging cataracts of their own unconscious desires.

Such desires are seen to imbrute those outside the hegemony of the code, such as the burlesque actors and actresses to whose "outlawry" Basil is so strongly and guiltily attracted. Especially enticing is the actress in a mermaid costume, whom Basil espies "in dishabille" when he accidently barges into her room. Howells had "some qualms" that this scene "might appear coarse" (*SL*, 1:386), even though, as John K. Reeves shows, it was considerably less suggestive in print than in manuscript draft, where Howells had been more explicit about the physical endowments of the actress and about her questionable virtue. He had implied that the actress might be, in fact, a prostitute, thereby linking her to the two whores that the Marches encounter on the Hudson River night boat.[14]

Garbed, respectively, in widow's black and bride's white, these two women are "both alike awful in their mockery of guiltless sorrow and guiltless joy" (*TWJ*, 45). Their threatening intrusion into the world of respectability parallels the intrusion of the nightmare accident into the pleasant dreams of the passengers. The night boat rams a skiff; a man is scalded and thrown overboard; the alarms ring; the crew scurries to the rescue; the victim is carried aboard in mortal anguish. The tragedy disrupts the civilized order of things: "Isabel had emerged into a world of dishabille, a world wildly unbuttoned and unlaced, where it was the fashion for ladies to wear their hair down their backs, and to walk about in their stockings, and to speak to each other without introduction. The place with which she had felt so familiar a little while before was now utterly estranged" (*TWJ*, 46). In this defamiliarized "topsy-turvy world," there is little to distinguish Isabel and the other ladies in dishabille from the burlesque actress—or the prostitutes. Although she does not know it, that is precisely why Isabel commands Basil to lock her into her cabin, out of harm's way from what is "utterly estranged." It is marriage, finally, that is seen to set Isabel above the whore in the bridal white; the true bride has the advantage of a husband to keep her safely locked up.

Pointing out a subtle link between marriage and prostitution was one of the provocations of radical feminists in the late nineteenth century; and Howells' narrator sarcastically alludes to such repugnant notions at one point, in describing Isabel's conversation with a married friend. "Mrs. Leonard beheld in her friend's joy the sweet reflection of her own honeymoon, and Isabel was pleased to look upon the prosperous marriage of the former as the image of her future. Thus, with immense profit and comfort, they reassured one another by every question and answer, and in their weak content lapsed far behind the representative women of our age, when husbands are at best a necessary evil, and the relation of wives to them is known to be one of pitiable subjection" (*TWJ*, 25).[15] Without intending it, Howells supported the feminists' case. As *Their Wedding Journey* makes clear, the "representative women" were wrong only so far as they saw marriage in terms solely of the woman's subjection. Rather marriage required mutual subjection: Isabel and Basil divide the labor of enforcing the Victorian proprieties upon themselves and each other.

Despite their conscious adherence to sexual restraint, however, both the Marches exhibit repressed passions. As Gary A. Hunt discerns, the novel suggests that Isabel's "overwrought fears," as in her hysterical attack at Niagara Falls, are "a distorted expression of desire, that her exaggerated dependence masks a teasing kind of aggressiveness, that her allegiance to strict decorum is superimposed upon a fascination with the wild, unregulated and even destructive element in the landscape of Niagara" (p. 23). Although Basil is more conscious of his sexuality and therefore more capable of concealing and controlling its urges in accordance with Victorian mores, he still suffers frustration and feels ambivalence toward his marriage. The effect of the moral code on Basil's personality is, as Hunt says, "to drive his forbidden impulses underground, as it were, where they continue to exist in the shape of fantasies that contradict its emphasis on a passionless manly reserve and its insistence upon the disciplined and ascetic life of purposeful activity" (p. 28). By the end of *Their Wedding Journey*, "we are left with the distinct impression that neither Isabel nor Basil is likely to arrive at a satisfying rapprochement with the moral code and that, moreover, it will come to play an increasingly divisive role within their marriage" (p. 24).

The lines of division between Basil and Isabel are evident in their quarrels. Theodore Dreiser once commented that *Their Wedding Journey* was a "fine piece of work . . . not a sentimental passage in it, quarrels from beginning to end, just the way it would be, don't you know, really beautiful and true." Some scholars hypothesize that this was a slip of the tongue, that Dreiser meant to praise *A Modern Instance*, since, as Kenneth S. Lynn says, "there is only one quarrel that amounts to anything" in *Their Wedding Journey* (p. 208).[16] But Dreiser may have been right despite himself: there may be only one pitched battle between Basil and Isabel, but the novel is full of their skirmishing and sniping.

Each of the Marches is pent up with half-conscious discontents that find release in unconscious aggression toward the other. We have already seen how Basil's eating irritates Isabel and how she retaliates by chiding him for his appetite. That her provincial Bostonian snobbery piques him is clear from his needling her about it at the Rochester hotel (*TWJ*, 64), and from his smugly exposing her mistaken identification of a commonplace New Yorker for a foreign nobleman (*TWJ*, 116–18). He is also annoyed by her domineering attitude—she habitually treats "her own decisions as the product of their common reasoning" (*TWJ*, 5)—and by the confounding irrationality in her behavior. How much he does not understand about Isabel becomes clear to Basil in their conversation about the whimsies of Mrs. Ellison:

> Basil stared. "O, certainly," he said. "But what an amusingly illogical little body!"
> "I don't understand what you mean, Basil. It was the only thing that she could do, to invite the young lady [Kitty Ellison] to go on with them. I wonder her husband had the sense to think of it first. Of *course* she'll have to lend her things."

"And you didn't observe anything peculiar in her way of reaching her conclusions?"

"Peculiar? What *do* you mean?"

"Why, her blaming her husband for letting her have her own way about the hotel; and her telling him not to mention his proposal to Kitty, and then doing it herself, just after she'd pronounced it absurd and impossible." He spoke with heat at being forced to make what he thought a needless explanation.

"O!" said Isabel, after a moment's reflection. "*That!* Did you think it so very odd?"

Her husband looked at her with the gravity a man must feel when he begins to perceive that he has married the whole mystifying world of womankind in the woman of his choice, and made no answer. But to his own soul he said: "I supposed I had the pleasure of my wife's acquaintance. It seems I have been flattering myself." (*TWJ*, 83–84)

Of course Howells intends for us to chuckle at the husband's bafflement over the dizzy illogic of his childish wife: such has long been the grist of situation comedy. But the sexist humor of this exchange lays bare Howells' aggression toward the inner workings of Victorian marriage. The wife, who is not bound to the logic of the male world, is seen to take credit for everything that goes well and to blame her husband for everything that goes badly. Thus the husband is invariably the guilty party to any quarrel, and it is the man's place always to give in. After their fight in Montreal over Isabel's perverse insistence on having a two-horse carriage, Basil yields. Having "made all the concessions," he cannot "enjoy the quarrel as she did, simply because it was theirs" (*TWJ*, 132). At times, Basil's yielding to Isabel extends to his abetting her dishonesty. "At heart every man is a smuggler," the narrator avers, "and how much more every woman!" (*TWJ*, 136). Isabel fills her trunks with contraband in Canada and then expects Basil to deceive the customs inspector. The narrator sardonically describes the double bind she puts him in: "'You mustn't fib about it, Basil' (heroically), 'I couldn't respect you if you did' (tenderly); 'but' (with decision) '*you must slip out of it some way!*'" (*TWJ*, 174–75).

Isabel's irresponsibility may be interpreted as a form of displaced anger: a passively aggressive resistance to the subjection of a Victorian woman in a patriarchal marriage, and a vengeance upon the nominally all-powerful man. If a wife is to be ruled by her husband, then he must drink the cup of his power to the lees—so her actions imply. Basil has more active methods of aggression, such as teasing. A subtler and more sadistic one is his shaking Isabel's fragile composure with hair-raising tales of death and violence, such as the over-the-cataract drownings of Sam Patch and Avery.

A typical example of antagonism between the Marches is the scene in which Isabel is paralyzed with fear on the island at Niagara and refuses to recross the suspension bridges that would take her to shore. Basil guiltily wonders if he has not "overwrought Isabel's nerves by repeating that poem about Avery, and by the ensuing talk about Niagara, which she had seemed to enjoy so much" (*TWJ*, 92). Very likely he has upset her, but Isabel denies that her dread has any cause except her belief in the unsafety of the bridges. This apprehension is irrational; and Hunt is right to see in Isabel's attack a "perfect instance of 'female hysteria'" (p. 20), of a piece with that of Freud's early patients, whose terrors included sheer sexual fear. Basil sees none of this, of course. He feels frustrated by Isabel's recalcitrance and bewildered by her sudden recomposure at the sight of Mrs. Ellison. Afterward he gets even for the trouble she has caused him by treating Isabel "with a superiority which he felt himself to be very odious, but which he could not disuse" (*TWJ*, 98). Tit for tat, she cuts him down to size a few pages later when he proffers the gift of a feather fan in colors so hideous that she can only wonder about *his* mental state. She promises to keep the object as a monument to his folly and bad taste. "And she deposed him, with another peal of laughter, from the proud height to which he had climbed in pity of her nervous fears of the day. So completely were their places changed, that he doubted if it were not he who had made that scene on the Third Sister" (*TWJ*, 100).

This scene was based, in fact, on Howells' own vertigo attacks at Niagara in 1860, when he had understood his own hysteria no better than Basil understands Isabel's. If so, in writing the novel a decade later, how much did he understand then of the psychological patterns I have been discussing? No doubt Howells was alert to the undercurrents of hostility between the Marches, but it is unlikely that he grasped the deeper psychosexual implications of his characterizations of them.

The "dark side" of *Their Wedding Journey* was as invisible to Howells as to his contemporary readers, blinded as they all were to the cultural codes they shared. Howells was telling the repressed truth about Victorian marriage in spite of himself; and, as in his earlier *Suburban Sketches* (1871), he was using his wits to defend against disturbing intuitions. What Lynn says of "Flitting" is true also of *Their Wedding Journey*: "Even though Howells had not suffered a nervous collapse for more than half a decade, he nevertheless lived on such a narrow margin of psychic health that he was very reluctant to undertake a sustained and serious examination of any subject that lay close to the bone of his personal life. Only by controlling autobiographical materials with a comic outlook could he dare to use them" (p. 207).

As Howells mastered the rudiments of fiction writing during the 1870s, he did not gain a commensurate mastery of his hidden conflicts. Although he dared more and more to loosen the controls on his use of autobiographical material and to express a less comic outlook, the psychological preoccupations of his fiction remained, as in *Their Wedding Journey*, largely submerged. Howells drew characters more psychologically complex than the Marches, but until *A Modern Instance*, these characters remained safely alien to himself. Like the American Girl, to whom he returned again and again in the 1870s, Howells retained a certain innocence that, like hers, was vulnerable to the encroachment of a threatening world within, which he often symbolized in the psyches of her suitors. The pattern is exemplified by Howells' first treatment of the American Girl.

III

When Henry James read *A Chance Acquaintance* (1873), he immediately recognized that Kitty Ellison was something new in American fiction. Later he praised Howells for creating women who are "always most sensibly women," whose motions, accents, and ideas "savor essentially of the sex." Howells was, according to James, "one of the few writers who hold a key to feminine logic and detect a method in feminine madness."[17] This neat (and somewhat sexist) formulation looks beneath the surface of Howells' portraits of the American Girl, for whose invention he shares credit with James.

During his New England pilgrimage in 1860, tête-à-tête with Hawthorne, Howells had heard the creator of Hester Prynne and Zenobia, with "the abrupt transition of his talk," begin "somehow to speak of women." Hawthorne said he had "never seen a woman whom he thought quite beautiful. In the same way he spoke of the New England temperament, and suggested that the apparent coldness in it was also real, and that the suppression of emotion for generations would extinguish it at last" (*LFA*, 49–50). Hawthorne's "abrupt transition" implied a connection that Howells was to make more explicit in his own work: between the suppressed emotion of the New England type and the "imperfection" of women. If Howells regarded the American Girl, in Paul John Eakin's phrase, as "a *precedented* heroine" who evinced the moral authority of antebellum New England in post–Civil War America,[18] he also saw her as the heiress to New England frigidity; and, like the fatally flawed Georgiana in Hawthorne's tale, she bore to his eyes the birthmark of suppressed emotion. This is the "taint" that William Wasserstrom detects in the Howellsian Girl. Like Hawthorne, Howells was "unable wholeheartedly to admire any woman because none were immune from the disease of passion. . . . And he better than anyone knew its symptoms."[19] Howells recognized at some level that the "method in feminine madness" was repression and that the "disease of passion" was often marked by neurotic symptoms. To see passion as a "disease" was itself a neurotic symptom that Howells shared with those of his contemporaries who subscribed to the genteel code.

In *A Chance Acquaintance*, Kitty Ellison and Miles Arbuton, the American Girl and her suitor, are usually seen as cultural symbols: Eriecreek versus Boston, the democratic West versus the aristocratic East. But in their courtship they also enact a psychodrama. The conflict between Western and Eastern values stands for the conflict between Howells' wish for emotional freedom and his need for emotional control: Kitty's passion versus Arbuton's repression.

In Arbuton, Howells shows how the neurotic perception of passion as a "disease" can, as Wasserstrom says, "turn even an American lady into a terrible caricature of her superb self" (p. 491). Such a transmogrification occurs in *A Chance Acquaintance* when Arbuton, having proposed to Kitty, is anxiously awaiting her answer. As he descends the steps from his attic room, he sees her at the window: "He was not a man of quick fancies; but to one of even slower imagination and of calmer mood, she might very well have seemed unreal, the creature of a dream, fantastic, intangible, insensible, arch, not wholly without some touch of the malign"—a veritable Lady Macbeth, as her uncle has seen her to be just a moment before. What accounts for this "elfish transfiguration," which makes Arbuton groan "over her beauty as if she were lost to him forever" (CA, 129)? Kitty has taken the shape of Arbuton's unconscious fears.

From the start of the novel, it is plain that this scion of New England Puritanism—named, appropriately, after Miles Standish—is tortured by suppressed emotions that he keeps in check by a fanatical adherence to the code of the Bostonian gentleman. The presence of these emotions is betrayed by Arbuton's unconscious impulses, which override his snobbish disdain for Kitty and the Ellisons and lead him into an inextricable involvement with them, an involvement he secretly desires. He "unwittingly" overtakes the Ellisons after having resolved "to follow them back to the boat at a discreet distance" (CA, 17); he offers his card to Colonel Ellison "by an impulse which he would have been at a loss to explain" (CA, 19); he hears the "sad news" of Kitty's aunt's confinement to Quebec "with a cheerful aspect unaccountable in one who was concerned at Mrs. Ellison's misfortune" (CA, 52); he feels "a formless hope" that "something might entangle him further" and compel his own stay in Quebec (CA, 54); he entertains marital fantasies about Kitty despite her social unsuitability (CA, 95).

Kitty represents to Arbuton the possibility of an emotional liberation that is proscribed to his Bostonian temperament—the "sense of freedom" that comes in an exultant "moment of frenzy" when he spontaneously hurls a pebble at the prisonlike cliff walls of Cape Eternity and hears it strike the target "with a shock that seemed to have broken all the windows on the Back Bay" (CA, 46). What he has broken are his "defences" (CA, 47): "It was as if for an instant he had rent away the ties of custom, thrown off the bonds of social allegiance, broken down and trampled upon the conventions which his whole life long he had held so dear and respectable." At this moment the "spirit of his college days, of his boating and ball-playing youth, came upon him" (CA, 46).

Arbuton has regressed, in other words, like an adolescent in the throes of an identity crisis; and like some of Erikson's severest cases, Arbuton goes so far as to choose a "negative identity,"[20] trying to become the antithesis to what he is by attempting to throw off his heritage as if it were sewn into the overcoat that, in a later scene, he gives away to a befuddled bystander. This coat is the sign of his "self-respect," his "condition" (CA, 99); by divesting himself of it, Arbuton hopes to shed the skin of his Bostonian customs and to escape the maze of his conflicted feelings toward the forbidden object, Kitty. In the heat of his passion for her, he even deludes himself into believing that these customs *are* merely skin-deep. When Kitty tries to show him how different their backgrounds really are, he loses "the sense of what she said in the music of her voice," and deflects her every dart of reason with an incanted, "'I love you!'" (CA, 141–42). Arbuton has not really changed. His cold puritan face is still visible at times behind the mask of his desperate jollity.

In *A Modern Instance*, Eustace Atherton distinguishes invidiously between Bartley Hubbard, the "natural man," and Ben Halleck, the morally refined flower of Bostonian civilization: "'The natural man is a wild beast, and his natural goodness is the amiability of a beast basking in the sun when his stomach is full. . . . No, it's the implanted goodness that saves,—the seed of righteousness treasured from generation to generation, and carefully watched and tended by disciplined fathers and mothers in the hearts where they had dropped it'" (MI, 416–17). According to Kitty's commonsense psychology, which resembles Atherton's, Miles Arbuton lacks a vital connection "'between his heart and his manners,'" which seem "'to have been put on him instead of having come out of him'": "'He's very well trained, and nine times out of ten he's so exquisitely polite that it's wonderful; but the tenth time he may say something so rude that you can't believe it. . . . [H]is training doesn't hold out, and he seems to have nothing natural to fall back upon'" (CA, 90). That is, within "'the mere husk'" of Arbuton's "'well-dressed culture and good manners'" (CA, 92), the seed of righteousness has died, leaving him devoid of a goodness so deeply implanted in his heart as to seem "natural." On that one occasion in ten when he does not act upon his training, Arbuton lacks even the "natural goodness" of the amiable beast. But what then governs his behavior?

Kitty's psychology falters at this point because, no less than Atherton himself, she shrinks from defining what lies within the "heart" when the concentric husks of "implanted" and "natural goodness" have been stripped away. What she calls Arbuton's unbelievable "rudeness" is the core of violent instinct that erupts on the occasion of his pebble throwing and, more importantly, on the occasion of his saving Kitty from a charging dog, which leaps suddenly out of a darkened doorway and sinks its teeth into the breast of Arbuton's overcoat as he clutches its throat in a murderous embrace. Significantly, Howells' narrative perspective in this scene is warily detached; he never tells what happens from within Arbuton's consciousness. Rather Howells describes what Kitty sees after the dog has leapt; she does not even know, until she is later told, that the dog meant to attack her. "It had all happened so suddenly, and in so brief a time, that she might well have failed to understand it, even if she had seen it all. It was barely intelligible to Mr. Arbuton himself" (CA, 104).

It is no more intelligible to Howells; hence his narrative evasion. The vicious dog, which had been the emblem of his own neurotic boyhood terrors, signifies the destructive menace of unconscious impulses. It represents an unsayable analogue to "natural goodness"—what Howells, had he named it, might have called "natural evil": the beast lurking in the shadows when its stomach *isn't* full, crouched in readiness to leap. As the dog tears Arbuton's overcoat, so bestial passion rends the fabric of civilized life: manners, morals, rationality itself. Because Arbuton has repressed his "natural evil," he cannot recognize it except as he projects it upon Kitty. Likewise, Howells could not acknowledge his own repressed self except through an imaginative complicity with Arbuton. What Arbuton fears in Kitty is his own sexuality, mirrored in what he unconsciously recognizes as her sexuality. Whenever this recognition threatens to become conscious, Kitty becomes transformed before his eyes into the fantastic and malign creature he sees at the window. She becomes another avatar of the dog-beast who must be kenneled.

Once the beast has leapt, once Arbuton has unleashed himself from the Bostonian code, he must still find a way to control his desire, lest it annihilate him. That is, once he has projected his passion upon Kitty, it is imperative for him to muzzle her as he has formerly muzzled himself. This need explains why, as part of his apparent change of character after the dog incident, Arbuton feels a "new sense of possession" of Kitty (CA, 105). She shrewdly perceives: "'Ever since then he's been extremely careful of me, and behaved—of course without knowing it—as if I belonged to him already'" (CA, 125). Psychologically, she does "belong" to him, insofar as she now embodies what Arbuton has disowned.

All the while he is trying to take possession of Kitty, Arbuton is unconsciously resisting himself. The voice of his strict social conscience (what Freud was to call the "super-ego")[21] tells him to see her as a degraded object to which he is both shamelessly and shamefully attracted, as he is to her gloves lying on the parlor table. "Keeping the shape of her hands," they are "full of winning character"; and "all the more unaccountably they touched his heart because they had a certain careless, sweet shabbiness about the finger-tips"

(CA, 112). However desirous he is of her "sweet shabbiness," Arbuton can-not marry Kitty unless she becomes other than herself, unless she is made over into a proper lady, the female double of his Bostonian self. In secret rev-eries he imagines that he will find a way to weaken her ties to her past; "a year or two of Europe would leave no trace of Eriecreek; without effort of his, her life would adapt itself to his own, and cease to be a part of the lives of those people there" (CA, 115). Kitty must be unsexed, as it were, so that she re-sembles the safely androgynous young lady whose "peculiar restraint of line" and "temperance of ornament" stamp her with "the unmistakable character of Boston": the "look of independent innocence, an angelic expression of ex-tremely nice young fellow blending with a subtle maidenly charm" (CA, 154).

The authority of Arbuton's super-ego is more powerful, after all, than his erotic desires. He fulfills Kitty's prediction—that he will be ashamed of her "'before those you knew to be my inferiors'" (CA, 142)—by ignoring her in the presence of the ladies from Boston. All that is needed to break the spell of his infatuation, to snap him back to moral attention, is a hint that Kitty is other than a nice young maiden-fellow. This hint is provided by the older Bostonian, who bitchily teases Arbuton for having taken up with "'some fair fellow-wanderer in these Canadian wilds,—some pretty companion of voy-age.'" Arbuton starts "like one thrilled for an instant with a sublime impulse" (CA, 156). He looks at Kitty, recognizes at last that she, dressed now in her own plain clothes, can never become worthy of the "sublime" ideal; hers is a cheaper thrill that must be renounced. To the end Arbuton sees himself as "the helpless sport of a sinister chance" (CA, 160); he feels no more respon-sible for his rejection of Kitty than for his earlier attraction to her. This is true insofar as both are the results of powerful unconscious forces.

It is important to recognize that the catalyst of Arbuton's betrayal, the "lady of more than middle age," is Kitty's inferior. She is a vulgar parvenu whose manner is "full of the anxiety of a woman who had fought hard for a high place in society, and yet suggested a latent hatred of people who, in yielding to her, had made success bitter and humiliating" (CA, 154). In contrast, her young companion is a different sort, a person whom Kitty fancies she could easily befriend "if they met fairly." Kitty wonders how these two Bostonians came to be together, "not knowing that society cannot really make distinc-tions between fine and coarse, and could not have given her a reason for their association" (CA, 156). Howells' point is that Bostonian society has been corrupted; no more does Boston live up to the moral ideals it exemplified dur-ing its abolitionist days, when its social manners sprang from well-tended seeds of righteousness. As it has been rotted by caste snobbery and suppressed hatred, the "implanted goodness" of Boston has changed into "implanted evil."

Despite the subtlety of his portrayal, Howells in a letter to James dismissed

Arbuton as a "simulacrum" (SL, 2 : 17). He shared James's preference for Kitty, who, unlike Arbuton, speaks her mind and vents her feelings freely. Her pertness (which James found a trifle overdrawn) derives from Kitty's fiercely democratic upbringing in Eriecreek, under circumstances that closely resemble those of Howells' own youth in Ohio. Like him, she has a jaundiced eye for pretension and a smiling eye for the incongruities of life. This comic sensibility enables her to banish gloom even at the worst of times. But there is sometimes a nervous edge to Kitty's sense of humor. After the dog attack, feeling strangely uncomfortable in the presence of the "new" Arbuton, she bursts into "a sudden, inexplicable laugh, interrupted and renewed as some ludicrous image seemed to come and go in her mind" (CA, 105). Here laughter is her defense against inner apprehensions.

Kitty is by no means so neurotic as Arbuton, but she is no less psychologically complex. If she shares some of Howells' background, if she represents an idealized and feminized version of his healthier-minded younger self, she also embodies his youthful self-division. Kitty recognizes that in Eriecreek, as in Jefferson, there is little "to touch the heart or take the fancy; that the village was ugly, and the village people mortally dull, narrow, and uncongenial." On the day before the "ordeal" of her rejection, for the "guilty space of a heat-lightning flash," she "wickedly" entertains the notion of marrying Arbuton simply to escape the village (CA, 145). She immediately repents, but her having this thought at all shows that, as Mrs. Ellison says, one "'needn't pretend that a high position and the social advantages'" that Arbuton offers "'are to be despised'" (CA, 164). Kitty is, in short, more than a simple country girl; she recognizes a side of herself that is different from, and somewhat in conflict with, the world of Eriecreek.

This doubleness in Kitty is most apparent at the times she stops to think over "the problem of [being] a young lady who despised gentlemen, and yet remained charming to him" (CA, 102). As in the passage just quoted, Kitty often juggles psychologically, regarding herself "with a kind of impersonal compassion" (CA, 91). While enduring her humiliation by Arbuton, as she later says, "'I seemed to be like two persons sitting there, one in agony, and one just coolly watching it'" (CA, 162).

The growth of Kitty's self-consciousness is measured by her perception of the Ursuline nuns whom she often watches from her boardinghouse window. At first they seem as phantasmal as the personages of the romances she is always concocting in her literary fantasies. Later she "adopts" two of these silent sisters and begins to imagine a history and character for each: "'one is tall and slender and pallid, and you can see at a glance that she broke the heart of a mortal lover, and knew it, when she became the bride of heaven; and the other is short and plain and plump, and looks as comfortable and commonplace as life-after-dinner.'" Kitty identifies herself, when the world is bright, with the statue-like sadness of the beautiful nun; in darker hours she prefers the jolly fat one. "'But whichever I am, for the time being, I am vexed with the other; yet they always are together, as if they were counterparts'" (CA, 76–77). They are Kitty's counterparts as well, upon whom she projects her divided self and then reads her own life into the "allegory of Life" she imagines for them (CA, 115).[22]

One Kitty is the girlish enthusiast who goes about Quebec "'in a perfect haze of romances,'" casting the people she passes as potential heroes and heroines (CA, 78). This Kitty, who wears her aunt's fine dresses, is susceptible to the deluding passion of her love for Arbuton. She feels the pressure of his "superior" taste; she learns "the shame of not being a connoisseur in a connoisseur's company," and feels the dread of committing "hitherto unseen and unimagined trespasses against good taste" (CA, 66–67). She is given to seriousness and, occasionally, to irrationality. The other Kitty, who wears her own homespun clothes, is a droll and practical realist, who is naturally at ease and psychologically astute. She would write a Howellsian sort of novel called *Details*—"'just the history of a week in the life of some young people who happen together in an old New-England country-house; nothing extraordinary, little, every-day things told so exquisitely, and all fading naturally away without any particular result, only the full meaning of everything brought out'" (CA, 98).

This second self ultimately prevails. Kitty can no more permanently put on the clothes of gentility than Arbuton can permanently put them off. All along she senses that Arbuton would "'deny me the right to be what I believe I am'" (CA, 85); and she catches herself at times giving voice to her unconscious misgivings, as when she wishes, with "a pang of surprise at words that seemed to utter themselves, 'that he would go away'" (CA, 92). By refusing to make herself over to suit him, Kitty fulfills this wish and retains her independence—but at a cost. As her uncle realizes, Kitty may be the wiser for her experience, but "'she won't be the happier'" (CA, 163). Gone is her naive faith in Boston's civilized supremacy, but gone also is her chance to gain what the East does have to offer over the West. Kitty's turning her back on Arbuton is, as Colonel Ellison says, "'a sign she wasn't fit'" for Boston's social advantages (CA, 164). But she is now too sophisticated and civilized to fit contentedly in Eriecreek. Like her creator, the Boston-plated exile from Jefferson, Ohio, Kitty is a culturally displaced person.

Although *A Chance Acquaintance* has the reputation of being an attack on Boston, it was, as Lynn observes, an attack only on Boston's failure to live up to its ideals, which still lived in the mind of Kitty's uncle in Eriecreek and also perhaps in the hearts of certain denizens of Beacon Hill. Howells was "merely performing the conservative task of calling a community back to its noble past." The Brahmins really had no cause to be angry with their Western pro-

tégé because, "like Polonius, he was only asking them to be true to themselves" (Lynn, 220–21).[23] But unlike Polonius, the unquestioning servant of
a rotten social order, Howells was aware that he risked being compromised
himself if Boston should prove to be incorrigible in its present ignobility. That
Howells was no more secure inside Boston than Kitty is outside of it is suggested by the deliberately vague ending of A Chance Acquaintance, in which
Kitty is leaving Quebec to "'work out her destiny some other way'" (CA,
164).

Readers of the novel had their own ideas about what that destiny should
be. Despite the enormity of the mismatch between Kitty and Arbuton, which
Howells stressed from first to last, readers of romantic taste chose to overlook
Howells' realistic intentions and to hope against hope that he would find a
way to marry the lovers. When he did not, some complained of their frustration and demanded at least a more satisfactorily connubial sequel.[24] Howells,
after all, had left the door open a crack. If Arbuton was "a Bostonian, not the
Bostonian," as he placated Oliver Wendell Holmes (LFA, 127), then there
still might be a suitable Eastern mate for the likes of Kitty.

This faint hope quelled Howells' own fear of cultural displacement, which
was partly a metaphor of his psychological self-alienation. In his fiction of the
1870s, using the symbolic geography of East versus West, America versus Europe, Howells figured the homelessness of his repressed desires, the incompat-
ibility between sexuality and the civilized code to which he consciously
subscribed.

IV

This is the underlying theme of The Lady
of the Aroostook, in which the American Girl makes the match that Kitty does
not. But in this most idyllic of Howells' novels, the ostensibly sunny outcome
is shadowed by unconscious implications that seem dissonant with the writer's
intentions.

At first glance Howells appears to be playing a variation on the international theme, such that his heroine Lydia Blood recalls Daisy Miller rather
than Kitty Ellison. Annette Kar, for example, sees both Howells' and James's
novels springing from "a common impulse to examine the European versus
the American solutions to a major problem of social morality"; and she classi-
fies Lydia and Daisy as American Girls abroad, whose "natural manner" is a
peculiarly American combination of "inviolable innocence" with "instinctive
moral judgment."[25] But read strictly as an international novel, The Lady of the
Aroostook is bound to be disappointing. Not only does Howells postpone
Lydia's arrival in Europe to the last quarter of the novel, but then he car-
icatures European society.

Howells treated Europe reductively because, as Higginson saw, *The Lady of the Aroostook* was really an "interoceanic episode," implying "a dialogue between the Atlantic and Pacific slopes." Howells made this dialogue literal in the novel by having Lydia born in California, raised in rural New England, courted by a scion of Europeanized Boston, and settled with him in her native West. Under the guise of an international novel, Howells was reconsidering the problem of interoceanic American displacement that he had left unresolved in *A Chance Acquaintance*. He did so with characters whose courtship involved the same sort of psychological interaction that I have discussed in regard to Kitty Ellison and Miles Arbuton.

Like Kitty, Lydia Blood is an outsider to the elite Boston society of her suitor (James Staniford), but she is a natural aristocrat nonetheless. She possesses, as Staniford sees, "'the genius of good society'" (*LA*, 72) as well as a "'supernatural innocence'" (*LA*, 57) that gives her mind the delicious wholesomeness and thrilling freshness of spring water (*LA*, 92). Like Hawthorne's Phoebe Pyncheon, whom she also resembles, Lydia personifies "the stern old stuff of Puritanism, with a gold thread in the web." [26] But like Hawthorne's seamstress Hester Prynne, who adorns the scarlet letter of her shame with golden thread, Lydia is a decidedly dark Puritan. With her olive hue and her sloe-black eyes, Lydia is unmistakably sexual.

Howells stresses Lydia's sexuality most obviously in her surname. "'I should have liked it better if her name hadn't been Blood,'" Staniford's friend Dunham remarks (*LA*, 58). "Blood" discomfits Dunham, who resembles Arbuton in his preference for bloodless women like Miss Hibbard, "the most exacting of her sex," to whose invalidism Dunham's manhood will be "perfectly sacrificed" (*LA*, 74). Later in the novel, Lydia's aunt Mrs. Erwin explains why she failed to introduce her to Lady Fenleigh: "'but it didn't seem as if I *could* get the Blood out. It *is* a fearful name . . . it sounds so terribly American'" (*LA*, 260). "Blood" suggests a fleshly frankness incompatible with Mrs. Erwin's gentility of manner and her Europeanized view of virginal sex. While she can blithely condone the sexual looseness of her European friends, Mrs. Erwin hypocritically dreads the appearances of her niece's unchaperoned but perfectly innocent shipboard romance with Staniford. That Lydia can be both sexual *and* innocent is what makes her a displaced person in Europe, Europeanized Boston, or degenerately Puritan New England.

Lydia's chaste sexuality is most strikingly dramatized in the scene where she appears for Sunday breakfast in her black silk dress. Howells has already established that Lydia has "the slim and elegant shape which is the divine right of American girlhood" (*LA*, 7), and Thomas the cabin boy has approvingly noticed her figure. "'I tell you,'" he says after she comes on board, "'I shall like to see you with that silk on'" (*LA*, 31).

She came out to breakfast in it, and it swept the narrow spaces, as she emerged from her state-room, with so rich and deep a murmur that every one looked up. She sustained their united glance with something tenderly deprecatory and appealingly conscious in her manner, much as a very sensitive girl in some new finery meets the eyes of her brothers when she does not know whether to cry or laugh at what they will say. Thomas almost dropped a plate. "Goodness!" he said, helplessly expressing the public sentiment in regard to a garment of which he alone had been in the secret. No doubt it passed his fondest dreams of its splendor; it fitted her as the sheath of the flower fits the flower.

Captain Jenness looked hard at her, but waited a decent season after saying grace before offering his compliment, which he did in drawing the carving-knife slowly across the steel. "Well, Miss Blood, that's right!" Lydia blushed richly, and the young men made their obeisances across the table.

The flushes and pallors chased each other over her face, and the sight of her pleasure in being beautiful charmed Staniford. "If she were used to worship she would have taken our adoration more arrogantly," he said to his friend when they went on deck after breakfast. (*LA*, 110–11)

Like the flushes and pallors on Lydia's face, the impressions she makes in this scene alternate between sensuousness and chasteness. Lydia is "appealingly conscious" of the men's admiration but as a sister, not a siren, would be. Thomas's sexual excitement is balanced by his apt exclamation, "'Goodness!'" Captain Jenness's suggestive drawing of the knife across the steel is juxtaposed to his saying grace. And what charms Staniford is that he can adore as well as desire her.

Indeed Staniford must overcome the prudery he initially shares with Dunham in order to become a worthy mate for Lydia. Early in the novel Staniford's acerbic wit and analytical habit of mind are shown to be defenses against dealing with women any more intimately than with "an elder-brotherly kindness for the whole sex" (*LA*, 97). Although he professes to Dunham, "'I have the noble earth-hunger; I must get upon the land'" (*LA*, 65), he is literally at sea, unable to fulfill his pastoral dreams. Dunham correctly guesses that his friend hesitates to go West alone. "'Now, if you were taking some nice girl with you!'" he speculates. "'What nice girl would go?'" Staniford retorts, and then adds in a revealing literary allusion, "'I will take some savage woman, she shall rear my dusky race'" (*LA*, 66). This line derives from the part of Tennyson's "Locksley Hall" where a frustrated lover yearns to retreat to "Summer isles of Eden lying in dark-purple spheres of sea": "There the passions cramp'd no longer shall have scope and breathing space; / I will take some savage woman, she shall rear my dusky race."[27] Like Arbuton's, Staniford's own passions have been cramped, and his "earth-hunger" starved, by the same repression that prompts him in punning on "take" to conceal its sexual connotations under persiflage. But unlike Arbuton, who never escapes the grip of repression, Staniford gradually learns to accept Lydia as both a domesticating angel and as the "savage woman" he desires.

His recognition of Lydia's dual nature parallels his discovery of her true name. When he first resolves with Dunham to protect Lydia's reputation, Staniford as yet knows her only as Miss Blood, an "'up-country schoolmarm'" (LA, 57). He speculates snobbishly that her first name is probably Lurella. Later, his patronizing attitude leads to his embarrassment:

> "but I—I—I thought your first name was"—
> "What?" asked Lydia sharply.
> "I don't know. Lily," he answered guiltily.
> "Lily *Blood!*" cried the girl. "Lydia is bad enough; but *Lily* Blood! They couldn't have been such fools!"
> "I beg your pardon. Of course not. I don't know how I could have got the idea. It was one of those impressions—hallucinations"—Staniford found himself in an attitude of lying excuse towards the simple girl, over whom he had been lording it in satirical fancy ever since he had seen her, and meekly anxious that she should not be vexed with him. (LA, 101)

The jarring contrast of "Lily" with "Blood" reflects the dichotomy in Staniford's "hallucinations" between innocence and sexuality. While he can admit to Dunham that "'Lurella Blood has a very pretty figure'" (LA, 69), such thoughts are seemingly at odds with his commitment to guard "Lily's" purity. They can be indulged in her presence only in a fantasy, which he hastens to suppress. Staniford realizes "that here suddenly he was almost upon the terms of window-seat flirtation with a girl whom lately he had treated with perfect indifference, and just now with fatherly patronage. The situation had something more even than the usual window-seat advantages; it had qualities as of a common shipwreck, of their being cast away on a desolate island together. He felt more than ever that he must protect this helpless loveliness, since it had begun to please his imagination" (LA, 102).

The sexual urges implicit in this fantasy, which is linked associatively to Tennyson's poem, become increasingly insistent. When Staniford hears Lydia sing, he feels "in his nerves the quality of latent passion in it" (LA, 120); and later, after a long walk on deck, he finds himself "carrying her hand towards his lips; and she was helplessly, trustingly, letting him" (LA, 131). This impulse he ruthlessly checks; but he encounters her the next day with commingled desire and shame: "As she lifted her glance to him, she blushed; and he felt the answering red stain his face" (*LA*, 133).

The stronger his attraction to her grows, the more fiercely he resists it. During another moonlight promenade, he finds that talking with Lydia about "the familiar project of a pastoral career in the far West" invests it "with a color of romance which it had not worn before" (*LA*, 166). As he presses her against him, drawing her shawl around her shoulders, he makes an unconscious leap between the pastoral idyll of the West and his erotic fantasy of shipwreck. "His mind wandered; he hardly knew what he was saying,—'but the one utterly inexorable calamity—the same now as when the first sail was spread—is a shipwreck'" (*LA*, 167). The fantasy has turned threatening because the repressed desires it signifies are threatening to surface. And for a delirious moment, despite the indecorously late hour, he yields to them. "Once Staniford had thought the conditions of these promenades perilously suggestive of love-making; another time he had blamed himself for not thinking of this; now he neither thought nor blamed himself for not thinking. The fact justified itself, as if it had been the one perfectly right and wise thing in a world where all else might be questioned" (*LA*, 167). Staniford's habitual restraint suddenly returns at the appearance of the dissolute Hicks, aboard for an alcoholic cure, who is carrying a book that Staniford gave to Lydia. By the next morning, Staniford has "hardened his heart" to Lydia: "He would not admit to himself any reason for his attitude, and he could not have explained to her the mystery that at first visibly grieved her, and then seemed merely to benumb her" (*LA*, 170).

The "mystery" is partly explained by Staniford's earlier anger with Lydia's "ignorance and inexperience": "It was shocking to think of that little sot, who had now made his infirmity known to all the ship's company, admitted to association with her which looked to common eyes like courtship" (*LA*, 156).[28] He seeks to punish Lydia for consorting with someone so obviously disreputable, but he also seeks to punish himself. His moral indignation masks both his jealousy of Hicks and his guilt for feeling jealous. He realizes that the same standards of propriety by which he judges Hicks condemn his own attentions to Lydia. To Dunham, and later to Mrs. Erwin, Staniford's behavior appears to be as questionable as Hicks's behavior appears to him. In both cases, the European rule applies: "'to treat men . . . as if they were guilty till they prove themselves innocent'" (*LA*, 280).

Howells suggests that both Hicks and Staniford really *are* innocent in their courtship of Lydia. What attracts them is not just her sexuality but her irrefragable purity, which transmutes their base passions into golden virtue. Hicks knows his alcoholism disqualifies him as Lydia's suitor, and he never makes improper advances even when he is drunk. If he could ever reform—and this seems unlikely—Hicks would do so for her sake. Similarly, Staniford learns from Lydia the difference between pure and impure passion after she sees him riding about Messina with a married woman. When he confronts her later on deck, he feels ashamed of his companion and himself: "But the sense of her frivolity—her not so much vacant-mindedness as vacant-heartedness—was like a stain, and he painted in Lydia's face when they first met the reproach which was in his own breast" (LA, 206). He feels ashamed also of the European double standard that permits him to flirt with a married woman but makes a "'beautiful young girl . . . as improperly alone in church as she would have been in a café'" (LA, 209).

Although Staniford realizes now that his feelings for Lydia are as loving as they are lustful, he is still trapped by social conventions that make no such distinction. By hewing to convention, by waiting to declare himself until Lydia reaches her aunt's home in Venice, he almost loses her. Staniford finally must trust his feelings, in which passion and principle are intertwined, to guide his actions; and he hastens to propose. Before answering him, however, Lydia asks "'what you thought when you found me alone on that ship with all of you.'" She fears, rightly, that Staniford had raised his own eyebrows to her ingenuous indiscretion. "'I want to know whether you were ever ashamed of me, or despised me for it; whether you ever felt that because I was helpless and friendless there, you had the right to think less of me than if you had first met me here in this house.'" Determined to win her hand against any scruple, Staniford seizes upon a "loop-hole of escape" in this "terrible question," and replies evasively, "'I will leave you to say.'" Rather coyly, the narrator interjects at this point: "Let those who will justify the answer. . . . A generous uncandor like this goes as far with a magnanimous and serious-hearted woman as perhaps anything else" (LA, 314–15). And he goes on to explain how Staniford has rationalized his deceit to himself.

Howells' narrative evasion here is essentially the same thing as Staniford's uncandor: both are trying to beg the question of Lydia's "respectability." Howells does so on the level of plot construction. The problem is that, as Lydia's question implies, there will always remain some doubt about her virtue—if not in Staniford's mind, then in the mind of everyone else in the societies depicted in the novel. In cultural terms Lydia brings to her marriage the stern old stuff of Puritanism without its sexual impoverishment; Staniford brings the aesthetic sensibility and the moral intelligence of the Europeanized East, but refined of its pretension and some of its sexual inhibition. But Howells is at a loss to imagine a place for his ideal couple to inhabit. Certainly Europe is out of the question. Mrs. Erwin's friends are incapable of overlooking the "singular facts" of Lydia's courtship, which Mrs. Erwin drapes with "decorous fictions" (LA, 318). Europeanized Boston is no better. Its exemplar Miss Hibbard feels nothing but contempt for "'a country girl, with country ideas, and no sort of cultivation,'" especially one whose vibrant beauty affronts her Bostonian bloodlessness (*LA*, 320). That leaves South Bradfield, Lydia's home town.

Although Howells endows Lydia with Yankee virtues, he leaves no doubt that she cannot survive in rural New England. At one point Staniford inveighs against the "'arid and joyless existence'" of country life—its paralyzed social customs, its moribund academies, its decay of the religious sentiment, its "banquets" of apples and water (*LA*, 70–71). Howells' depiction of South Bradfield largely confirms this impression. Although Aunt Maria frets about Lydia's departure for "'Venus,'" as she calls it, she can barely thaw out her reserve long enough to say goodbye, and on two occasions her attention to Lydia's affairs is distracted by her evidently greater concern with 'Mirandy Holcomb's funeral. Such morbid curiosity is matched by Aunt Maria's fetish for petty discipline and self-denial. After routing some "cowering conscience-stricken" hens from under her lilacs, she rewards herself with a cup of Japanese tea, which country people prefer, the narrator deadpans, "apparently because it affords the same stimulus with none of the pleasure given by the Chinese leaf" (*LA*, 9). When Lydia returns to the village in the winter after her marriage, the snow-buried landscape wears "an aspect of savage desolation" (*LA*, 321). The only source of heat is a sheet-iron stove in the parlor, on which Lydia's doddering grandfather keeps resting his fingers "till he burnt them, and then jerked them suddenly away, to put them back the next moment" (*LA*, 324). This pathetic, unconscious reaching for warmth contrasts to Staniford's caressing Lydia's waist—much to the dismay of Aunt Maria, who concedes only grudgingly that it might be "'natural'" for a husband to put his arm around his wife (*LA*, 325).

What Europe, Boston, and South Bradfield have in common as unsuitable homes for Staniford and Lydia is a neurotic attitude toward human sexuality, an attitude that reflects Howells' own ambivalence toward his American Girls. As William Wasserstrom remarks, Lydia Blood is typical of Howells' heroines in being "an angel who is also profoundly tainted." Although she is clearly superior to the stuffy Bostonians and the hypocritical Europeans who reject her, still Lydia seems somehow to have lost her virtue—for which offense, says Wasserstrom, Howells "exiled her to the antipodes" of California (p. 487). The major weakness of *The Lady of the Aroostook* is that although Staniford posits the existence of a "'Paradise of women'" in the "'Promised Land'" of America (*LA*, 229), Howells cannot give it imaginative form. He tells us in the sketchy final chapter that Staniford buys a ranch and finds "occupation if not profit in its management," that Mrs. Erwin abandons Europe and finds repose in the life of San Francisco and the climate of Santa Barbara, that her English husband finds a rich lode of "philological curiosities" for his

Hand-Book of Americanisms (*LA*, 319). That is all. If California is the "Paradise of women"—and we hear nothing of Lydia's fate there—we must accept it on faith.

More precisely, we must participate in Howells' narrative act of wish fulfillment, hoping against the grain of the entire novel that Lydia will find acceptance in the real world, that the sexual taint of the "savage woman" will not bar her from civilized society. Or, to put it differently, that Howells' own illicit attraction to female sexuality—an attraction that finds its expression in Staniford, Arbuton, and all the other suitors of the American Girl—will not put *him* at odds with his conscious values and civilized self-image. At this stage of his career, Howells was simply incapable of confronting the psychocultural dilemmas he was raising in his own novels. The result, as in *The Lady of the Aroostook*, was fiction that seems mysteriously attenuated, at least to any reader who looks beneath the polished surface of a book "universally accepted as a delightful trifle with untrifling implications." [29]

Such a reader was Henry James, whose judgment of *The House of the Seven Gables* is relevant here: it seems "more like a prologue to a great novel than a great novel itself"; the *donnée* of the story "does not quite fill it out"; we get "an impression of certain complicated purposes on the author's part, which seem to reach beyond it." [30] In fact, James was writing *Hawthorne* at the time he read *The Lady of the Aroostook*, and he seemed to be echoing it in his reaction to the novel. "It is the most brilliant thing you have done," he wrote to Howells, "and I don't see how your own manner can go farther." But then he said how: "I sometimes wish in this manner for something a little larger—for a little more *ventilation*, as it were. . . . You are sure of your manner now; you have brought it to a capital point and you have only to apply it. But apply it largely and freely—attack the great field of American life on as many sides as you can. Plunge into it, don't be afraid, and you will do even better things than this." [31]

Howells was about to take the plunge that James prescribed—first in *The Undiscovered Country*, which he had completed in draft before he began *The Lady of the Aroostook*, and then in *A Modern Instance*, which had been germinating in his imagination since 1875. These novels heralded Howells' entry into the "great field of American life," but they also plunged him more deeply than ever into the vertiginous seas of his inner life, where Howells could not avoid dealing with "certain complicated purposes."

CHAPTER FIVE
COMPLICATED
PURPOSES

In *Their Wedding Journey*, *A Chance Acquaintance*, and *The Lady of the Aroostook*, Howells confined himself by and large to the interactions of two main characters. As he told Warner, he was satisfied that "the real dramatic encounter" in fiction was dyadic, or involved three or four characters at most (*SL*, 2:103). It was the latter possibilities, of triangular or rectangular relationships, that shaped such novels as *A Foregone Conclusion* (1875) and "Private Theatricals" (1875–76), and the play, *A Counterfeit Presentment* (1877). Unlike *The Lady of the Aroostook*, which looked backward toward Howells' earliest fiction, these works forecast *The Undiscovered Country* (1880) and *A Modern Instance* (1882), in which Howells dealt with subjects broader than the courtship of the American Girl.

I

In *A Foregone Conclusion*, there is the first instance of what became a typical Howellsian triangle, consisting of two men and a woman, whose relationship to one of her parents is a subsidiary but important concern.[1] In this case, the men are Henry Ferris, the American consul to Venice, and Don Ippolito, a disaffected Italian priest; they are rivals for the love of Florida Vervain, who is traveling in Europe with her mother. As often happens in Howells' fiction, the characters engage in a round of psychological analysis and speculation about each other, which contributes to a certain ambiguity in Howells' portrayal of any one of them. Ferris tells Florida at one point, "'I'm the dog that fetches a bone and carries a bone; I talked Don Ippolito over with you, the other day, and now I've been talking you over with him'" (*FC*, 88). Such talk results, ironically, in profound mutual misunderstanding. In part because of cross-cultural prejudices, in part because of personal biases, each character's view of the others is more or less distorted.[2] Florida mistakes Ferris's affectionate teasing of Mrs. Vervain and herself as insolence. Ferris mistakes Florida's defensive pride as hauteur and misconstrues her compassion for Don Ippolito as seductiveness. He mistakes Don Ippolito's ingenuousness for craftiness and underestimates the sincerity of the priest's belated religious conversion. Florida mistakes Don Ippolito's amateurish tinker-

ing for inventive genius and misinterprets his love for her as friendship. Don
Ippolito mistakes Ferris's rivalry for sympathy and Florida's mothering as womanly attraction to him.

Originally titled "The Tragedy of Don Ippolito," A Foregone Conclusion
shows how the priest is victimized by his entrapment in a false role and by
the misjudgments of his American companions. Ferris, especially, is all too
eager to psychologize Don Ippolito into a neat case of neurotic conflict. Not
recognizing that he is describing himself as much as the priest, Ferris asks
Florida: "'Why mightn't it be that all his doubts came from anger and resentment towards those who made him a priest, rather than from any examination of his own mind?'" Don Ippolito is ruled, according to Ferris, by "'sub-
consciousness of his own inadequacy'" (FC, 263–64). But so is Ferris, who is
an aspiring artist incapable of painting a true picture. In his portraits of Florida and Don Ippolito, he fails to capture the essential innocence of either;
unable to recognize his own inadequacy, Ferris reduces his subjects to the narrow limits of his vision and talent. Like that of the other suitors of the American Girl, Ferris's perception is warped by his unconscious fear of sexuality.
Guilty about his unacknowledged desire for Florida, he reads his own lust into
the priest's motives and attributes to him a nonexistent "lurking duplicity"
(FC, 82). At the same time he fails, as Don Ippolito tells him, to distinguish
in Florida between "'a woman's love'" and "'an angel's heavenly pity'" (FC,
238). Ferris shares the bifurcated vision of Staniford and Arbuton by which
women are seen to be either angels or whores and by which virtue cannot
be reconciled with desire.[3]

Like Ferris, and much more than Kitty Ellison or Lydia Blood, Florida Vervain has her own psychological problems. Indeed, she is the first in a series of
overtly neurotic American Girls that leads to Marcia Gaylord in A Modern
Instance. Florida is a mass of contradictions. She is characterized oxymoroni-
cally by "violent submissiveness," "tigerish tenderness," "haughty humility,"
and "unfathomable innocence" (FC, 153, 261–62). Howells implies that
Florida's ambivalence toward her mother underlies her conflicts. At one point,
as she watches Mrs. Vervain sleeping, Florida looks into her face "with an
expression of strenuous, compassionate devotion, mixed with a vague alarm
and self-pity, and a certain wondering anxiety" (FC, 41). Her devotion and
some of her anxiety arise from Florida's conscious concern for the welfare of
her mother, whose frequent brushes with death in her family have left her
nervously delicate. Mrs. Vervain herself is a strange mixture of languor and
energy, common sense and foolishness, compassion and bigotry, sweetness and
vinegar. Although Howells does not fully develop the idea, he suggests that
Mrs. Vervain is also somewhat tyrannical—a parent who extorts obeisance
from her child by falling ill, by threatening subtly to withdraw from her (perhaps even by dying) and thus to leave her truly alone and unloved. For her

part, Florida unconsciously resents her mother's manipulations, but she cannot admit her anger to herself for fear of its emotional consequences. Resentment appears obliquely as "vague alarm and self-pity." As Ferris observes, Florida, whose tropical name suggests the heat of her passions, has "the air of being embarrassed in presence of herself, and of having an anxious watch upon her impulses" (FC, 19). Hence she is apt to displace or project her angry impulses by lashing out at Ferris instead of her mother and by attributing her own rage to him. Her loving impulses, which are often compensations for her unconscious aggression, are expressed in "the greatest excesses of self-devotion," which Ferris perceives is "merely the direction away from herself of that intense arrogance of nature which, but for her power and need of loving, would have made her intolerable" (FC, 261).

No less than the American characters, the Italian Don Ippolito is riddled with self-doubts, most importantly about his sexual identity. A priest without a strong vocation, Don Ippolito is an unwilling and frustrated celibate who seeks to escape the "'life-long habit of a lie'" (FC, 137) by falling in love with Florida. But just as Ferris tries to deny the woman he sees in her, so she denies the man she refuses to see beneath his clerical robe. If anything, this talare, which falls "about him like a woman's skirt" (FC, 146), makes Don Ippolito appear feminine. On several occasions the narrator calls attention to this aspect of the priest, as when he describes him moving about a room "with his sliding step, like some tall, gaunt, unhappy girl" (FC, 192). Later, when Florida encourages his fantasies of a new life in America, Don Ippolito yields to her plans for him with a tearful enthusiasm that gives pause to Mrs. Vervain. "'But, shedding tears, now,'" she remarks to Ferris; "'it's dreadful in a man, isn't it? I wish Don Ippolito wouldn't do that. It makes one creep. I can't feel that it's manly; can you?'" (FC, 203). This unmanly man, who finally embraces the celibacy he once detested, is the first of several sexually ambiguous, nearly androgynous, male characters in Howells' fiction.

Howells was soon to elaborate upon the homosexual implications in his love triangles—the way the two males are intimates as well as rivals—and also upon the passional bonds of children and parents. That is, he would become bolder in exploring psychosexual issues that were merely implicit in A Foregone Conclusion. But this novel, like most of those written in the 1870s, seems inchoate and confused in its treatment of material that Howells could not keep out of his fiction but that he could not keep in clear focus.

II

Perhaps the blurriest of all these early works is "Private Theatricals," the only one of Howells' novels not to appear in book form immediately after its serialization (in 1875–76). One literary rumor has it that Howells feared a lawsuit from those who thought themselves to be the models of some of his minor characters. Others, such as Carl Van Doren, believe that Howells "suppressed" the novel out of expedient commercial regard for his women readers, who would be apt to resent, as did Charles Dudley Warner's wife, what Howells called "my little freedoms to my great honor and reverence for her sex" (SL, 2:117).[4] But, as Edwin H. Cady observes, publication in the widely read *Atlantic Monthly* "was anything but suppression" (p. 192); and there is good evidence that Howells meant to challenge his readers, female or not. "It's more of an experiment upon my public than I've ever ventured before," he told his publisher, Fields, "and I shall not consider it successful till I have their approval of it in book-form" (SL, 2:110). Other letters imply that "Private Theatricals" was not republished because Howells came to recognize its artistic flaws—the flatness of the characters and the problematical ending—but could not revise it to his own satisfaction.[5]

If "Private Theatricals" was an "experiment," albeit a failed one, then what was experimental about it? Howells was not specific in his letter to Fields, but the novel itself offers some clues. First, it contains more major characters and depicts more romantic entanglements than any of Howells' early novels. There is a slightly manic quality about the multiplication of character interrelationships, to the point where it becomes difficult, given the plethora of interlocking love triangles, to keep track of who is falling in or out of love with whom. "Private Theatricals" may be imagined, diagrammatically, as a pentagon, at each point of which stands one of the major characters (Belle Farrell, Wayne Easton, William Gilbert, Susan Gilbert, Rachel Woodward). Within this pentagon one may connect virtually any three points and thereby draw a love triangle that operates in the novel.[6] Second, Howells seems to have extended his efforts in *A Foregone Conclusion* to render characters with a complexity and mystery worthy of Turgenev's example, such that their motivations are bafflingly ambiguous. Although the title is usually taken to refer to Mrs. Farrell, a seductive young widow with a theatrical flair for erotic charades, the idea of "private theatricals" applies to all the major characters, who engage one another in a repertoire of misleading roles. The keynote to the novel is struck by Mrs. Gilbert in her shrewd observation to her brother-in-law William: "'when will men learn that the boomerang is the natural weapon of woman? We're all cross-eyed when it comes to love-glances; you can't tell where we're looking'" (PT, 105). Third, Howells treated the whole matter of love glances more frankly than in any novel before *A Modern Instance*, and he dared to suggest that aggressive as well as sexual passions often serve as weapons in the war between the sexes. Mrs. Farrell and Mrs. Gilbert each in her way plays masterfully upon the emotions of the other characters to achieve her ends, which often have more to do with power than with love. The two

men in the novel, Gilbert and his boon companion Easton, are less adept
love warriors than the women; but they too cast cross-eyed glances—at Belle,
at the ingenuous Rachel, and, not least of all, at each other. Howells seems
to recognize that the sexual currents in his love triangles may flow in any
direction.

"'It's quite like a love-affair'" (PT, 133), quips Mrs. Farrell about the mutual devotion of these former comrades in arms, who resemble Damon and
Pythias and who treat each other, like the biblical David and Jonathan, with
a "delicacy, passing the love of women" (PT, 99).[7] To Belle, one of them is
"'so mightily, so heroically manly, that the other necessarily womanizes in
comparison. Isn't that it? But which is which?'" (PT, 91). To Gilbert, Easton
is "'a man's man'" (PT, 30), across whose shoulder he may lay his arm in a
gesture that is "the nearest that an American can come to embracing his
friend" (PT, 158). This gesture patches up the first of their quarrels over
Belle, who jealously connives to destroy a closeness between them that
squeezes her out. Later, when Gilbert and Easton come to trampling their
friendship under foot "with the infernal hate that may have always lurked, a
possible atrocity, in their hearts," they are saved from "the final shame" of
exchanging blows only by their "instinctive" sense of "the personal sanctity in
which they had held each other" (PT, 164). When Easton accidentally in-
jures himself, Gilbert leaps to his aid, groaning with "the anguish of the sex
which our race forbids to weep" (PT, 165).

There is nothing explicitly homosexual about this friendship, but Howells
plainly hints that the intimacy between Gilbert and Easton has an erotic element that exacerbates—by reminding women of their exclusion—the combat between the sexes that rages in this novel. "'Why is it that there isn't
some common ground for men and women to meet on, and be helpful to each
other?'" Belle laments to Easton, with as much conviction as she ever has
about anything. "'Must they always be either lovers or enemies? Yes, enemies;
it's really a state of almost warfare; there can't be any kindness, any freedom,
any sincerity'" (PT, 96). The novel implies that kindness and sincerity are
emotional luxuries to those women, like Belle and Susan Gilbert, who acutely
feel their lack of freedom, that is, their dependence upon men for purpose
and power and identity.

Belle Farrell is an "'inspired flirt'" (PT, 78), a "well-millinered wood
nymph not the least afraid of satyrs" (PT, 17), a "stylish Florence Nightingale
with a dash of Lady Macbeth" (PT, 173). She is, as Gilbert says, at once "'so
deep and so transparent. She does everything for an effect, and she isn't at
peace with herself for a moment'" (PT, 78). Belle herself confesses: "'It
seems to me that I know how to feel, but that I never feel. It seems to me that
I am always acting out the thing I ought to be or want to be, and never being
it'" (PT, 180). She is the victim, in short, of an "'*extreme unconsciousness*'"

(*PT*, 60) that impels her to act upon impulses, often destructive ones, that she does not understand. Belle aspires, as Susan Gilbert puts it, to do "'something vivid, stunning; and that isn't quite what society smiles upon—in Boston'" (*PT*, 36).

In her voluptuousness and flamboyance, Belle resembles Hawthorne's Zenobia; but, unlike Zenobia, Belle has never taken up "the Cause of Woman" because "'*that* requires self-sacrifice, too, in its way; and Mrs. Farrell doesn't like women very much, and she does like men very much; and she couldn't bear to be grotesque in men's eyes'" (*PT*, 36). Not a true radical, Belle is a feminist-*manqué* who prefers to live in a "'demi-semi-Bohemian way'" (*PT*, 35). Her lack of intellectual force and self-consciousness makes her all the more dangerous; she embodies, in fact, a distillation of the female sexuality that makes all of Howells' American Girls more or less threatening to men. She is Basil March's actress "in dishabille" and Kitty Ellison as Lady Macbeth and Lydia Blood as the "savage woman" all rolled into one: so completely the incarnation of poisonous passion that she seems more and less than human. Belle is called a sorceress, an enchantress, a witch, a Babylonian priestess. Her black magic accounts for the horror in Easton's "deep reverie" in which he imagines Gilbert and Mrs. Farrell talking and laughing together, he dressed "in his suit of white flannel," but she in "a gown of dark crimson silk, stiff with its rich texture, and trailing after her on the gray rocks and over the green ferns." Bare-headed Belle conceals "in the dark folds of her hair . . . a string of what seemed red stones at first, like garnets in color, but proved, as she came nearer, to be the translucent berries of a poisonous vine" (*PT*, 153). Even brotherly love provides scant protection from the intoxicating crimson woman.

Yet, for all her sexual menace, Belle is treated with surprising sympathy by Howells. Even at a moment when she is reveling in her power over Gilbert and Easton, the narrator intrudes to extenuate her motives: "A light of triumph burned in her dark eyes, but one could not have said that as a woman she had not a right to the few and fleeting triumphs that love gives her sex, on which it lays so many heavy burdens" (*PT*, 137–38). The overall effect of "Private Theatricals" is much as Kenneth S. Lynn describes: "For most of the story, Mrs. Farrell inspires in the reader the same sort of vengeful desire that Mrs. Kemble felt." Fanny Kemble had written during the serialization of the novel to urge Howells, "for pity's sake give her the Small Pox—she deserves it." "But in the end," says Lynn, "we are made to feel a half-respectful compassion for her" (p. 234).

Such compassion is easier to feel because Howells so carefully distances the reader (and himself) from Mrs. Farrell, making her seem to be an aberrant case of female pathology, someone to be pitied for her very excesses. He also tries to counterbalance her character, as Hawthorne did Zenobia's, by presenting a woman worthier of admiration. Howells' Priscilla is the shy and asexual

Rachel Woodward, "'the manliest girl'" Mrs. Gilbert has ever known (*PT*, 108), who, with her sisterly "'pale charm'" (*PT*, 240), strikes Gilbert and Easton each as perfectly suited to the other. Like Lydia Blood, but bleached of her dark sexuality, Rachel is the quintessence of Yankee virtue. Gilbert tells his sister-in-law: "'I don't think I've understood, before, just the sort of feminine goodness that the unbroken tradition of your New England religiousness produces. Puritanism has fairly died out of the belief . . . but in such a girl as Rachel Woodward, all that was good in it seems to survive in the life'" (*PT*, 184). Rachel's goodness is no match for Belle's wiles; and although she ends up keeping company with one of the men Belle desired (Gilbert), she loses the one *she* desired (Easton). What remains for her is the hope of becoming a good painter. Like Howells' later women artists, such as Alma Leighton in *A Hazard of New Fortunes* (1890), and Cornelia Saunders in *The Coast of Bohemia* (1893), Rachel seems likely to succeed only if she can learn to do without a man. Like Margaret Vance, who becomes an Episcopal nun in *A Hazard of New Fortunes*, Howells' purest women have a vocation for solitude and celibacy.

Only once again, in Bessie Lynde of *The Landlord at Lion's Head* (1897), was Howells to create a vamp like Belle Farrell; and in that later novel he also used a Puritan virgin (Cynthia Whitwell) as a foil. This was the narrative equivalent to "splitting of the object" as a defense mechanism.[8] Howells usually expressed his bifurcated view of women by drawing an American Girl who is tainted by sex and toward whom male characters feel ambivalence; but sometimes, as in "Private Theatricals," he divided women into virginal and whorish characters and then attempted to disown his attraction to the latter. Having isolated purity from passion, he could treat the "good" woman with unreserved approval and the "bad" one with a judicious compassion born of protective detachment. However, the vital fire of a Belle Farrell or a Bessie Lynde burns so much brighter than the votive candle of a Rachel Woodward or a Cynthia Whitwell that the "bad" woman tends unduly to dominate the novels in which she appears. Despite his use of narrative splitting in "Private Theatricals," Howells shows male characters being attracted to Belle against their (and his) better judgment. In the final chapter, for example, Mrs. Gilbert's very respectable husband is clearly fascinated by Mrs. Farrell despite his thorough disapproval of her. Evidently, so was Howells. One reason he could not revise the novel satisfactorily may be that he could find no way to prevent Belle Farrell from taking it over, such that it refused allegiance to its author's conscious values.

The third woman in "Private Theatricals," Susan Gilbert, represents another type that was to become more prevalent in Howells' fiction: the predatory mother, whose ruthlessness seems directly proportional to the degree of her invalidism. Mrs. Vervain, in *A Foregone Conclusion*, manipulates her daughter psychologically, but she lacks either the calculation or the debilitation of Susan Gilbert, or of Mrs. Breen and Mrs. Maynard in *Dr. Breen's Practice* (1881), or (worst of all) of Mrs. Mavering in *April Hopes* (1888). Technically, Mrs. Gilbert is not anyone's mother; but she has raised her orphaned brother-in-law William from his boyhood, and she clings to him with the possessiveness of a "'childless woman'" for a "'motherless boy'" (*PT*, 216). His trusting devotion and his suggestibility to her advice give her the leverage she needs to control him in "the dangerous and important matter of marriage, for she was both zealous and jealous that he should marry to the utmost advantage that the scant resources of her sex allowed" (*PT*, 32). Mrs. Gilbert's sphere of influence may be small, but she is very resourceful within it, as she deftly maneuvers to "protect" her surrogate son from her rivals for his love. She draws Belle into "daughterly" confidence in order to pry from her an admission of her disloyal preference for Gilbert over Easton. Later she purposefully pricks Gilbert's conscience in order to induce him to renounce Mrs. Farrell.

For meddling in romantic business, Mrs. Gilbert is equaled by General Wyatt in *A Counterfeit Presentment* (1877), who coerces his daughter Constance's lover into jilting her but neglects to tell Constance what he has done and why. This man, a forger and an adulterer, is an unmitigated cad in Wyatt's opinion; and Wyatt regards his actions and his later silence about them as the natural responses of a father protecting his girl's "'pure heart'" from "'a sense of intolerable contamination'" (*CP*, 37). But, contrary to his expectations, Constance blames him for the loss of her lover—she wonders, "'Does papa really like me?'" (*CP*, 71)—and she sinks into a depression that leaves her feeling so worthless and enervated that, as her mother says, she seems to take "'a dreadful pleasure in torturing those who love you.'" Falling ill is partly a vengeance upon her father: the sadistic phase of her masochism. "'I know now that I am a vampire,'" Constance says, "'and that it's my hideous fate to prey upon those who are dearest to me. He [the cad] must have known, he must have felt the vampire in me'" (*CP*, 69).

But if Constance is vampirish, so too is her father in his incestuous attachment to her. Constance can vividly recall, in a memory that seems to epitomize her happy girlhood, how she once ran down the street to her dashing officer on horseback. "'He was all tanned and weather-beaten; he sat his horse at the head of his troop like a statue of bronze.'" When he saw her coming, he leapt from his mount and "'caught her in his arms, and hugged her close and kissed her, and set her all crying and laughing in his saddle.'" Throughout her school days, Constance's father showered upon her "'presents and feasts and pleasures'"; he took her everywhere and wanted to give her everything (*CP*, 73). Such proofs of her father's love make it painfully difficult for Constance to accept that he could ever have thwarted her. When she learns the truth, she flies at him in a rage that prefigures Marcia Gaylord's tantrum at her father's dismissal of Bartley Hubbard: "'And after all these days and weeks and months that seem years and centuries of agony, you tell me that it was *you* broke my heart! No, no, I never *will* forgive you, father!'" (CP, 146). But she immediately does, as soon as General Wyatt pulls the stop of paternal self-pity: "'I had hoped something, everything, from my girl's self-respect, her obedience, her faith in me'" (CP, 149).

Melting before Wyatt's distress, Constance becomes a pliant papa's girl again; but her submission to her father is partially displaced in her yielding also to a substitute lover—a man, indeed, who bears so uncanny a resemblance to the cad that he seems to be his "*doppelgänger*" (CP, 117). (His face is the "counterfeit presentment.") But Bartlett is also the double of General Wyatt in his quick temper and worshipful devotion to Constance. In marrying Bartlett, the girl is achieving a safe resolution of her Electra complex; she is choosing a man who resembles her father (as the cad did also), but one whom it is not taboo for her to desire.[9] "'I'm rather a deep and darkling villain myself,'" jokes Bartlett at the end. "'You?'" replies Constance, "'Oh, you are as nobly frank and open—as—as—as papa!'" (CP, 153). In light of Wyatt's less than frank and open dealings with her, Constance's statement has chillingly ironic overtones.

It is unclear if Howells intended them to be heard, however, because despite his use of the incest theme, he seems to have envisioned A *Counterfeit Presentment* as a comedy suitable for an evening of light entertainment at the theater. The last two acts, one of which was added after book publication in order to increase the chances for stage success, effectively gloss over the psychosexual issues raised in the first two acts.[10] As Oscar W. Firkins notes, A *Counterfeit Presentment* is tonally incongruous: "There are three grades of seriousness in the play: the coincidence [of Bartlett's resemblance to the cad] is inherently light; the situation of Constance is essentially tragic; but the treatment occupies a middle zone, lightening and darkening as occasion serves. As often happens in Mr. Howells, the depth of the suffering exceeds that of the story."[11] This last phrase brilliantly sums up the weaknesses of Howells' work in the 1870s. Only when he began to explore the depths of his characters' suffering did Howells give that "ventilation" to his manner that James felt was lacking in The *Lady of the Aroostook*. And since the characters' suffering so often derived from unconscious sources, Howells could not avoid, in writing his more ambitious novels, exploring the undiscovered country of his own inward terrain.

III

"In an intimate sense it is a very deeply interesting piece of autobiography," wrote Charles Eliot Norton to the author of *The Undiscovered Country* (1880). "You would rightly protest against the public critic who should look at your book in this way; but you will not be troubled that the friend discovers in it what the critic has no right to surmise."[12] As one of Howells' oldest Bostonian friends, Norton was in a position to recognize the disguised self-portraiture in Howells' novel of spiritism and Shakerism. The character of Ford, for instance, was drawn from Howells' own experience as a self-exiled Westerner who felt no more at home in the elite social circles of Boston than in the village he had left behind. Like Howells, Ford is also a writer, though not a successful one, interested in the decaying fabric of New England rural life. Dr. Boynton, the fanatical and quixotic quester for revelations from beyond, owed much to Howells' own father and also to Robert Dale Owen, whose writings on spiritism had occasioned a public embarrassment for Howells as editor of the *Atlantic*.[13] A major literary source of *The Undiscovered Country* was *The Blithedale Romance*, Howells' personal favorite among Hawthorne's books.[14] The long section of the novel set in Vardley was based on Howells' visits to the Shaker community at Shirley, Massachusetts. He felt obliged, in fact, to insist in a footnote that his Shakers were "imaginary in everything but their truth, charity, and purity of life, and that scarcely less lovable quaintness to which no realism could do perfect justice" (*UC*, 161n).

The Undiscovered Country had taken a long time for Howells to write, longer than any of his early novels; and by the end of it he was feeling "pretty well used up," as he told C. D. Warner.[15] Howells must have known that he had used himself in more intimate a sense than even Norton could recognize; for *The Undiscovered Country* had engaged its author at the deepest personal levels. The central theme of the novel—the erosion of traditional morals and beliefs—reflected Howells' own religious doubts and his "anguish over the impact of science as a severe blight on man's hopes for immortality."[16] Furthermore, he recognized that spiritism was intimately related to unconscious motivation, a subject very much in the American intellectual air in the 1870s and one that Howells had explored tentatively in his early novels.

Oliver Wendell Holmes, for example, was restating a commonplace when he said in *Mechanism in Thought and Morals* (1871): "The more we examine the mechanism of thought, the more we shall see that the automatic, unconscious action of the mind enters largely into all its processes. Our definite ideas are stepping-stones; how we get from one to the other, we do not know: something carries us; we do not take the step."[17] Howells, who had reviewed Holmes's book in the *Atlantic*, might have been remembering these remarks when he wrote in *The Undiscovered Country*: "The origin of all our impulses is obscure, and every motive from which we act is mixed. Even when it is simplest we like to feign that it is different from what it really is, and often we do not know what it is" (*UC*, 106).

Without his knowing it, Howells' own mixed motives had informed his writings of the 1870s. These obscure impulses were present too in *The Undiscovered Country*, but here they were treated more forthrightly and consciously, as if Howells were capitalizing in this novel on the self-knowledge he had earned in the writing of his earlier ones. *The Undiscovered Country* was a pivotal novel that gave definitive expression to the themes of his earlier work and at the same time pointed toward the more ambitious work to come.

In the configuration of characters, for example, Howells used the familiar triangle of the American Girl, her suitor, and his rival; but he gave equal stress to the triangle of the American Girl, her suitor, and her parent. For the first time in his fiction, Howells was making explicit the intersection of these triangles: how the parent often resembles the rival, how the psychodrama of courtship is played out in more than one generation. He also introduced a variation into each triangle that showed his growing awareness of psychological complexities. Egeria's relationship to Dr. Boynton was an augmented version of the father-daughter complex he had first explored in *A Counterfeit Presentment*; but Howells also took into account the "missing" parent, by showing how Egeria's mother exerts an influence from beyond the grave. In the other triangle, Howells split the figure of the male rival into heterosexual and homosexual components, represented by Hatch and Phillips—a split that had been implicit in the androgynous Don Ippolito. Thus not only must Ford contend with Hatch for Egeria, but Egeria must contend with Phillips for Ford.

This latter rivalry appears less prominently in the novel itself than in the drafts that led up to publication.[18] In the galley proofs for the *Atlantic* serial, which Howells revised heavily, there were unmistakable signs that Phillips was meant to be, as Ford says, "'an example to our generation of the Greek ideal of life.'" This comically foppish gentleman, known in Boston for "his taste for bricabrac in human nature as well as objects of art," is valued socially as an "introducible man who could be presented to puzzling novelties of either sex, and help get them safely through the evening, and could afterwards be trusted for a graphic account of them." The novelty of the rugged Westerner is so great that, as Phillips remarks to Ford after tracking him to Mrs. Le Roy's boardinghouse, "'I'm always looking for you, my dear fellow.'" Earlier he explains:

> "I think one of the advantages of another life—a new departure—may be that we shall be able to resist the fascination of such characters as yours."
>
> "And,—I'm fascinating?" asked Ford.
>
> "O yes,—to women, and to undecided men like myself. Didn't you know it?" . . .

"Now you *are* flattering me," said Ford with an ironical smile. "Be frank: you don't mean it."

"I'm doing you simple justice," returned Phillips. "And can't you see what an irresistible attraction you must naturally have for a man like me?"

"I've never been at the pains to formulate you," said Ford[.] "I don't know what sort of man is like you."

Howells himself evidently thought better of formulating Phillips too plainly for he deleted from the novel all of the passages I have just quoted.[19] But he did retain enough to make it clear that Phillips's interest in Ford is homo-erotic.[20] As the narrator says: "Such men as Phillips consorted with were of the feminine temperament, like artists and musicians (he had a pretty taste in music); or else they were of the intensely masculine sort, like Ford, to whom he had attached himself. He liked to have their queer intimacy noted, and to talk of it with the ladies of his circle, finding it as much of a mystery as he could" (*UC*, 37).

This "queer intimacy" does not mystify Egeria, who shrewdly perceives that Phillips is the major obstacle to the progress of her love for Ford. During the early stage of their courtship at Vardley, Egeria raises the subject of Phillips, as if out of the blue:

"Does Mr. Phillips write, too?" asked the girl.

The abruptness of the transition was a little bewildering; but Ford answered, "My Phillips? No; he talks."

"But hasn't he any business?"

"None of his own. Did he amuse you?"

"I don't think I understood him," said Egeria.

"He would be charmed with your further acquaintance. He would tell you that he could meet you on common ground,—that he didn't understand himself." (*UC*, 322–23)

In effect, Egeria is testing the strength of Phillips's hold on Ford, which re-sembles Dr. Boynton's mesmeric hold on her; and it is essential to her interests that Phillips's charm be dispelled.

Howells arranges the plot so that a rift occurs between the two men, leav-ing the field clear for Egeria. Phillips is jealously shocked to learn at second hand of the seriousness of Ford's attachment to the "'Pythoness,'" as he per-sists in calling Egeria:

"Going to marry her!" cried Phillips.

"Why, of course. Did you think anything else? Is marriage such an unnatural thing?"

"No. But Ford's marrying is." (*UC*, 383)

Phillips has a premonition that he has done his "'last talking'" to Ford. This fear is realized when Ford seizes upon a pretext to break with his friend; he blames Phillips unfairly for the malicious gossip of Mrs. Perham. Later, after his marriage, Ford is able "to see Phillips's innocence in what occurred"; but the two men "could never have been easy in each other's presence after that scene, though they have met on civil terms" (*UC*, 416). What stands in the way of any other terms, of course, is Egeria; and Phillips salves the sting of Ford's rejection by backbiting his wife, spreading the rumor that domestic life has softened Ford's rough appeal and transformed him from "'bricabrac'" to "'part of the world's ordinary furniture.'" "'When he married the Pythoness,'" Phillips intimates, "'I was afraid there was too much bricabrac; but really, so far as I can hear, they have neutralized each other into the vulgarest common-place'" (*UC*, 417).

Even in the censored form in which it got into the novel, the homoerotic desire of Phillips for Ford is more vitally imagined than the heterosexual at-traction of Hatch toward Egeria. Hatch is drawn so mechanically that it seems that Howells was merely going through the motions in creating him. Hatch's attentions to Egeria produce little or no suspense about the marital outcome of the novel, and he is finally dispatched by the clumsy device of Howells' revealing an offstage engagement to some woman out West. Indeed, it seems that Hatch's devotion to the Boyntons was always inspired less by a love interest in Egeria than by his fondness for her father.

Here another part of the homosexual motif becomes perceptible. Howells implies that Phillips is replaced in Ford's life not just by Egeria but also by Dr. Boynton, who becomes a rival to his daughter. After regarding Ford as his worst enemy for most of the novel, the old man suddenly adopts him as a surrogate son, thereby displacing Egeria (who has failed him) from his bedside intimacy. As with Phillips's attentions, Ford is acquiescent to Boynton's, which nearly monopolize his time as the doctor nears his death. "As the days passed, a curious sort of affectionate confidence grew up between Ford and the fan-tastic theorist, and the young man listened to his talk with a kindliness which he did not trouble himself to reason" (*UC*, 288).

Lynn calls Boynton "the spitting image of William Cooper Howells" (p. 246); and, in light of Howells' attachment to his father, the "affectionate confidence" that Ford does not "trouble himself to reason" may be recognized as the homoerotic aspect of an Oedipus complex. The heterosexual links of an Oedipal triangle are also present: in the incestuous bond between Boynton and Egeria, in which the young woman figures as Boynton's lost wife and mother as well as his daughter; and in the love of Egeria and Ford, which is also figuratively incestuous insofar as Ford is a replacement for Egeria's father.

That Egeria is bound to her father in an Electra complex has been convinc-ingly demonstrated by Kermit Vanderbilt; and I will not remake this case or

review the plentiful evidence for it, evidence that may be found in the published novel and also in the manuscript.[21] As Vanderbilt concludes, Dr. Boynton's mesmeric designs mask his own forbidden feelings: "His spiritualist ardor
acts as a censor; it gives him a respectable excuse for controlling Egeria and
rebuffing Ford, all in the name of spiritual progress for the race. What becomes poignant through it all is the more deeply buried motive—Boynton's
desired reunion with the wife he had loved" (p. 30).

The death of Boynton's wife is the key to his behavior, as Vanderbilt says.
But it should be added that Boynton's poignant attempt to replace his wife
with his daughter has also a distinctly sadistic side that resembles the cruelty
of Austin Sloper toward Catherine in James's *Washington Square* (serialized the
same year as *The Undiscovered Country*). Like Dr. Sloper, Dr. Boynton is
driven by rage as well as by grief. Unconsciously, he feels betrayed by his wife,
whose "abandonment" of him he avenges by controlling their child so forc-
ibly. He punishes Egeria as well for having been, as the manuscript makes
clear, the direct cause of her mother's death.[22] In his mastery of Egeria, Boynton also seeks a belated compensation for his lack of control over his wife's
fate; he is unconsciously assuring himself that he will never be so helplessly
abandoned again. Spiritism promises to Boynton the even stronger assurance
that he has not really been abandoned at all, that his wife may comfort him
from the world beyond.

Boynton's hunger for certainty is itself a neurotic symptom; his voracious
need for emotional security makes him childishly gullible. As Olov W.
Fryckstedt remarks, "Faced with new 'facts' or 'phenomena' he is instantly
ready to formulate new and sweeping theories. He displays a misguided and
undisciplined intellectual ingenuity as he builds new fantastic theories on the
ruins of old ones he has discarded. His enthusiasm when he thinks that he has
found a new lead is of a feverish intensity which suggests a nervous disorder."[23] Obsessive theorizing is Boynton's way of containing a volcanic inner
violence—an annihilating infantile rage—that erupts now and then in out-
bursts of vituperation, apoplexy, paranoid delusion, and murderous fantasy.
Waiting for the northbound train at the Boston station, he observes the rail-
road bridges outlined against a darkening sky. "'They look like so many gib-
bets,'" he remarks matter-of-factly to Egeria. "'It's a homicidal sight,—or suicidal'" (*UC*, 112).

The destructive/self-destructive urges implicit in this bizarre comment find
expression also in Boynton's hysterical hatred for his dead wife's father, who
quite sensibly opposed Boynton's scheme for making a mesmeric spectacle of
Egeria. As Vanderbilt suggests, Boynton's rivalry with his father-in-law is rep-
licated psychologically in his rivalry with Ford, his prospective son-in-law.
Howells does surely sense how Oedipal antagonisms are regenerated. He also
shows, in the partial cure of Boynton's neurosis, how the unconscious cycle of

violence may be ended by bringing its sources into consciousness. Boynton's crucial recognition that he "'played the vampire'" toward Egeria (*UC*, 319) allows him to seek reconciliation both with his wife's father and with Ford.

In his depiction of Boynton, Howells himself was making more fully conscious what had been implicit in his earlier novels: the connection between neurosis and repression, between irrational acts and forbidden impulses. As Boynton comes to realize about Egeria, her gift as a medium, "'a condition of the highest clairvoyant force'" (*UC*, 68), was "'the perishable efflorescence of a nervous morbidity'" (*UC*, 317), and his attempts to perpetuate and to exploit her neurosis had recklessly endangered "'her health and her sanity'" (*UC*, 361). Egeria too is eventually released from the coils of the Electra complex by a growth of self-awareness; but what she discovers in herself is not incestuous desire—that remains unconscious—but a powerful instinct for human love.

IV

The romance of Ford and Egeria Boynton is the culminating courtship of the American Girl in Howells' novels of the 1870s. Like Rachel Woodward, Egeria is a flower of New England's Indian summer, a virtuous and unpretentious country girl; like Lydia Blood, she combines the graces of a natural aristocrat with a sylvan spirit that makes her seem, after her recovery at Vardley, "a part of the young terrestrial life that shone and sang and bloomed around her" (*UC*, 191). An artist or a poet might have "figured her in his fancy as the Young Ceres: she looked so sweet and pure an essence of the harvest landscape, so earthly fair and good" (*UC*, 213). And so sensual, as Howells had made clearer in a sentence he deleted from this passage: "her grand height was filled to the proportions of ripe womanhood, and had lost the girlish slenderness that had once made her look frail." In a later scene, also deleted before publication, this Young Ceres had displayed her fecundity with a suggestiveness seldom equaled in Howells' writing. Egeria is strolling in the edenic Shaker garden with Ford, "looking dreamily" (*UC*, 300) at the beds of prince's feather, coxcomb, bachelor's button, mourning bride, marigold, and touch-me-not, when she notices some seed pods from a balsam fir. "She stooped down and carefully gathered one, which she flung into his hand. There was no result. 'It isn't quite ripe enough,' she said. She gave the pod a little push with her finger and it sprang open with antic fury, and tossed its seeds out upon the ground. He smiled at it [in] transport, and she said, 'It ought to have done that of itself[.]' [H]e felt glad that it had not. But her part was so far from coquetry that if he had been a much gallanter man he could not have said what he felt."

What Ford feels is implicit from the very start, in Mrs. Le Roy's parlor, when he sets eyes upon Egeria's "beautiful, serious face," her alert blue eyes, and her blonde hair, which has "a plastic massiveness" and which lies "heaped in a heavy coil on her neck, where its rich abundance showed when she turned her profile away" (*UC*, 4). Ford is enticed by the sexual magnetism of this bewitching creature, and he finds himself pursuing her against his will. She, likewise, is unconsciously attracted to him, as when early in the novel she hurriedly smoothes her hair and arranges her dress and rushes downstairs to a visitor she thinks is Ford, her supposed enemy, "with such eagerness as a girl might show in hastening to greet her lover" (*UC*, 76).

As Ford later tells her, "'we all control one another in the absurdest way.'" For most of the novel, this idea—as Egeria phrases it, "'that we can have power over others without knowing it, and even without wishing it'" (*UC*, 323)—is an all too threatening reminder of her father's mesmeric control. Having escaped so narrowly from him, Egeria has no wish to be enslaved by Ford; she fears there may be truth in Ford's joking description of himself as "'some malignant enchanter'" who has "'the power of casting an ugly spell'" over her (*UC*, 332). This fear is allayed at last when Ford and Egeria discover that the force that draws them together is nothing ugly after all, only the beneficent "spell" of love (*UC*, 411)—the kind of love that the Shaker elder Elihu describes as "'the master-feeling of the human heart; it flourishes in the very presence of death; it grows upon sorrow that seems to kill. It knows how to hide itself from itself. It takes many shapes, and calls itself by many other names'" (*UC*, 349).

The Freudian name for this "master-feeling"—which Elihu calls this "supreme passion" in the manuscript—would be Eros. In Freud's usage, Eros connotes much more than the purely genital function of human sexuality; it encompasses the transformations (or sublimations) of libido into nongenital forms of life-giving human love and even into the religious idea of divine love. But however ethereal a shape Eros might take, it remains connected *au fond* to sexuality.

This is precisely the point that Elihu tries to make to Ford when he tells him why it is impossible for the celibate Shakers to tolerate the presence of the young lovers in their midst: "'Nothing . . . is so hard to combat in the minds of our young folks as the presence of that feeling ["this passion" in the manuscript] in others who consider it holy and heavenly, while we teach that it is of the earth, earthy'" (*UC*, 348). To Elihu, there is a sharp distinction to be made between Eros, which masks the unholy earthiness of sex in a counterfeit presentment of heavenly holiness, and true heavenly love, which is purely spiritual. To the Shakers, Eros, insofar as it involves sexuality, is incompatible with and antagonistic to divine love.

Howells himself regarded such a distinction as problematical because the logic of splitting Eros from divine love could lead only to the celibacy of the Shakers, whose refusal to regenerate themselves is treated in the novel as the fatal defect in their otherwise admirable way of life. In fact, the most admirable of the Shakers, such as Sister Frances, find ways to circumvent the strict rule, at least vicariously.[24] Elihu, by contrast, is portrayed as a stiff and sapless dogmatist; and, tellingly, among the non-Shakers, only Boynton, whose fanaticisms are shown to be neurotic, approves of the celibate life. When Boynton implies that Egeria should join the Vardley community, Ford is understandably horrified, as if in an "odious dream," by the "image of Egeria in the Shaker garb, with her soft young throat hidden to the chin, and the tight gauze cap imprisoning her beautiful hair" (UC, 292). To him, celibacy is "'begging the question'" (UC, 291). Egeria agrees. In a deleted passage, she expressed plainly what was Howells' own opinion: "'Why don't they get married and live together naturally? I think that is the best way.'"[25]

Yet in The Undiscovered Country, as in The Lady of the Aroostook, there is ambiguity in Howells' conception of what is "natural." Like Elihu, he was wary of the sexual component of human love; but whereas Elihu distinguishes between human love (Eros) and heavenly love, Howells distinguishes between the heavenly and earthly aspects of Eros. For Elihu, human love cannot resemble divine love because it involves sexuality; for Howells, human love, even in its genital/reproductive aspects, does resemble the divine love that he saw reflected in the regenerative cycles of nature. For Howells the earthiness of Eros—what makes it unheavenly—lies not in sexuality per se, but in the unsublimated forms that sexuality takes in the unconscious.

That is, Howells was haunted by a profound, unresolved fear of repressed Eros: the perverse urges, including incestuous desires, that threatened his own fragile psychic stability and his firmly held ideas of civilized order. But he feared just as much the violent impulses of the unconscious—what Freud was to call the aggressive instincts and later would postulate in the form of a death instinct (Thanatos). Sex and aggression, Eros and Thanatos, are so tightly intertwined, according to Freud, that it is extremely difficult to distinguish the workings of one from those of the other. Howells made no distinction at all, calling both unconscious forces by the same name, usually "passion," by which he meant the anarchic and irrational part of human nature, whether in its sexual or aggressive form. Thus for Howells the ideal of human love is not Eros minus genital sex, but Eros purified of passion.

Even more than Lydia Blood, Egeria represents the embodiment of this ideal. For all her eroticism, which exceeds that of any of Howells' American Girls before Marcia Gaylord, Egeria is meant to be seen as untainted by passion. She is earthy but unsoiled. At the same time, as her name implies, she has a quasi-mythological stature that raises her above down-to-earth heroines like Lydia.[26] Among Howells' early women characters, only Belle Farrell is comparably archetypal. But Egeria is the antithesis to Belle, the dark sorceress of passion. Egeria is the white goddess of purified Eros. Even Ford, who is so transfixed by her bodily presence, envisions his intercourse with her in sacred, not profane, terms. Contrary to what Elihu thinks, her purified human love *is* heavenly. "'You talk of your angelic life!'" Ford exclaims to the elder. "'Can you dream of anything nearer the bliss of heaven than union with such tenderness and mercy as hers?'" (*UC*, 352).

But just as Lydia Blood appears tainted to everyone but Staniford—and even to him—so Egeria does not escape misapprehension. When, after their harrowing night journey from the Egerton station, she and her father arrive at the country inn, which obviously doubles as a whorehouse, the sinister landlord becomes suspicious of them. "'She's no more your daughter than she is mine,'" he sneers at Boynton. "'I'd know where you picked her up, but she's one of the girls that's escaped from the reform school'" (*UC*, 153). In other words, unless she were a recent fugitive, the landlord, as local pimp, would have recognized her, assuming as he does that she and Boynton are no different from the prostitute and the client who is picking her up in a buggy as the Boyntons are arriving at the inn.[27] This outrageous misperception nonetheless stirs some unconscious recognition in Egeria because later she awakes from a "'horrible dream'" in which "'the house seemed full of drunken men— and women—like that girl in the buggy; and we couldn't get away, and you [Boynton] couldn't get to me, and—oh!'" (*UC*, 157). The terror in Egeria's dream arises from her sense of entrapment in a degraded sexual identity, the one assigned to her by the landlord.

The full destructive force of what she imagines is figured not in her report of the dream but in the terrifying presence that sweeps through the inn while she is sleeping—a power that seems to redden the sky and wrench the branches of the trees, to lift a marble top from a table and send objects flying across the room, to shoot thunder and lightning and rattle the very fibers of the house. "The room was full of it, whatever it was; every part of the wood-work—doors, window casings, cornice, wainscot—was now voluble with a muffled detonation" (*UC*, 156).

These occult phenomena, the perception of which Howells is very careful to attribute only to Boynton, are interpreted by him as a miraculous visitation of spirits called up by the sleeping Egeria. By dissociating his narrator from Boynton's point of view, Howells, in the manner of Hawthorne, calls the reality of the events into question. It is possible that they are nothing more than a paranoid delusion, materialized by Boynton's desperate wish for conclusive spiritistic evidence and by his repressed rage at the landlord's mistreatment of him.

But Howells also implies that Boynton may be correct to relate the events to Egeria's occult power. The strange phenomena may express *her* unconscious thoughts, transmitted psychically to the physical world around her. It is clear that the force carries the same sexual and aggressive charges that pervaded the séance in Mrs. Le Roy's parlor and that animate Egeria's dream. What the drunken men and women are doing—something too fascinating for her not to watch but too horrible for her to describe—is displaced into the uncannily erotic noises in the walls: "Presently this straining sound, as if the fibres were twisting and writhing together, was heard in the wood-work of the room" (UC, 156).[28]

What the novel implies, despite Howells' attempt to portray Egeria as a white goddess, is that even she bears the mark of dangerous passion—literally, the bloody mark of her mother's ring, with which Ford accidentally pierces her finger in the opening scene. This ring, as Vanderbilt says, is the sign of Egeria's Electra complex; it implicates her in the unconscious family romance that extends over three generations in the struggle involving her grandfather and mother, as well as her father, her lover, and herself. Egeria is not a whore, as the landlord believes; but, as her own dream testifies, she has human ties of blood to "that girl in the buggy."

In the manuscript, Howells made this affinity even clearer in a (deleted) scene in which the landlord called Egeria "'Some dumn huzzy he picked up on the road som'er's, and passed off for his da'hter. Great da'hter!'" After overhearing this slur, Ford finds himself clutching at the man's throat and shivering a stick over his shoulders. The suddenness of the attack is as astonishing to Ford as to his victim: "Ford was not aware of passing from his mood of dazed inquiry to any other." He feels "unspeakably degraded" by a violence completely "foreign to the whole habit of his life." He is ashamed not only to discover such hidden violence in himself but also to recognize that "he had avenged in the man's person very much the same sort of outrage that his own attitude had done them from the beginning." The motives behind Ford's assault on the landlord are mixed. His righteous indignation is a reversal of what he denies: his own suspicions of Egeria and her father, who had once seemed to him, as much as to the landlord, like a "'couple o' cussed tramps!'" Like Howells' other suitors, Ford is unconsciously disgusted by the passion that he perceives in the American Girl and that he refuses to perceive in himself.

Ford's capacity for passion—both sexual and aggressive—means that he too is susceptible to unconscious influences; and like Egeria he bears his own mark of blood: the self-inflicted wound he receives accidentally when he drives the blade of his knife into his palm while he is cutting maple boughs for her. Egeria binds up his hand with a handkerchief, reciprocating the healing gesture that Ford made her in the opening scene, after he had pierced her finger. Howells underlines the connection between the two wounds. "'I was thinking that it must have seemed as if some savage beast had torn you,'" Ford says to Egeria, and then looks "at the hand on which she wore her ring," which she self-consciously hides in the folds of her dress (*UC*, 296). That Egeria's wound resulted from an act of love—Ford, after all, was trying to rescue her from the depraved atmosphere of the dark séance—implies that love and blood are inevitably linked.

V

Blood, as we have already seen with Lydia, is associated with repressed Eros in Howells' fiction; it is also associated with repressed aggression. Blood is drawn by the "savage beast" which, in *A Chance Acquaintance*, Howells saw lurking in the unconscious, ready to strike at any moment. But, as we have also seen in *A Chance Acquaintance*, Howells believed in the existence of a quasi-instinctive force for goodness. This is the "implanted goodness" of love, whose "spell" is cast upon Ford and Egeria and which overcomes, in their case at least, the power of the beast—or, as I have called it by analogy, "natural evil."

Howells' idea of "implanted goodness" reflects the optimistic strain of evolutionary philosophy that is associated with his friend and Cambridge neighbor John Fiske, the most influential American disciple of Herbert Spencer.[29] As Vernon L. Parrington remarks, Fiske had a more religious cast of mind than the inveterately agnostic Spencer, and he boldly "took high theistic ground, asserting that evolution implies the existence of a creative mind, vaster than the anthropomorphic conceptions of theology and far nobler, whose cosmic plan unfolding in the material universe compels a belief in a benevolent God, and a belief also in the 'eternal source of a moral law which is implicated with each action of our lives, and in obedience to which lies our only guarantee of the happiness which is incorruptible.'"[30] "Implanted goodness" is rooted in the "eternal source of a moral law," that is, in the providential unfolding of the evolutionary process.

Part of that process, according to Fiske, is the gradual extinction of the animal part of human nature—the beast of "natural evil." As he wrote in *The Destiny of Man, Viewed in Light of His Origin* (1884):

> Man is slowly passing from a primitive social state in which he was
> little better than a brute, toward an ultimate social state in which his
> character shall have become so transformed that nothing of the brute
> can be detected in it. The ape and the tiger in human nature will
> become extinct. Theology has had much to say about original sin. This
> original sin is neither more nor less than the brute-inheritance which
> every man carries with him, and the process of evolution is an advance
> toward true salvation.[31]

Thus, as Henry Steele Commager says, Fiske's theory obviated the problem of evil; "for evil, which was now seen to be but a maladjustment to nature, was destined inevitably to disappear in that larger harmony which was good." Furthermore, Fiske solved in principle "the problem of the sanctions behind those moral and religious teachings which for centuries had guided the footsteps of men along paths of righteousness to salvation."[32] Morality was given a "scientific" foundation in the theory of evolution.

Putting morality on a new scientific basis is exactly what Boynton is trying to do in his spiritistic experiments, even though for a time he perceives himself as an enemy to science. In his oration to the Shaker meeting, the doctor touches upon concerns that were equally serious to Fiske and to Howells:

> "You who dwell here, in the security, the sunshine, of this faith, have little conception of the doubt and darkness in which the whole Christian world is now involved. In and out of the church, it is honeycombed with skepticism. Priests in the pulpit and before the altar proclaim a creed which they hope it will be good for their hearers to believe, and the people envy the faith that can so confidently preach that creed; but neither priests nor people believe. As yet, this devastating doubt has not made itself felt in morals; for those who doubt were bred in the morality of those who believed. But how shall it be with the new generation, with the children of those who feel that it may be better to eat, drink, and make merry, for to-morrow they die forever? Will they be restrained by the morality which, ceasing to be a guest of the mind in us, remains master of the nerves? Will they not eat, drink, and make merry at their pleasure, set free as they are, or outlawed as they are, by the spirit of inquiry, by the spirit of science, which has beaten down the defenses and razed the citadel of the old faith? I shudder to contemplate the picture." (UC, 235–36)

Boynton hopes that if spiritism can be proven, there will be a new source of revelation to replace the fading inner voice of traditional conscience. Spiritism, as the basis for moral action, would save humankind from the terrible reign of immorality that scientific materialism threatens to establish.

But The Undiscovered Country explicitly rejects spiritism as a means to moral order. Boynton himself comes to realize that it is merely a "grosser" form of the materialism it ostensibly opposes: spiritism too is "'a materialism that asserts and affirms, and appeals for proof to purely physical phenomena.'" Furthermore, "'If it has had any effect upon morals, it has been to corrupt them'" (UC, 366–67).

Howells was not a true believer in Fiske's providential evolution. But neither was he so firm a disbeliever as Freud, who was to write in 1920: "It may be difficult, too, for many of us, to abandon the belief that there is an instinct towards perfection at work in human beings, which has brought them to their present high level of intellectual achievement and ethical sublimation and which may be expected to watch over their development into supermen. I have no faith, however, in the existence of any such internal instinct and I cannot see how this benevolent illusion is to be preserved." [33] In this matter, as in many others, Howells was agnostic, suspended painfully between a wish to believe in Fiske's cosmic optimism and a dark suspicion, foreshadowing Freud's, that Fiske's theory was a benevolent illusion.

Howells achieved an uneasy compromise in *The Undiscovered Country* by affirming the existence of "implanted goodness" (love) and by implying the existence of "natural evil" (passion). The novel was, in part, a pastoral in which the new Adam and Eve (Ford and Egeria) reverse the Fall by reentering an edenic natural world. [34] "Natural evil," conceived as in Fiske's philosophy as the evolutionary equivalent to original sin, is seemingly erased by the love that purifies Ford and Egeria of repressed Eros and aggression, as if they have already reached the golden age that lies ahead, according to Fiske's alchemical idea of evolution.

But Howells severely qualifies the pastoral vision by showing that Vardley is a cloistered environment, surrounded by the fallen world of the city and the decaying countryside, and also by showing how the characters—even Ford and Egeria, except for a brief time at Vardley—are fallen creatures, slaves of passion. Spiritism itself, even that of the Shakers, is exposed as a benevolent illusion that in its blindness to the destructive element in human nature threatens to become a necromancy that would loose upon the world the power of devils rather than angels. In her resistance to her father's mesmerism, Egeria is trying to prevent the release of this demonic force, which has proven its destructive potential in the occult rampaging at the inn.

Like Freud, Howells recognized that the condition of general uprightness, what Freud would call the "untiring impulsion towards further perfection," is achieved by "the instinctual repression upon which is based all that is most precious in human civilization." [35] Also like Freud, Howells intuited that repression itself is based upon human allegiance to social and moral codes, and he sensed that the operation of unconscious forces threatened to undermine these codes by making morality completely relative, no longer referable to any permanent standards of decency and no longer subject to precise measurements of responsibility. Should guilt be attached to these unconscious urges? What degree of self-consciousness is necessary before moral judgment is relevant or even possible?

Such problematical questions arise in *The Undiscovered Country* when Boynton confesses to Ford that he has "'played the vampire'" toward Egeria, thereby blaming himself for the harm he has done her unwittingly. Ford protests against the alarming implications of Boynton's statement: that he is morally culpable for his mixed motives, including, by implication, his incestuous desires for his daughter. "'The harm is less than you think,'" Ford responds. "'I don't believe that any one but ourselves can do us essential injury here. We may make others unhappy, but we can't destroy the possibility of happiness in them; we can only do that in ourselves. Your conscience has to do with your motives; it judges you by them, and God—if we suppose Him—will not judge you by anything else. The effect of misguided ["misjudged" in the manuscript] actions belongs to the great mass of impersonal evil'" (*UC*, 319).

Ford is defending here the same position taken by Holmes in *Mechanism in Thought and Morals*, in which he railed against "the mechanical doctrine which makes me the slave of outside influences" (p. 303)—whether defined Calvinistically as original sin or psychologically as unconscious motivation. According to Holmes, "The moral universe includes nothing but the exercise of choice: all else is machinery. What we can help and what we cannot help are on two sides of a line which separates the sphere of human responsibility from that of the Being who has arranged and controls the order of things" (pp. 301–2). Every human act to which the standards of moral judgment may reasonably be applied is dependent on choice and "is in its nature exclusively personal"; and "its penalty, if it have any, is payable, not to the bearer, not to order, but only to the creditor himself" (p. 304). To Holmes, as to Ford, "natural evil" is wholly "impersonal," beyond the boundaries of individual human responsibility.

Howells was no more comfortable with this view than he was with Fiske's cosmic optimism.[36] Although it seems he was siding with Ford against Boynton, Howells was doing so less out of philosophical conviction than out of psychological self-defense. For he was not yet prepared to face the disturbing conclusions that were implicit in Boynton's confession: that unconscious wishes might not belong to the "great mass of impersonal evil," that "natural evil" might be deep within himself.

Throughout the 1870s, Howells projected his unconscious life into his characters and portrayed their psychological depths with increasing sophistication, but he did not allow himself to recognize their passional life as his own. His precarious mental balance, in fact, was based upon his *not* fully making this recognition. Should Howells have lost the protective distance between his inner life and his art, he would have imperiled his very sanity. That is exactly what he did in writing *A Modern Instance*.

CHAPTER SIX

A
MODERN
INSTANCE

In November 1881, after enjoying many stable and prosperous years, Howells fell into a "long sickness" (*LFA*, 176) while he was writing *A Modern Instance*, his most ambitious novel to date and perhaps the best he would ever write. Like his adolescent breakdown in 1854, this collapse was linked to the eruption of his inner conflicts.

On the whole, Howells' life, between his return from Venice in 1865 and his resignation from the *Atlantic Monthly* in 1881, had been far from distressing. The familiar story, which I need not rehearse, of his rise from literary free lance to editor in chief of America's premier magazine has an archetypal quality, captured in the headlines for Theodore Dreiser's article on Howells in 1898: "How He Climbed Fame's Ladder . . . His Long Struggle for Success, and His Ultimate Triumph" (*INT*, 59). Among the signs of success during Howells' Cambridge years were a prestigious position that afforded him literary power and a comfortable standard of living; critical and popular recognition as a writer; an invitation (which was especially flattering to an autodidact) to join the faculty of Union College; a lectureship at Harvard, which also granted him an honorary M.A.; a cozy domestic life, blessed by the addition of two more children; a vast network of friends and admirers, including the older Cambridge intellectuals and his own literary contemporaries. Everything was conducive to Howells' peace of mind, and his equanimity showed. Norton remarked to Lowell in 1874 that Howells "looks so much at ease, and his old sweet humour becomes ever more genial and comprehensive."[1] To "envious observers," as Kenneth S. Lynn says, Howells appeared "to be almost intolerably happy, successful, and well-adjusted" (p. 194).

On at least three occasions, however, between 1865 and 1881, Howells was brushed by the kind of anxiety that had overwhelmed him in youth and would unbalance him again. Early in 1870, while he was writing the lectures he was to present to the Lowell Institute, he complained frequently of a sore wrist. "I'm dragging on very slowly . . . but it's a terrible job, and I long to see the

end of it," he told his father. "I have no heart in it; and the work is propor-
tionately tiresome." In February, Howells was stricken with an abcess in his
bowels, and for the first time in ten years he was confined to bed (for a week)
and to the house (for a month). Upon his recovery he had to redouble his
efforts—as he would twelve years later with A Modern Instance—and his wrist
pains persisted until the lectures were done. "My hand seems a trifle better—
and I suspect it has spells," he reported in May.[2]

Howells' sore wrist may have been a simple case of writer's cramp, caused by
an especially heavy workload. But it may also be interpreted as a hysterical
symptom, akin to his rheumatic pains in 1857, which had rendered him unable to "handle my knife and fork deftly, let alone a pen" (SL, 1:15). Deliver-
ing the Lowell Lectures was a signal honor for Howells, one proof of his acceptance by the Cambridge intellectuals he wanted so much to impress. He
must have been anxious about rising to the occasion. A subtler anxiety may
have come from his feeling that the Lowell Lectures were something of a command performance, a reminder of his vassalhood to the Brahmins toward
whom he harbored mixed feelings. Howells clearly felt no enthusiasm for a
commission he could not very well refuse—except symptomatically.

In the following summer of 1871, Howells accompanied his father on a trip
to the elder's childhood home in Steubenville, Ohio. Although William
Cooper Howells had not set foot there for fifty years, he "knew every inch of
the road, even after dark." In sharp contrast, his son pondered his alienation
from "this queer Ohio River country, where I was born, and where I find myself more of a stranger than I would anywhere else in the world."[3] Raking up
his own past likely contributed to Howells' anxiety during this journey. He
was in "an awful state" from the heat and loss of sleep. As he later told his
father: "I wish we had taken some time for our trip when it would have been a
less sacrifice for me to go; for I felt that I unkindly made you conscious that I
had left my interest behind me. However, a pleasure attaches even to the
remembrance of drawbacks of such an experience, and except the hot weather,
and my resulting depression, I'm glad of everything that happened."[4]

In 1876, while he was on vacation in Shirley, Massachusetts, temperatures
soaring above 100 degrees induced an ominous "oppression" of Howells' nerves
that reminded him of the dreadful summer of 1854: "I suffer a terror like that
of my old monomania about hydrophobia. However, I expect to worry
through." Ten days later he collapsed while escorting a relative to the train
and was treated for prostration by a local physician. "My nerves have not yet
recovered their tone, and I feel considerably shaken," he wrote to his father.
"I suppose I had been gradually weakening under the heat which has been
really terrible here, and that the reaction necessarily comes slowly."[5]

These psychic rumblings were quite exceptional during Howells' Atlantic
years, but physical enervation became chronic under the weight of his edi-

torial duties. As he had done in his adolescent language studies, he worked harder than was needed, that is, obsessively; and sheer exhaustion was one of the major reasons for his resignation early in 1881. As he explained to his friend Horace E. Scudder, "I have grown terribly, inexorably tired of editing. I think my nerves have given way under the fifteen years' fret and substantial unsuccess [in terms of the magazine's eroding solvency]. At any rate the MSS., the proofs, the books, the letters have become insupportable" (SL, 2:274).

Howells entered the year of his 1881 breakdown in a weakened condition, but still in better health than his wife and elder daughter, whose baffling illnesses were a constant source of worry for him. If, as Howells once grimly put it, American society "sometimes seems little better than a hospital for invalid woman," his own household was depressingly typical.[6]

I

In the third month of his marriage, Howells joked to his father about Elinor's dosing herself for a cold: "I think it is well to begin taking medicine in the family at once, and as I do'nt like it myself, Elinor is obliged to carry out the principle" (SL, 1:140). In light of her subsequent medical history, it seems that Elinor took this "principle" all too seriously. This is not to trivialize her later years of suffering, both physical and mental, but to suggest how her case fits a pattern common to American women of her time, for many of whom, as for Elinor Howells, invalidism became a way of life. Feminist scholars have observed that the history of nineteenth-century "female complaints" is inseparable from the history of Victorian sexual codes: by seeming to confirm the idea of female "inferiority," invalidism was often a symbolic and unconscious expression of woman's submission to patriarchal authority. For women of an elite background, frailty was also a mark of caste; such female invalids constituted a perversely literal kind of "leisure class." As Ann Douglas remarks, "ill health in women had become positively fashionable and was exploited by its victims and practitioners as an advertisement of genteel sensibility and an escape from the too pressing demands of bedroom and kitchen."[7] Invalidism, in other words, was as much a cultural as a medical phenomenon—the result as much of the socialization as of the biology of women. In any given case, as Freud discovered in his hysterical patients, organic and psychoneurotic symptoms intertwined.

Henry Ferris, in A Foregone Conclusion, notices that "all his countrywomen, past their girlhood, seemed to be sick, he did not know how or why; he supposed it was all right, it was so common" (FC, 126). Women writers and women married to writers were no exceptions. Sophia Hawthorne, Olivia Clemens, Marian Hooper Adams, Alice James, Constance Fenimore Woolson, Elizabeth Stuart Phelps, Louisa May Alcott, Charlotte Perkins Gilman,

Edith Wharton—this is a partial roster of those who were "ailing," some for most of their lives. Wharton, who largely overcame the debilitation of her early married life, later epitomized one type of the invalid in Zeena Frome, who wastes away most of her life dabbling in patent cures and cultivating her "condition," but who then, showing unexpected vitality, rises from her sick bed to nurse her crippled husband and his erstwhile lover.

The paradox of Zeena Frome—that her apparently enfeebled body conceals an inner reserve of energy—also describes Elinor Howells (who, it should be added, did not share Zeena's querulous self-absorption). When Samuel Clemens learned in 1880 that Elinor, supposedly as a result of a back injury, was "drifting into invalidity as a settled thing," he exclaimed to her that both he and Livy had always looked upon her "as a sort of Leyden jar, or Rumkoff coil, or Voltaic battery, or whatever that thing is which holds lightning & mighty forces captive in a vessel which is apparently much too frail for its office, & yet after all isn't." Howells was quick to praise the aptness of this metaphor, replying, "She never *does* quite go to pieces, but it always looks like a thing that might happen" (MT-HL, 323, 328).

Elinor first gave the appearance of going to pieces in 1867, during a pregnancy that eventuated in miscarriage. Despite another apparent miscarriage two years earlier in Venice, she had retained her vitality throughout the Howellses' European years.[8] Elinor had kept to a brisk pace of shopping, visiting, entertaining, touring, and working on her sketches. In 1867, however, her recovery was slow; and when she gave birth to a son, John Mead Howells, on 14 August 1868, it was Howells' "reasonable hope" that her health might "at last be firmly reestablished" (SL, 1:298). In the following months, she mustered enough strength to be "better than she has been since her miscarriage" (SL, 1:319). But in the summer of 1869, when she hastened to her dying father's bedside in Brattleboro, Howells worried that she would overdo. "I suspect that your strength is nothing but nerve," he warned her, "and I beg you to keep the fact of your own poor health in mind, as far as you can consistently with present duty" (SL, 1:333). Squire Mead died in early July, and Elinor "felt it deeply" (SL, 1:329). She was still feeling low four months later when Howells confided to Norton that her "ill-health is our one great drawback, for it is hard for her to bear and for me to see" (SL, 1:345).

As Lynn says, beginning in 1869, Elinor's "reduced strength was recognized in the Howells household as an irrevocable condition" (p. 191). It was also a "curious" one, as Howells explained to his father in 1871: "no positive disorder, and yet this continued feebleness, which nothing seems to help. The only consolation is that she does not lose ground" (LinL, 1:163). At times she even gained a little ground, as when, in 1870, Elinor showed "faint aspirations" toward enjoying Cambridge society (SL, 1:355), or when she bloomed during her pregnancy with Mildred (born 26 September 1872), or when she involved herself with designs for their Redtop house in Belmont.[9] She did go to parties now and then; she did venture alone into Boston on the horse cars; she did manage the household affairs; she did travel with her husband. But then she always relapsed into an invalidism that had become so routine by 1875 that Howells could remark matter-of-factly to his father that "Elinor commonly has a break-down at this time of year" (SL, 2:92); and to Clemens, Howells could quip that since "Mrs. H. and Mrs. Clemens are both tearing invalids, don't you think it would be better not to give that ball *this* visit?" (SL, 2:91). Making a mordant private joke of their common situation offered comic relief to these friends whose wives were given to saluting each other most often "from the habitual sick-bed" (MT-HL, 141). "We know," Clemens wrote in 1880, "what it is to be busy & have a wife whose health requires peace, & rest from <intrusion.> social taxing" (MT-HL, 290).

Elinor's condition seems to have had a psychoneurotic base, Howells' understanding of which was refracted into his many fictional portraits of invalids.[10] Sometimes Elinor's mental distress was exacerbated by purely physical problems, as when she injured her back in a fall in late 1879. Even then, however, the resulting symptoms were partly psychological. Howells told Norton that Elinor was suffering "the sort of nervous pain and depression which results from such injuries." In February 1880, she was distracted from her back problem by "a terrific carbuncle" that "kept her in agony night and day."[11] But the spinal pains continued over the summer, and Elinor finally found relief from a specialist in New York.

Meanwhile, as if taking a cue from her mother, Winifred Howells was breaking down.

From birth Winifred (or Winny, as she was always called) enjoyed the doting attention that new parents often give their firstborns. In her "Venetian Diary," Elinor recorded the minutiae of Baby's mundane triumphs: her sleeping and eating habits, her teething, her first words, her (somewhat belated) first steps. Elinor went so far as to compose, as if from the infant's point of view, a day-by-day journal of the "Weaning of Winifred." She was a pudgy and healthy and pretty girl—altogether "cunning," as people used to say. Howells wished his mother could only see "how sunnily her little life has issued from my gloomier nature" (SL, 1:203). There was no shadow upon the happiness of this "beaming and blooming" child (SL, 1:250), and nothing to adumbrate her later misfortune.

Just as Howells' father had kindled his son's literary passions, so he encouraged Winifred's. Well before she learned to write, she would coax her father to record the precocious rhymes she made up. Later Winny imbibed the bookish air at home, and she mingled almost daily with the Cambridge literati. She naturally identified herself with them and with her father and began to fantasy a future as a poet, confiding to her journal, as her father had done in his own youth, her ambition "to be a great writer." [12] As I have argued elsewhere, the conflicts aroused by Winifred's literary hopes contributed to her emotional turmoil in adolescence and to her subsequent invalidism, which ended in her death at the age of twenty-five. [13] But I am concerned here only with the effects on Howells of his daughter's initial collapse.

In 1880, as Winny entered her seventeenth year, Howells must have recalled the dreadful significance of his own sixteenth birthday, on which date he had expected to die. Instead he had succumbed a year later to "nervous prostration." Understandably, he would have been alert to anything ominous in his daughter's behavior at the same age. But the day before his own forty-third birthday, Howells assured his father that Winny was having her "triumphs at school" and was "growing up a strong, tranquil nature" (SL, 2:245). This hope seemed to be vindicated throughout the spring, as Winifred began the social ritual of becoming a young lady by attending her first grownup luncheon and a girls' dancing party in Cambridge. In late June, feeling "rather fagged from her school" (SL, 2:257), she left home for a fortnight's stay on the coast, where she did some sketching. "She has a marked talent in that way," Howells noticed. "For the present her literature seems to be in abeyance." [14] Perhaps there was a hint of inward changes in Winifred's shift of identification from her literary father toward her artistic mother. That something was wrong is suggested by the poem she wrote that summer, in which she alluded to having been "of late . . . full sore oppressed / Vext with some trifling trouble hard to bear." The rest of "Magnolia" concerns the poet's taking consolation from the sea, whose breakers seem like "our troubles sore, / Which darken ever with their gathered weight," until "we cease to strive against our fate" and behold the troubles dissolve like waves upon the shore. [15] These healthy-minded sentiments may have provided the "uncommon pleasure" that H. W. Longfellow felt in reading the poem (SL, 2:268); but, as in Longfellow's own work, there is a hollowness in the optimism of "Magnolia" that makes it seem like a stay against confusion—against the undertow of psychic troubles that had dragged Winifred under by the time the poem appeared in October.

On 1 December 1880, Howells wrote to President Rutherford B. Hayes (his cousin by marriage) to decline an invitation for Winifred to visit the White House. "At present she is not at all well, and we could not accept for her without fearing that she might break down with the excitement and fatigue of the journey. She has been obliged to leave school on account of continual vertigo, and is now taking exercise in a gymnasium, and we hope for a speedy improvement." [16] In her chief symptom, at least, Winny was still very much her father's child. He too had suffered vertigo in his youth, and the idea of prescribing physical therapy for Winifred came from his Columbus days, when a gymnasium had given him "entire relief." [17]

At her worst Winifred was unable to "cross the room alone," but by February 1881 she had progressed far enough to take what amusement she could in Boston (*MT-HL*, 348). She was "unmistakably growing better" during the next months, but she was still not cured (*SL*, 2 : 279). Winifred's homeopathic physician, Dr. Walter Wesselhoeft, urged that the Howellses obtain a second opinion from Dr. James Jackson Putnam, an allopathic specialist in cases of nervous prostration. In his old age Putnam was to become Freud's most important American convert to psychoanalysis; but in 1881, he was still applying the standard remedy for nervous disorders: the "rest cure" developed by Dr. S. Weir Mitchell. As Ann Douglas describes it, the patient (nearly always female) was "confined to her bed flat on her back . . . permitted neither to read, nor, in some cases, even to rise to urinate. The massage treatment which covered the whole body lasted an hour daily. Becoming progressively more vigorous, it was designed to counteract the debilitating effects of such a prolonged stay in bed. Meanwhile the patient was expected to eat steadily, and gain weight daily." [18]

A full-time nurse was hired to enforce the demanding regimen of Winifred's rest cure. She was "bathed, rubbed, and *lunched* continually" (*SL*, 2 : 293). Her parents dubbed her "the Lunch Fiend" and felt lighthearted again, confident that they were "at last acting in the right direction" and that she was "really gaining in flesh and strength" (*MT-HL*, 367–68). There was no cause for worry; for her doctors agreed, if in nothing else, that it was "only a question of time as to her recovery" (*SL*, 2 : 295).

The tedium of the rest cure, however, soon undermined Howells' confidence in Putnam. The treatment was taking too long; and although it put flesh on Winny, it also sapped her vitality. "If she could have been allowed to read, I think the experiment might have succeeded," Howells complained; "but I think the privation has thrown her thoughts back upon her, and made her morbid and hypochondriacal" (*MT-HL*, 373). In September 1881, he told his father that he and Elinor now considered Dr. Putnam to be a failure and that they intended to put Dr. Wesselhoeft back on the case. In October, he ordered Winifred out of bed for the first time in three months, and the results were immediate and gratifying. "She is not strong yet; but she is down stairs, she walks out, is cheerful, and seems to be getting rid of her vertigo. Of course she has her ups and downs, and at times is very morbid; but still she is gaining, and gaining fast" (*SL*, 2 : 299).

Just as Winny was returning to health, Howells himself was collapsing. In mid-November 1881, he reported to his father that he was "down with some sort of fever—probably a short one. . . . It's the result of long worry and sleeplessness from overwork, nothing at all serious" (*LinL*, 1 : 303). Two days later Elinor elaborated: "Will has been threatened with gastric fever, but is better today. . . . Winnie is wonderfully improved. . . . She says she has not

felt so strong for two years as she does now."[19] By November 20, Howells'
fever had taken "the rheumatic form," such that he was "full of aches and
pains," sometimes localized in the heart and right arm. His physician ("an
acknowledged pessimist") warned of an extended illness of three or four
weeks ("he always mentions the very worst possibilities").[20] Howells' condition immediately became so grave that there was serious danger of his dying.
"Will has never been so sick before since I knew him as this time," Elinor
wrote to William Cooper Howells on 21 November, "but we hope it is all over
now." Three weeks later, feeling like "a diluted shadow," Howells crawled out
of bed and down to his library; he was "still really sick in some matters," but
"at least glad of my enlarged bounds."[21] The family moved to a boardinghouse
in Cambridge in December, so that Howells could be "handy to the doctor at
all hours." Apparently, there had been "a very persistent and tedious recurrence" of a "stricture" that required "courage and patience" and a few days of
treatment (SL, 2:302).

This sentence has led the editors of Howells' letters to speculate that his
"immediate physical symptom was a recurrent cystitis, so painful that apparently a doctor was needed to insert a catheter for urinating" (SL, 2:302n).
The evidence seems too slight to support so specific a diagnosis, especially
since "stricture" might as easily refer to the rheumatic pains in the heart and
arm. Howells himself mentioned that his sickness had left him "with a weakened action of the heart that makes it useless for me thinking of ever walking
up that hill [at Redtop] for an indifinite [sic] time to come" (SL, 3:7).

In any case, Howells recovered very slowly during the winter of 1882,
which he spent in a rented house in Boston. He told Clemens in January that
he was not himself by any means, but that he was "glad to be here on any
terms: not because this is a very good place, but because it's the only place
I'm sure of, and it is very fairish. (I mean this world; not 16 Louisburg Sq.)"
(MT-HL, 385).

Meanwhile Winifred was finding life at 16 Louisburg Square to be very fairish indeed. Her father remarked that she was "doing a great deal of gayety"
and "enjoying it immensely" in a "very Winnyish way" (SL, 3:9). In March,
he reported that Winny was "now quite herself again, and Mrs. Howells is
'usually well'" (LinL, 1:311). The whole family was fit enough by July to
undertake a long-postponed European vacation.

In the pattern of the Howells family's ailments in 1880 and 1881, a psychic
"economy of pain" seems to have been operating, such that Elinor, Winifred,
and Will Howells took turns, as it were, breaking down.[22] Winifred's collapse
in 1880 occurred just as her mother was recovering from a siege of especially
poor health and reaching a plateau of chronic, but stable, invalidism. Howells'
collapse in 1881 came just as his daughter was improving. Winifred's gains
were temporary, as it turned out; as soon as her father had recovered his

strength—and after her mother had completed her "annual spring collapse" (SL, 3:16)—Winny's condition deteriorated again. It was as if the Howellses were unconsciously adjusting their psychic states and timing their collapses and recoveries in order to preserve a delicate psychological balance within the family.[23] That balance seemed to require that someone, but not more than one person, be broken down at every moment. This was the family pattern for many years: throughout the 1880s, Winifred was the primary bearer of bad health; after her death in 1889, Elinor turned for the worse; and soon after her death in 1910, Mildred (the younger daughter) collapsed.[24]

I am suggesting that the Howellses' ailments, even when they were accompanied by organic symptoms, were at least partly psychoneurotic. Or, to put the matter in contemporaneous Freudian terms, the Howellses' breakdowns all exhibited "somatic compliance," in which somatic pain is "not *created* by the neurosis but merely used, increased and maintained by it." In his early cases in the 1890s, Freud recognized the difficulty of establishing "whether the symptoms of hysteria are of psychical or of somatic origin, or whether, if the former is granted, they are necessarily *all* of them psychically determined." He believed that, in fact, "every hysterical symptom involves the participation of *both* sides. It cannot occur without the presence of a certain degree of *somatic compliance* offered by some normal or pathological process in or connected with one of the bodily organs." There was always "a genuine, organically-founded pain present at the start," to which the neurotic symptom attached itself symbiotically. The pain, which was somatic in origin, then became "a mnemic symbol" of repressed thoughts struggling for expression and achieving symbolic expression in the somatic symptom itself.[25]

I am arguing, therefore, that somatic compliance was involved in Howells' "rheumatic" pains of 1881. Until the publication of the *Selected Letters*, scholars had always assumed that the breakdown of 1881 was psychological. The discovery of somatic symptoms does not make it any less so. Howells himself alluded to a symptomatic side effect of his illness as "another incident, which may or may not have its psychological value" (MLP, 178); and in 1881, there had been newspaper stories, possibly based on family statements, that Howells was "very ill with a nervous disease brought on by over-work." Charles Dudley Warner reported having read something to this effect in the *American Register* in Munich.[26] Howells confirmed the gist of the report when he replied three months later: "I was extremely sick—paying for a long immunity, and for follies of overwork committed in my anxiety to get off to Europe by the 1st of January" (SL, 3:16).

The timing of the European trip had depended on Howells' completing *A Modern Instance*, the composition of which had been interrupted at a critical juncture by his illness. He did not need Warner to remind him that "the novel, which was to be done by Jan 1st, is not yet finished, and that will add to

your worry and depression of spirits."[27] As Warner implied, there was a connection between Howells' breakdown and his writing of A Modern Instance,
but other stresses in his life had made him particularly vulnerable.

II

                                   In a letter to Clemens on 20 January
1882, Howells referred to feeling "five years older than I was <six> two
months ago" (MT-HL, 385). The cancellation of "six" suggests that, for a
moment at least, Howells associated his enfeeblement not just with the two-
month period of his illness, but with the months before that. Anyone who
reads through Howells' letters of 1881 is likely to sense pressures building
throughout the year toward the breakdown at the end of it.

There were, first of all, the continual strains of Elinor's and Winifred's inva-
lidisms, the treatments for which were often as taxing upon Howells as the
illnesses they were supposed to cure. It grieved him especially to see the days
of Winny's "beautiful youth slipping away, in this sort of dull painful dream"
(SL, 2 : 289n). It was as if, by the power of some familial curse, Winny were
fated to relive her father's adolescent suffering to the extent of reproducing, at
almost exactly the same age, one of his own neurotic symptoms. Helpless as
he was to prevent this tragedy, Howells still felt obscurely responsible for it, if
only for failing to recognize its warning signs or to discover the proper remedy
in good time. Like Clemens, who found it difficult to accept "the idea that
she has been really an invalid," Howells must have asked himself again and
again, "What can have brought her to this state, I wonder?" (MT-HL, 366).

Then there was the marked change in Howells' daily life that followed
upon his resignation from the Atlantic. He had felt restive for years under the
yoke of his editorship, and he had begrudged the sacrifice of his own work to
the exigencies of running the magazine. So when the publishers of the Atlantic dissolved their partnership in late 1880, amid acrimony about their division of assets, Howells seized the opportunity to establish himself as a full-
time professional writer. In exchange for the right to publish Howells' books,
James R. Osgood agreed to pay him a fixed salary. This arrangement left
Howells free to work on his own time and at his own pace, so long as he
fulfilled the contractual agreement of producing one novel a year for three
years.

Even this requirement must have seemed lax enough, for Howells had been
working on several different books since 1875. In early 1881, Doctor Breen's
Practice was finished and ready for serialization; A Fearful Responsibility was
nearing completion; half of A Woman's Reason was drafted; "The Children of
Summer," which became The Vacation of the Kelwyns, was at an early stage
(where it would remain until 1909); A Modern Instance, germinating since

1875, was now clearly in mind. Howells submitted an outline to Osgood in February. Other projects beckoned, such as Clemens's idea for *Mark Twain's Library of Humor*.

But the freedom that Howells had coveted for so long must have come as a shock to him, habituated as he was to the *Atlantic* routine. Before, for good or ill, his own work had existed in tension with his editorial tasks; writing fiction had been something he could regard almost as a diversion, an invigorating relief from the office grind. Now, writing novels was his full-time job, his declared profession, and his only source of income—a potentially risky business at which he could not afford to fail. He must succeed, moreover, without the advantages he had enjoyed as editor of the *Atlantic*: the power and security and fame that might be lost to him as a free lance. How much ambivalence Howells felt about quitting the *Atlantic* is suggested by his response to Horace Scudder's resignation as editor many years later. Howells could "quite understand" Scudder's misgivings and his final resolution; "for, as I told you, I am periodically visited in dreams with a longing to edit the Atlantic again, and yet I was glad to give it up" (*SL*, 4:179–80). As late as 1902, he was still working over his decision in a dream "of going into partnership with Osgood in the publishing business. It seemed all right" (*SL*, 5:32).

Having really gone in with Osgood in 1881, Howells knew that running the *Atlantic* could no longer serve as an excuse for not meeting the imaginative challenges that he, with nudging from Henry James, had set for himself. In his early forties now, a seasoned author of several books who was confident he had found his mature voice, Howells was ready to test himself, to attempt a more ambitious novel than any of those written in the 1870s. He was anxious about fulfilling both the letter of the contract with Osgood and the spirit of the contract with himself.

In 1879, while Howells was perfecting the travel book-romance in *The Lady of the Aroostook*, James was launching *The Portrait of a Lady* in full self-consciousness that this was to be a "big" novel; and in the letters he wrote during its composition, James exuded the confidence, even the arrogance, of a writer in complete command of his materials, who looks upon his work and sees that it is good. By contrast, Howells was nervous about beginning *A Modern Instance*, the novel that marked a parallel turning point in his career. He wrote to Clemens on 17 April 1881, "I don't know exactly how hard this work will be; but it wont be very light" (*SL*, 2:281). On the same day he told Osgood that he was having second thoughts about committing himself to *Mark Twain's Library of Humor*: "I ought to keep very fresh for my new story, which I fore-feel is going to be a drain on me" (*SL*, 2:280). Adding to Howells' apprehension was his struggle to finish *A Fearful Responsibility*, his problems with which gave him "a scare about loading up with more work" until he could see his way through *A Modern Instance* (*SL*, 2:281).

That process involved Howells' traveling to Indiana in late April to observe a divorce trial. His route took him through Xenia and Dayton, places
that were associated with old psychological wounds. From Xenia, he wrote to
Elinor that the town had reminded him of that occasion when "I was so terribly home sick when I came up to work in the printing office from Eureka"
(SL, 2:282). After a side trip to Eureka, he reported finding the Mills "almost
exactly as when I left them, thirty years ago" (LinL, 1:297). If visiting his
father's youthful haunts in 1871 had depressed him, it seems likely that the
sight of Eureka Mills after thirty years prompted some distressing recollections
as well. Upon his return, Howells felt an urge to do some writing about those
boyhood days, a subject he had put aside in 1867.[28]

Other memories must have been stirred by the shooting in July of President
James A. Garfield, whom Howells and his father had known and supported
politically for many years. It had been on Congressman Garfield's veranda in
Hiram, Ohio, in 1871, that Howells had spellbound an admiring crowd
of neighbors with tales of his literary friends and acquaintances. In 1874
Garfield had arranged William Cooper Howells' consular appointment in
Quebec, a favor that had largely relieved Howells of financial responsibility
for his father. Three years later, again thanks to Garfield, William Cooper was
transferred to Toronto; and early in 1881 the elder Howells was hoping for
yet another boon from the new President: promotion to the consulship at
Montreal.

While the mortally wounded Garfield lingered over the summer, Howells
shared in the general anxiety, "that deeply indwelling sorrow, which so possessed each of us that at any moment of that time we could have questioned
the lurking shadow in our lives, and found it a personal grief for Garfield's
suffering, a brooding fear of his death."[29] Howells worried that should the
President die, a new administration might not only fail to promote William
Cooper Howells, but might remove him from office, leaving him in need of
support at a time when the upkeep of the Belmont house, Winifred's expensive rest cure, and brother Sam's chronic indigence had combined to strain
Howells' resources (which would have been quite sufficient under ordinary
circumstances).

III

In a letter written during his convales-
cence in December 1881, Howells jokingly compared himself to Garfield's as-
sassin. "But now I am out of any first-class pain," he told Clemens; "I have a
good appetite, and I am as abusive and peremptory as Guiteau. These are said
to be good signs" (MT-HL, 382). It seems odd that Howells should have
identified himself with a deranged criminal, even in jest. It seems less odd,

perhaps, if we recall that Howells, thirty years later, perceived that "the false scoundrel" Bartley Hubbard had been drawn from himself (*SL*, 5:361); for one of the psychological risks that Howells took in *A Modern Instance* was to dramatize the "criminal" element in himself.

This aspect of the novel is illuminated by "Police Report," a long sketch that Howells completed in August 1881, after he had attended two sessions of Boston police court. He felt no more comfortable there than he had in the Cincinnati police station in 1857, when he had been so repelled by its luridness that he later quit his job as city editor. In the first half of "Police Report," a similar repulsion took the form of protective narrative distancing. Howells adopted a lightly ironic tone in his fanciful treatment of the proceedings as a "free dramatic spectacle" in several acts (*I&E*, 47). The very rapidity with which the cases followed one another—"as at a variety theatre, without any disagreeable waits or the drop of a curtain"—was proof against emotional involvement (*I&E*, 54–55).

Howells' tone begins to modulate toward the middle of the piece, however, as he begins to recognize the "actors" as being more complex than the characters he was creating for his own comedies of this period. Watching a complicated case involving the estrangement of a Negro man from his wife, Howells observes that "if the actors in the little drama were of another complexion how finely the situation would have served in a certain sort of intense novel" (*I&E*, 78–79). In recounting another case, he tells his readers not to suppose "that I did not feel the essential cruelty of an exhibition that tore its poor rags from all that squalid shame, and its mask from all that lying, cowering guilt, or did not suspect how it must harden and deprave those whom it daily entertained" (*I&E*, 82). There is a moral price to pay for such voyeurism, Howells implies: "it was impossible not to feel that here in degree were the conditions that trained men to demand blood, to rave for the guillotine, to turn down the thumb" (*I&E*, 82–83).

If one danger for the spectator at police court is to become dehumanized through detachment, an opposite but equal danger is to become morally disoriented through compassion. Howells describes his reactions to a case involving a Madame (euphemistically called the "fallen spirit"), one of her prostitutes (the "lost soul"), and a client (the "old fool"), who was robbed in the whorehouse. To his surprise, they seem to Howells "rather subjects for pity than abhorrence," and he asserts that "one could not doubt that a distorted kindliness and good-nature remained to them in the midst of their depravity." It seems, in fact, that the "divine life" present in these poor creatures is "struggling back to some relation and likeness to our average sinful humanity" (*I&E*, 87).

Here are the glimmerings of Howells' doctrine of complicity, not to be fully articulated until *The Minister's Charge* (1887). Here also is a clue to Howells' problems in writing *A Modern Instance*. As Kermit Vanderbilt points out,

Howells was discovering possibilities for self-redemption in these sinners at the same time he was creating an irrevocably depraved Bartley Hubbard, who can choose only self-damnation.[30] A conflict is obvious in "Police Report," as in A Modern Instance, between Howells' will to believe in free moral choice and his deterministic sense of the predestined evil of the born villain. In emotional terms this conflict is between his pity and his abhorrence toward the criminal.

Howells retreats in both the sketch and the novel from a conscious acknowledgment of these conflicts. In "Police Report," he fears that it is "not a wholesome feeling, this leniency that acquaintance with sinners produces" (I&E, 88). As if to compensate, he concludes the essay with some somber reflections on the irradicability of criminal behavior. The police court is futile, he says; it is "a mere suppression of symptoms in the vicious classes, not a cure." For all the good it does to send criminals to jail or to work houses, the police might just as well dynamite the Black Maria that backs up daily to the courthouse to "receive its dead." As Howells himself recognizes, "dead" is a slip of the pen. "The word came inevitably," he adds; "it is not so far wrong, and it may stand" (I&E, 91–92). In accepting this slip, Howells gratifies an urge to do what the police will not: to kill off the criminals who have aroused his sympathy.

The ending of "Police Report," with Howells' fantasying the explosion of the Black Maria, links the piece to A Modern Instance. In both, a grim and violent "justice" arose from Howells' need to repudiate acts of imaginative leniency that his acquaintance with sinners had produced. Just as his identification with the prostitutes and their victim was not "wholesome," neither was his identification with Bartley Hubbard.

As George M. Spangler notes, A Modern Instance is pervaded by a "moral anxiety" that derives from Howells' unwilling oscillation "between identifying himself with Bartley and rejecting him fiercely."[31] Although he clearly intended "the career of his ambitious young villain to embody a cautionary analysis of the moral quality of American life," Howells failed "to make Bartley and his crimes appear as wretched as the narrator, not to mention . . . half a dozen seemingly reliable characters, insists they are" (pp. 239–41). Furthermore, he consistently subverted the credibility of all those who join in the "chorus of condemnation" of Bartley. "In forcing Bartley's degeneration and heaping punishments on him," Howells made his protagonist, as Spangler says, "a scapegoat for his own confusion and anxiety" (p. 249).

Beginning with an anonymous British reviewer of the novel, many critics of A Modern Instance have complained that Bartley's downfall is rigged. Olov W. Fryckstedt puts it bluntly: "As the novel proceeds we suspect that Bartley is sliding downward because the author deliberately pushes him."[32] This pushing, often by a censorious and intrusive narrator, becomes more strenuous and, it seems, more arbitrary in the part of the novel that was written just before Howells' breakdown.[33] In the part he wrote afterward, he virtually shoved Bartley out of the novel, allowing him to appear just once after Chapter 31, and only then to serve as a target for the narrator's and the characters' recriminations. As if he had learned a lesson from his collapse—that it was too dangerous to place this character at the center of the novel—Howells banished him to the periphery. By this ultimate narrative punishment of turning the plot away from Bartley, Howells seems to have atoned for any earlier "leniency" toward this avatar of his own "average sinful humanity."

We can begin to understand, now, the mysterious aversion Howells felt after his breakdown to reading "anything of a dramatic cast." He recalled that although he had been able to read the most hair-raising travel narratives without ill effects, "the mere sight of the printed page, broken up in dialogue, was anguish. Yet it was not the excitement of the fiction that I dreaded . . . it was the dramatic effect contrived by the playwright or novelist, and worked up to in the speech of his characters that I could not bear. I found a like impossible stress from the Sunday newspaper . . . which with its scare-headings, and artfully-wrought sensations, had the effect of fiction, as in fact it largely was" (*MLP*, 178).

This reaction seems all the more baffling in light of the therapeutic effects of Howells' reading after his breakdown in 1854. Then the strong plots of Dickens' novels had befriended him and "formed a partial refuge" (*YMY*, 80). Fiction had provided substitute defenses, and Howells later had learned to protect himself from threatening impulses by practicing "a psychological juggle" (*YMY*, 81).

In 1881 the juggle failed him; it was no match for the force of his repressed fears. Now there was impossible stress, not relief, in reading the fiction of others—just as there was in the writing of his own novel, in which the speech of his characters became expressive of cacophonous inner voices, of conflicts unbearably unresolved. Before, Howells had made his fears "alien" by disowning them, by giving them to his characters through projection. Now, as the juggle failed to work, as he began to recognize the source of his characters within his own psyche, the recognition was so terrible that he was forced to deny what he was glimpsing. The dramatic effect, no longer serving to combat Howells' fears, was unleashing a dread so powerful that it forced him to stop writing. Breaking down was a sure but costly way for Howells to escape the anxiety of his own artfully wrought sensations.

IV

In 1886, when asked by his brother-in-law to select something for a reading from his work, Howells singled out the closing episodes of Chapters 7 and 8 of *A Modern Instance* as the "strongest passages I ever wrote . . . but they shake my own nerves when I read them, and I don't believe other people would stand 'em" (*SL*, 3:168). Whatever fretted Howells about these passages may indicate what had terrified him in 1881.

In the first of the nerve-shaking scenes, Bartley confides in Squire Gaylord about his altercation with Henry Bird. The sharp lawyer wastes no time cutting to the heart of the matter, leading Bartley to confess that the quarrel was instigated by old man Morrison's charge that he had "'made love to his confounded girl'" (*MI*, 77). Then Gaylord bears down, as if he were grilling a hostile witness:

> "And you never had made up to the girl at all?"
> "No."
> "Kissed her, I suppose, now and then?" suggested the Squire.
> Bartley did not reply.
> "Flattered her up, and told her how much you thought of her, occasionally?"
> "I don't see what that has to do with it," said Bartley with a sulky defiance. (*MI*, 78)

Bartley's silence and his evasiveness convict him in Gaylord's eyes and, more importantly, in Marcia's. She has been a witness to the cross-examination —part of the time, she has been sitting in Bartley's lap—and her father has conducted it for her benefit. "'I wanted her to understand just what kind of fellow you were'" (*MI*, 79), he sneers at Bartley: the kind capable of "'fooling with a pretty girl, when you get a chance and the girl seems to like it'" (*MI*, 80). It matters not at all that Bartley has been loyal since his engagement to Marcia. Gaylord even agrees with him that her "'retroactive legislation'" (*MI*, 80), blaming him for a flirtation before he was committed to her, is unfair.

Bartley's deepest offense is not that he trifled with Hannah Morrison or struck Henry Bird, but that he has luxuriated selfishly upon his knowledge of Marcia's blind passion for him. "This was the point that, put aside however often, still presented itself, and its recurrence if he could have known it, was mercy and reprieve from the only source out of which these could come" (*MI*, 84). As Henry Nash Smith observes of this narrative intrusion, "Howells is pressing too hard . . . his moral indignation takes over, and he all but steps out on the stage in order to speak directly to the reader over the head of his character."[34]

The more Bartley ponders his case, the more it appears to him that he has been punished "out of all proportion to his offence" (*MI*, 83). In fact, this punishment and all his later ones *are* disproportionate unless we accept the proposition, as Gaylord tells Marcia in the second nerve-shaking scene, that Bartley has "'the making of a first-class scoundrel in him.'" To her question,

"'Do you think he's a scoundrel now?'" her father replies, "'He hasn't had any great opportunity yet'" (*MI*, 93–94). According to Gaylord, the emergence of active villainy in Bartley is only a matter of time. "'Don't you see that the trouble is in what the fellow *is*; and not in any particular thing that he's done? He's a scamp, through and through; and he's all the more a scamp when he doesn't know it'" (*MI*, 96). Prior to his committing any culpable act, he is already guilty by the very definition of his inherently defective character. As Oscar W. Firkins says, "We have to presume a latent wickedness which events successively uncover rather than a nascent wickedness which they successively induce."[35]

Orphaned at a young age, Bartley was "an extremely pretty child, with an exceptional aptness for study" (*MI*, 27). His guardians pampered and petted him, and encouraged him to trade on his "smartness" (*MI*, 20). It may be, as Ben Halleck says, that Bartley possesses "'no more moral nature than a base-ball'" (*MI*, 213), but it is Bartley's fate rather than his fault that he lacked a disciplined father and mother to drop into his heart the seeds of "implanted goodness." He has "civilized himself as rapidly as his light permitted" (*MI*, 26), and he has received little help from the supposedly more civilized people around him. "A chief cause of Bartley's fate," says Spangler, "is that he lacks 'principles' and 'traditions' to guide his conduct, and it is soon clear that society, whether in rural Equity or urban Boston, is in a similar predicament and can offer nothing to counteract his basic amorality" (p. 240).

The episode from Chapter 7 dramatizes one philosophical crux in the novel. If Gaylord is right that the "'trouble is in what the fellow *is*; and not in any particular thing that he's done,'" that Bartley is "'all the more a scamp when he doesn't know it,'" then on what basis can Bartley be judged at all? "Implanted goodness," which Atherton defines as the socially imbued prerequisite for individual moral choice and moral responsibility, belongs only to a civilized elite. Creatures like Bartley and Marcia, who possess merely "natural goodness," are damned one way or another.

"'In some sort they chose misery for themselves,'" avers Atherton about the Hubbards; "'we make our own hell in this life and the next,—or it was chosen for them by undisciplined wills that they inherited.'" Atherton ignores the apparent contradiction in this statement. Or, rather, he finds the question of whether the Hubbards are damned by free will or by fate to be irrelevant. With chilling puritanical conviction, he adds, "'In the long run their fate must be a just one'" (*MI*, 417). The same contradiction is evident in Howells' treatment of Bartley's flight from Boston, the scene that was written probably just before the breakdown. Having stolen the money he borrowed from Halleck, and having run out on Marcia after a particularly nasty quarrel, Bartley impulsively boards the westbound train. Hours later, as he steps upon the railway platform in Cleveland, he begins to regret his hasty action and feels an impulse to go home. But when he looks for the money to buy a return ticket, he finds that his wallet has been lifted. "Now he could not return," says the narrator; "nothing remained for him but the ruin he had chosen" (*MI*, 348).

The arresting illogic of this sentence reflects the general confusion in Howells' characterization. Although he has shown Bartley's character to be at least as much the product of his upbringing and environment as of his free choices, and although his flight from Boston is described as the unreflective panic of a man moved by deep psychic forces, and although Bartley's fate is sealed by the chance loss of his money, still Howells holds him to full moral account for "the ruin he had chosen." As Vanderbilt says, "Even the reader unacquainted with Howells' conflicts over moral freedom and scientific naturalism will bolt at this rupture in the tragic consistency of the action, and suspect that what lies here is some form of lacerating doubt over man's ability to choose and control the design of his life" (p. 81).

Other critics agree that Howells' collapse must have been related to the contradiction between freedom and fate he had expressed in this baffling sentence. "As Bartley Hubbard's flight into the anonymous West draws near," observes Smith, "the fictive universe comes to present more and more clearly the aspect of an unbreakable sequence of causes and effects. Bartley and Marcia seem to have been hopelessly (and therefore, it might seem, blamelessly) doomed from the start—as if by a Calvinistic inevitability without the alleviating force of divine grace" (p. 94). So strong was Howells' will to believe in free will that he was unable to accept the bleak philosophical implications of his own novel, unable to grant, as Vanderbilt says, "that complex environmental and psychological forces can obliterate the moral distinction imputed to human activity" (p. 81).

Howells' reaching this philosophical impasse may well have contributed to the lacerating psychic stress that broke him down. But if we return to the second of those nerve-shaking scenes, another factor becomes apparent.

At the end of Chapter 8, frantic that she has sent Bartley away, Marcia is trying to persuade her father by any means to get him back. Sitting on his knee, as she earlier sat upon Bartley's, Marcia alternately implores and demands, dissolves into tears and flies into rage, all the while trying to exploit her father's special fondness for her. The emotional dynamics of the scene, which are accentuated by suggestive physical details—Marcia's fondling her father, pressing his hand upon her breast, pushing against him in her wrath— indicate the incestuous nature of this fondness.[36] The scene depicts figuratively an attempted seduction of Gaylord by his daughter, and it builds with great emotional power to Marcia's climactic swoon into a "dead faint," and her father's lifting her limp body and then laying it down "like one that fears to wake a sleeping child" (*MI*, 97). Throughout their encounter, Squire Gaylord is discomposed by the intense passion of his "'poor, crazy girl'" (*MI*, 96), against which he defends himself by exhorting her to control herself. The emotional assault upon him has been so wrenching that he finds "a kind of relief," after she faints, "in looking at her lifeless face" (*MI*, 97). It seems likely that one reason the scene shook Howells' nerves is the same reason it shakes Gaylord's: the sexual tension is almost unbearable.

For his portrait of Marcia, Howells drew upon his understanding of Elinor's profound attachment to Squire Mead, especially pronounced at the time of his death in 1869. He also used, as Lynn says, his "literary knowledge of the sexually tense relationships between older men and younger women in Hawthorne's fiction, his personal observation of Mark Twain's fierce devotion to his daughter Susy, and his secondhand information about Mrs. Henry Adams's remarkable closeness to her father" (p. 257). Moreover, Howells was developing a theme present in such earlier works as *A Counterfeit Presentment* and *The Undiscovered Country*.

What has more immediate bearing than either of these on *A Modern Instance* is *A Fearful Responsibility*, which Howells completed during the winter of 1880–81, the period of Winifred's initial collapse; for this story shows Howells' deepening, if still subliminal, awareness of his own implication in the incestuous entanglements of fathers and daughters.

Ostensibly, *A Fearful Responsibility* is a reprise of the international theme: a minor variation on *The Lady of the Aroostook* by way of *A Foregone Conclusion*. Owen Elmore, a bumbling but earnest professor, goes abroad to Venice when his college closes at the start of the Civil War. Elmore feels guilty, as Howells had, about not enlisting; but his friends assure him that his work, a projected history of Venice—Howells too had intended to write such a history—is a higher form of service. Elmore's war guilt fades after the opening chapters as he finds something else to worry about. Lily Mayhew, a young friend of his wife, arrives from America to stay with the Elmores. Looking after Lily is the "fearful responsibility." She steps off on the wrong foot by ingenuously encouraging the attentions of an Austrian officer; like Lydia Blood, she innocently risks compromising her virtue in European eyes. Acting in loco parentis, Elmore spends most of the novel trying to save face for Lily by fending off Ehrhardt (the Austrian) and a gaggle of other suitors who flock to the American Girl. But Lily continues to carry a torch for Ehrhardt, whom she scarcely knows, and she eventually returns home unengaged to anyone. For a while she falls ill, seemingly from unrequited love, but she ultimately recovers enough to marry a clergyman and to live more or less happily ever after.

Elmore, however, is haunted to the end by the guilty fear that he ruined Lily's life by breaking off her relations with Ehrhardt, by putting social appearances and his scruples before her heart's desire. It may be that Howells intended to satirize Elmore's punishing conscience, which continues to stab him even after he realizes that to "connect her fate any longer with that of Ehrhardt was now not only absurd, it was improper" (FR, 163). Or he may have meant to reveal Elmore as a victim of his own lack of romantic readiness.[37] But it is unclear, finally, what Howells intends because he never clarifies why Elmore feels so guilty—despite his hinting here and there that the guilt arises less from Elmore's conscious actions than from his unconscious perceptions.

So preoccupied is he with being a surrogate father to Lily that Elmore neglects to notice at first her womanly charms. Like Lydia Blood, Lily exudes a moral integrity that is infused by sexual vitality. Although her "simple, fresh, wholesome loveliness" catches the eye of everyone else, Elmore looks at her "with a perfectly serene ignorance of her piquant face, her beautiful eyes and abundant hair, and her trim, straight figure" (FR, 39). Later, as he begins to feel "proud of having her in charge," Elmore also begins to see that she is "pretty" (FR, 52)—but only with the oblique vision of a doting parent who takes "a childish pleasure in having people in the streets turn and glance at the handsome girl by his side, of whose beauty and stylishness he became aware through the admiration looked over the shoulders of the Austrians, and openly spoken by the Italian populace" (FR, 62).

Gradually Elmore's pride is eroded by an uneasy feeling that there is something dangerous about such beauty: "Take her in one way, especially in her subordination to himself, the girl was as simply a child as any in the world,—good-hearted, tender, and sweet, and, as he could see, without tendency to flirtation. Take her in another way, confront her with a young and marriageable man, and Elmore greatly feared that she unconsciously set all her beauty and grace at work to charm him; another life seemed to inform her, and irradiate from her, apart from which she existed simple and childlike still" (FR, 98).

It seems that Elmore's guilt has much to do with his fear of Lily's nascent womanhood: the power it gives her over all those eager suitors and the threat it represents to his control over her and over himself. Like all of Howells' American Girls, Lily is simply too seductive for her own good; and like all the American Girls' suitors, Elmore is no more capable of accepting her adult sexuality than his own, which he projects upon her. He much prefers the simple child he sees in Lily to the "unconsciously" flirtatious young woman.

I have made this underside of Elmore's character seem more realized than it is in the novel, where the psychosexual aspects are revealed haphazardly, as if in breach of Howells' defenses. Howells clearly grasped some of the psychological implications of A Fearful Responsibility. His use of the word "unconsciously" in the passage just quoted is explained by a scene in which Elmore and his wife are discussing how the American sculptor Hoskins, who is secretly in love with Lily, can have modeled a Hellenic goddess upon her without quite knowing what he was doing:

> "Owen!" cried his wife, with terrible severity. "You don't think that Lily would *let* him put her into it?"
>
> "Why, I supposed—I didn't know—I don't see how he could have done it unless—"
>
> "He did it without leave or license," said Mrs. Elmore. "We saw it all along, but he never 'let on,' as he would say, about it, and we never meant to say anything, of course."
>
> "Then," replied Elmore, delighted with the fact, "it has been a purely unconscious piece of cerebration."
>
> "Cerebration!" exclaimed Mrs. Elmore, with more scorn than she knew how to express. "I should think as much!"
>
> "Well, I don't know," said Elmore, with the pique of a man who does not care to be quite trampled under foot. "I don't see that the theory is so very unphilosophical."
>
> "Oh, not at all!" mocked his wife. "It's philosophical to the last degree." (*FR*, 111–12)

Elmore implies that Hoskins has responded in kind to Lily's irradiating beauty and grace; that is, he has succumbed to her charms unconsciously. But to Mrs. Elmore, "unconscious cerebration" is a casuistical excuse for Hoskins's licentiousness. He *knew* what he duplicitously refused to "let on." Mrs. Elmore has the last word on this matter when Hoskins finally proposes. Elmore is shocked: "'I didn't dream of his—having any such—idea. . . . I trusted everything to him.'" "'I suppose you thought his wanting to come was all unconscious cerebration,'" his wife twits him. "'Well, now you see it wasn't'" (*FR*, 150).

Was it or wasn't it? Howells leaves Hoskins's motives as murkily ambiguous as Elmore's. Because he shared Mrs. Elmore's indignant skepticism as fully as Elmore's curiosity about the idea of "unconscious cerebration," Howells could take the notion philosophically enough to bring it into the novel.[38] But he could not permit himself to apply it consistently to his characterization of Elmore—because that would have meant applying it to himself as well.

As James L. Woodress remarks, "The most interesting thing about *A Fearful Responsibility* . . . is the autobiographical content." Woodress explains that the situation·in the novel was based on the experiences of Will and Elinor Howells in Venice in 1864–65, when Elinor's sister Mary Mead had come for a visit and had entangled herself romantically. But, Woodress adds, "it is hardly likely that Mary Mead's eligibility caused Consul Howells as much anguish as Lily Mayhew causes Professor Elmore."[39]

Such anguish must have had another emotional source: Howells displaced
the autobiographical content of A *Fearful Responsibility* that derived from his
family life during the time of its slow and symptomatically difficult composition, which, as I have said, spanned the period of Winifred's first breakdown.[40]
Elmore's ambivalence toward Lily reflects Howells' own uneasiness that his
child of Venice had reached the age when romance (and even courtship)
might become a reality for her and for her anxious father. As Winifred was in
1880, Lily is a "bright, intelligent girl" who, having "overdone a little at
school" (*FR*, 16), is given to adolescent mood swings from dreamy languor to
bounding gaiety. Also as Winifred had, Lily reacts to the pressures upon her by
falling ill, and she has an uncanny ability to inspire guilt. After her health
gives way, Lily sometimes visits the Elmores to reminisce about Venice. "But
often she sat pensive and absent, in the midst of these memories, and looked
at Elmore with a regard which he found hard to bear: a gentle, unconscious
wonder it seemed, in which he imagined a shade of tender reproach" (*FR*,
157). It is this look that triggers Elmore's guilt at the end of the novel—a look
that Howells may have read in the bewildered eyes of his nervously prostrated
daughter.

Writing *A Modern Instance* while Winifred was taking her rest cure, Howells
probed again into the mysteries of the Electra complex. In the only two
stories in which he had given his American Girl a father, the incest theme
had arisen, but never so dangerously close to the surface of the text as in *A
Modern Instance*; and neither Constance Wyatt nor Egeria Boynton possessed
Marcia Gaylord's sexual force, which, toned down as it was in revision, still
was made remarkably explicit. In this, Marcia closely resembles Belle Farrell,
the femme fatale of "Private Theatricals"; and it is the Belle Farrell in Marcia
that Ludwig Lewisohn sees as Howells' "unadmitted knowledge of her true
character": "a predatory and possessive female of a peculiarly dangerous and
noxious kind."[41]

Consciously, Howells knew nothing of the sort. He wished, as he told Osgood (*MI*, xxix), to hold the "undisciplined" Marcia and Bartley equally ac-
countable, "up to a certain point," for the ruination of their marriage; and
although he expected the reader's sympathy to be "chiefly with the wife because
she inevitably suffers most," Howells undercut Ben Halleck's absurdly romantic vision of Marcia as a holy innocent, martyred on the altar of her unholy
marriage. Rather, Marcia was conceived as a "less-than-saintly saintly girl,"
as Paul John Eakin calls her, flawed but fundamentally good.[42] After the novel
was published, Howells told a correspondent that he had "perfectly understood" his intentions about Marcia: "So many readers detest her; but to my
mind she had a generous soul with limitations that appeal only to my pity"
(*SL*, 3:29).

As with Belle Farrell, however, Howells' pity was a defense against some of his deepest neurotic fears: of women's passion and his own, of the incestuous roots of sexuality.[43] If he had a psychic need to try to make Bartley seem worse than he is, he had a corresponding need to try to make Marcia seem better. For Howells could not easily bear what he was glimpsing in Marcia's bond to her father: the horrifying paradox that the bourgeois family enforces a taboo against incestuous urges that its members inevitably and unconsciously play out with each other.

V

Lewisohn believes that the "vivid energy and impassioned skill" with which Howells drew Marcia Gaylord could have come "from nothing less than an experience, personal or intimately vicarious, of the type" (p. 249). Taking up this "shrewd insight," Lynn speculates that Marcia "sprang from Howells's experience of living with his wife" (p. 257). Lynn hastens to add that Marcia is far from an exact portrait of Elinor Howells. (Or of Winifred, for that matter, whom she more closely resembles physically and emotionally.) Howells' personal experience was necessarily disguised as he transformed it into fiction.

Nonetheless it is suggestive that Howells' wrath toward Bartley seems to be aroused most fiercely by his threat to marriage: not by his marital infidelity—for Bartley is a sexually faithful husband even, it seems, after he has deserted Marcia—but by his infidelity to the idea of marriage itself. After one of his early quarrels with Marcia, and again later in the novel, Bartley's thoughts wander "to conditions, to contingencies of which a man does not permit himself even to think without a degree of moral disintegration." In these "ill-advised reveries," Bartley muses upon his life "as it might have been if he had never met her, or if they had never met after her dismissal of him" (MI, 332). Bartley entertains the notion that Marcia might be better off should he abandon her; she would be free then to make a happier second marriage. The narrator explains that these "vague impulses, arrested mental tendencies" have nothing to do with Bartley's "sane and waking state" (MI, 333). They are the vagaries of an unconscious criminal in Bartley who is potentially even a murderer. A few pages later, when he foresees the "inconvenience" of trying to explain to Marcia why he was fired by Witherby, Bartley says to himself, "'Good Lord! . . . I wish I was dead—or some one'" (MI, 337).

It is for indulging such reveries at all, as much for acting upon them in deserting Marcia, that Bartley is so severely punished by Howells. Yet, as we have seen, this compensatory severity is a sign that he identified himself with Bartley. Lewisohn, who was the first to stress this identification, asserts that Howells "wanted Marcia deserted" (p. 250). If she reflected the worst part of Howells' life with Elinor and Winifred, did he wish literally to abandon them?

Lynn rightly insists that A Modern Instance is, after all, a novel. "As a roman à clef, the book might have exacted unbearable penalties" (p. 257). But such penalties, in the form of Howells' breakdown, were exacted, at least partly because he sensed that he was sharing in the "moral disintegration" of Bartley's reveries. What Howells wished to escape, however, was not a particular wife and daughter, but domesticity itself.

In August 1882, Howells wrote to Edmund Gosse, with whom he had kindled a warm friendship during the family's European sojourn: "I had such a lovely time last night that I would now like to cut the ties of a husband and father, and come to live with you. Is there not some law or privilege by which you could adopt an elderly foreigner of failing intellect? I would do chores about the house, run of errands, tell Theresa [Gosse's daughter] stories, and make myself generally useful. Think of it seriously: I mean business" (SL, 3:26). In light of A Modern Instance, the last serial proofs of which Howells enclosed with his letter, this was a remarkably bad joke. The playfulness of the letter only thinly concealed the same sort of "ill-advised reverie" for which Howells had condemned Bartley Hubbard. In fact, Howells outdid his character, who had contemplated merely the severance of domestic "ties"; Howells leapt ahead to envision the details of a life without them. Or, rather, he imagined an inverted domesticity, in which he would be not a husband and father, but an apparently female dependent: a servant or perhaps a wife! One unconscious implication of Howells' proposal was that the trouble with marriage for a man was the burden of male authority.

In Their Wedding Journey, as I have shown, Howells had demonstrated the effects of patriarchal assumptions upon the inner dynamics of Victorian marriage: how they bound the husband and wife to conflict and mutual repression. It is telling, then, that in the same month that he offered himself to Gosse, Howells finished a story in which, for the first time in ten years, he revived the characters of Basil and Isabel March, who were so often in his career to serve as fictional alter egos for himself and Elinor.

"Niagara Revisited," which was based closely on the Howellses' railway journey to Toronto by way of Niagara in June 1882, was the first new story that Howells wrote after his breakdown; and he seems to have projected into it some of the same threatening impulses that had disrupted his work on A Modern Instance (completed just before the family's trip). Like the rest of Their Wedding Journey, to which it was added as the final chapter in the edition of 1887, "Niagara Revisited" reveals beneath a comic veneer the disturbing tensions of Victorian marital life. Insofar as the Marches now seem to have much in common with the Hubbards, the story may be seen as a coda to A Modern Instance.

Howells' theme is the discrepancy between the romantic hopes of the Marches' youth and the unromantic actualities of their middle age. They are

retracing their wedding journey, after twelve years of marriage, in the company of their two children. Basil is now forty-two, with a salt-and-pepper
mustache and a Bartley Hubbardish paunch that strains the buttons of his
frock coat. His career in the insurance business has not been a financial success, and he regrets that he did not go into literature instead. Isabel is a pre-
maturely old thirty-nine, with rapidly thinning hair to which she vainly attempts to give "an effect of youthful abundance" by combing it over her
forehead (*TWJ*, 180). Her parochialism has intensified over the years, and so
has her neuroticism: "her nerves were more sensitive and electrical; her apprehensions had multiplied quite beyond the ratio of the dangers that beset
her" (*TWJ*, 181). Basil is hoping that their journey will have a tonic effect on
Isabel, but she worries about losing what is "'sacred to those dear young days
of ours'" if she should find that Rochester and Buffalo and Niagara itself do
not live up to her beautiful memories of them (*TWJ*, 185). Indeed, when they
arrive there, Niagara Falls resembles a ghost town; the bridal couples have
long since deserted it for more fashionable resorts.

More depressing than the physical changes in the Marches (or in the
America of their wedding journey) is the bleakness of their inner lives. They
seem to take little joy in their children, to whom their giving "the best of
everything" has kept them feeling pinched (*TWJ*, 181). The daughter, who is
scarcely mentioned, is said to take after her obstreperous brother who, like
any boy in "his actuality," has "very little to commend him to the toleration
of other human beings" (*TWJ*, 193).[44] Basil and Isabel take no more joy in
each other. They are still quarreling, more corrosively than ever.

Basil's attempt to forestall one such fight is a major incident in the story.
Having paid fifty cents each for his family to enter Prospect Park above the
American falls, Basil is determined to get his full money's worth by riding the
tram to the foot of the falls and exploring the man-made cave behind it.
Isabel, who has no sympathy for "this illogical spirit of economy," sends him
off with the children (*TWJ*, 190). Falling into a tourist trap, Basil manages to
get himself charged an additional and exorbitant three dollars for their use of
some raincoats and boots: "It was not so much the three dollars as the sense of
having been swindled that vexed him; and he instantly resolved not to share
his annoyance with Isabel. Why, indeed, should he put that burden upon her?
If she were none the wiser, she would be none the poorer; and he ought to be
willing to deny himself her sympathy for the sake of sparing her needless pain"
(*TWJ*, 191).

Clearly, Basil is less concerned with insuring Isabel's comfort than with escaping her righteous anger at his foolish expenditure. Harboring his guilty secret, Basil listens with Isabel to their coachman's tale of a French visitor to
Niagara who reported his wife had been swept over the falls and who enjoyed,
at first, the condolences naturally due a grieving widower. But his subsequent

refusal to return for the funeral, once the body had been found, aroused "a general regret that he had not been arrested":

> A flash of conviction illumed the whole fact to Basil's guilty consciousness: this unhappy Frenchman had paid a dollar for the use of an oil-skin suit at the foot of the Fall, and had been ashamed to confess the swindle to his wife, till, in a moment of remorse and madness, he shouted the fact into her ear, and then—
> Basil looked at the mother of his children, and registered a vow that if he got away from Niagara without being forced to a similar excess he would confess his guilt to Isabel at the very first act of spendthrift profusion she committed. The guide pointed out the rock in the Rapids to which Avery had clung for twenty-four hours before he was carried over the Falls, and to the morbid fancy of the deceitful husband Isabel's bonnet ribbons seemed to flutter from the pointed reef. He could endure the pretty arbor no longer. "Come, children!" he cried, with a wild, unnatural gayety; "let us go to Goat Island." (TWJ, 191–92)

There is a hint here—in the words "morbid" and "deceitful"—of the high dudgeon with which Howells had regarded Bartley's far less violent reveries. But the passage is clearly meant to be comic. What husband wouldn't understand, so the narrator implies, an urge to push a nagging wife over the falls? And, for that matter, what wife wouldn't understand Isabel's corresponding fantasy as, late in the story, she ponders the fate of Kitty Ellison:

> If she had married that man [Arbuton], would she have been any happier? Marriage was not the poetic dream of perfect union that a girl imagines it; she herself had found that out. It was a state of trial, of probation; it was an ordeal, not an ecstasy. If she and Basil had broken each other's hearts and parted, would not the fragments of their lives have been on a much finer, much higher plane? Had not the commonplace, every-day experiences of marriage vulgarized them both? To be sure, there were the children; but if they had never had the children, she would never have missed them; and if Basil had, for example, died just before they were married—She started from this wicked reverie, and ran towards her husband. . . . [S]he passed her arm convulsively through his, and pulled him away. (TWJ, 199)

In both instances, wishing one's spouse dead leads to a moral recoil and then to reconciliation. The pattern is the same as in one of the Marches' squabbles. He has called her "'a little wrinkled'"; she has called him "'very fat'"; they glance at each other "with a flash of resentment" and then turn their anger into tolerant laughter (TWJ, 197). For the Marches, divorce will never need to be contemplated so long as they can drain off their aggression in comic relief.[45]

Or in murderous fantasies? Howells' narrator does not need to berate Basil and Isabel for the "wicked" reveries as he had berated Bartley because the Marches are so much more capable of punishing themselves and each other. In *A Modern Instance* the narrator serves, in effect, as the conscience Bartley lacks, saying to the reader what a man more civilized than Bartley would say to himself. But the Marches are so full of "implanted goodness" that they may be trusted always to repress any desire to be free of their marriage. Their reveries, like Howells' fantasy in his letter to Gosse, ultimately do *not* "mean business." Yet "Niagara Revisited," like *A Modern Instance*, suggests that Howells felt strong ambivalence about the ties of domesticity; morally committed as he was to the institution of marriage, he felt secret sympathy toward Bartley's rebellion against it. Consciously, however, he could not permit himself to countenance divorce because he regarded marriage as the bedrock of civilization.

To Robert Louis Stevenson, this theme in *A Modern Instance* was all too clear: the novel was an attack, which Stevenson chose to take personally, on divorce. Mutual friends had been trying to bring the two writers together while Howells was abroad in 1882. But since, as Stevenson wrote to Howells, "My wife did me the honour to divorce her husband in order to marry me," he deemed it impossible to meet anyone "who considers himself holier than my wife" (*LinL*, 1:332–33). This "unanswerable letter," as Howells called it to Stevenson ten years later (*SL*, 4:49), has often been cited to suggest that any such interpretation of *A Modern Instance* is hopelessly reductive. Edwin H. Cady, for example, argues that Stevenson, before peremptorily cutting Howells' acquaintance, "would have been better advised to read the book carefully"; and Cady then quotes from Horace Scudder's perceptive review of the novel: "'It would be unjust to regard *A Modern Instance* as a tract against the divorce laws . . . it is a demonstration of a state of society of which the divorce laws are the index'" (p. 211).

But this broader reading of the novel does not, after all, gainsay Stevenson's narrower one. As Scudder implies, Howells sees the divorce laws as symptomatic of a society in moral disarray. He may be exploring the general state of that society, but he is also, implicitly, deploring divorce as a specific threat to the social order. As he told Osgood, the "moving principle" of the novel was to be "the question of divorce" (*MI*, xxix).[46]

In Atherton's diatribe, which may well have been what infuriated Stevenson, the lawyer denounces "'those scoundrels who lure women from their duty, ruin homes, and destroy society—not in the old libertine fashion in which the seducer had at least the grace to risk his life, but safely, smoothly, under the shelter of our infamous laws.'" The possibility of divorce, says

Atherton, tempts people "'to marry with a mental reservation'" that weakens "'every marriage bond with the guilty hope of escape whenever a fickle mind, or secret lust, or wicked will may dictate'" (*MI*, 397–98). Stevenson was one of the first of many readers to regard Atherton as Howells' *raisonneur*; and whatever ironic distance Howells sometimes puts between himself and Atherton's opinions, he never consciously differs with him on the idea that the Hubbards' divorce case, and Halleck's involvement in it, are portents of social decay.

Atherton's attitudes in *A Modern Instance* were anticipated in Howells' review in 1879 of Mary Wollstonecraft's letters to Gilbert Imlay, the American adventurer to whom she bore an illegitimate daughter before he deserted her, as Howells said, "for another and unworthier love." As if he saw the connection to the novel that was forming in his imagination, Howells called these letters a "tragic monologue," the expression of "a loving heart and a generous soul lavishing themselves in vain on an unstable and unworthy object." Part of the tragedy is that Imlay, like Bartley Hubbard, had a "restless and fickle nature" that ill fitted him to bear the stress of Wollstonecraft's "exacting and sometimes censorious devotion." Her letters show that, like Marcia Gaylord, she reproaches her lover and then "blames herself for reproaching him; she loses her trust in him, and struggles with self-upbraiding to regain it. But all the same she breaks her heart."[47]

The difference, of course, is that Wollstonecraft's heartbreak is the direct result of her "mistaken theory of faithful love without marriage." Feeling that she is somehow "pure in spite of her error," Howells is reluctant to blame her; but he "cannot regret that her suffering was signal, for she had tried to make herself a law against the law that holds society together." Like a latter-day Hester Prynne, believing that her adulterous liaison had a consecration of its own, Wollstonecraft misused her "strong but ill-regulated mind" and was punished accordingly. Giving herself to Imlay "without the sanction of law" proved to be in vain; and her sin was apparently visited upon her children: Fanny Imlay, who "died in her young girlhood, without having known any father's care except that of her mother's husband, Godwin"; and Mary Godwin, who eloped with Shelley while his "deserted wife was living," and who was "ready to live with him as her mother had lived with Imlay." Howells' defense of marriage in this review resembles Atherton's, and like Atherton he implies that the "signal" punishment of sinners against marriage is divinely ordained.

As Fred G. See remarks, marriage in the nineteenth century was "a moral and cosmological emblem," the "chief metaphorical sign of the continuous mediation between man and God."[48] For Howells and most of his contemporaries, marriage was not just "the law that holds society together," but a manifestation of the divine law that providentially guides human affairs. Divorce was feared as a rupture of what See calls "the ambiguous relationship between historical events and spiritual presence" (p. 388). The unpardonable sin of a Bartley Hubbard (or a Mary Wollstonecraft) was to personify the failure of marriage "to consecrate experience and therefore to structure it" (p. 388). When Bartley says of his marriage, "'I don't know that there's anything *sacred* about it'" (*MI*, 322), and when he later sues for divorce, he calls into question the existence of Providence itself and shakes the philosophical foundations of Victorian American society. *A Modern Instance*, as See argues, is "not only a psychological study of divorce but also of related fragmentations which extend from consciousness to social institutions and myths, to law, marriage, and theology" (p. 396). See credits Howells with deconstructing the "failed theological structure" of nineteenth-century ontology (p. 388), but he also wonders if Howells perhaps "could not face the demystified world that he had created" (p. 399).

It seems clear that he could not, at least in 1881, for the writing of *A Modern Instance* precipitated in Howells an emotional crisis. As I have tried at great length to suggest, there was a multiplicity of "causes" for Howells' breakdown, ranging from disruptions of his professional and domestic lives to the arousal of his unconscious fears. But his ambivalence toward marriage seems to have been a crucial element in his collapse if only because Howells' philosophical belief in this institution was so closely intertwined with his psychological defenses: marriage was the law that held both society and himself together.

For Howells, as for Freud, it was "impossible to overlook the extent to which civilization is built up upon a renunciation of instinct, how much it presupposes precisely the non-satisfaction (by suppression, repression or some other means?) of powerful instincts." Intuiting, again like Freud, that "civilized man has exchanged a portion of his possibilities of happiness for a portion of security," Howells dared, at the risk of his psychic balance, imaginatively to take the side of civilization's discontents.[49] But not for long; for by identifying himself with Bartley Hubbard, Howells jeopardized his own capacity for instinctual renunciation. It seems that Howells brought his collapse upon himself by lowering his defenses; and in completing *A Modern Instance* after his breakdown, as he rebuilt those defenses, he felt compelled to reaffirm that security, whatever its cost in possible happiness, was the greater portion.

VI

Howells faced the task of completing *A Modern Instance* with evident weariness and trepidation. (As if to signal his anxiety, his wrist began to pain him again.) Ironically, if he could not bear to read other novels during his recovery, he had no choice but to read his own, for it was already running serially in the *Century*. One installment had been stretched to two issues in order to give Howells more time, but the final chapters and the revisions of the earlier ones had to be finished at once. He was "working away all the time" at the story, he told Clemens on 31 January 1882: "I find that every mental effort costs about twice as much as it used, and the result seems to lack texture" (*MT-HL*, 391). He voiced a similar complaint to Warner two months later, as he was nearing the end of the novel, and he told George W. Cable that he was doing his best "to hide its faults from the reader" (*SL*, 3:16, 11).

That Howells himself found a lack of "texture" in the pages written after the breakdown implies an awareness that he was working under very different emotional conditions from those in which he had begun. He felt that his illness had aged him two or three years in four months, and he was "glad to have got well on any terms" (*SL*, 3:16). Because he intended to stay well, Howells needed to protect himself from the novel, to find a psychologically safe way to finish it. Therefore, he was not just completing *A Modern Instance* during the spring of 1882, he was "rewriting"—in fact, "unwriting"—the first part of it by "undoing" the imaginative sin of having made Bartley too sympathetic.

As Smith says, the concluding section of *A Modern Instance* "becomes in effect a different story," one that is unexpectedly and unfortunately dependent upon "outworn literary conventions . . . of exactly the kind of fiction that Howells attacked in his critical writing" (pp. 95–96). Of the quite typical passage, quoted above, in which Atherton fulminates against divorce, Smith writes: "Scoundrels luring women from their duty and ruining homes, a seducer risking his life (as Lovelace does in *Clarissa?*), secret lusts, and guilty specters shrinking through the world are not images one would expect to find in Howells's fictive universe. They belong to the detritus of sentimental popular fiction. But I believe these phrases are set down here without irony" (p. 98).

On the other hand, Don L. Cook, also perceiving that "Ben Halleck and Atherton step directly out of the moralistic romance of beautiful renunciation," assumes that Howells the realist must intend irony, but that "the parody of voracious conscience in the figure of Halleck and of irresponsible moral rigor in the case of Atherton seems not to have been drawn broadly enough to penetrate the minds of Howells' readers."[50] It would be more accurate to say that the "parody" did not penetrate Howells' own mind; for there is every reason to believe that he thought himself to be, as he told Cable of his efforts on the novel, "very much in earnest about it every way" (*SL*, 3:11). If Howells sometimes appears to undercut Halleck and Atherton, if he seems to debunk the sentimental conventions he is using, that is because the last section, like the rest of A Modern Instance, was written at emotional cross-purposes. Any "parody" in it is ultimately self-parody, accomplished by Howells' unconscious subversion of his conscious intentions.

To recognize just how much the ending of A Modern Instance resembles a romance of beautiful renunciation, we have only to look at one such story that he almost certainly had in mind. In March 1880, Elizabeth Stuart Phelps, author of The Gates Ajar, The Story of Avis, and other works in the sentimental mode, outlined to Howells a new novel that she hoped he would accept for the Atlantic.[51] Friends: A Duet was to be a psychological study (but "not a pathological treatment") of two ordinary (but "morally rather fine and strong") persons caught in one of "those indefined [sic] relations with which society is full, and over which it is always perplexed." Reliance Strong, a highborn and sensitive Bostonian lady, is brought the tidings of her husband's death by their close friend Charles Nordhall. The story consists of the development of an "ideal friendship" between these two: "he struggling to be loyal to his dead friend, John Strong, and a faithful comforter to his dead friend's widow; she, loyal without struggle, to her husband's memory":

> The Platonic friendship accelerates as it "usually" will; the man (of course) breaks down first. The contest wages till the very last line of the book; where with "an expression of entreaty, wild as an eternal regret," she yeilds [sic]—as "the usual" woman would. I trust that the ideal of a possibly poised friendship between woman and man, is suggested, and that while "it is natural to be happy," my readers will also feel that it "is natural to be true;"—that the artistic effect will be one of partial sadness at my heroine's acceptation of anything below the highest in the marriage relation. . . . The light-natured reader will be glad she married him. The other kind will almost wish she had not. So, at least, I hope.

With her desire to dwell upon "the refined moral problems" of her heroine, Phelps wished not to deal with "the great moral struggles" that she associated with adulterous liaisons. Although illicit passion may give "great intensity" to a story, she recoiled from "touching a position which has been so often soiled by writers of fiction." Thus there was to be "no moral impediment" between Reliance and Charles "other than that created by the affection of a delicate woman for a dead husband, whom it is the consequence of her religious faith for her to consider 'a live man.'"

Friends: A Duet was serialized in early 1881, and Howells was reading it while he was composing A Modern Instance. When Phelps sent him a copy of her novel in July, he replied with enthusiasm, telling her that he was "very greatly stirred up by your book, and thought a thousand things." He admired her working out of a "great and simple" but precious theme: "the texture is wonderfully delicate and wonderfully fine; but then if you *have* gold in your hand you can beat it out to any subtilty you like, and steel you can draw to the tenuity of a hair." Perhaps Howells was thinking here of his relatively greater artistic problem: how to achieve a subtle "texture" from the decidedly un-golden material of the basely metallic Bartley and the mercurial Marcia. He found, in any case, that he felt sorry for Charles Nordhall: "Women, I always think can take care of themselves in matters of the affections, and can be what they like; but men are helpless and must be Caesar or nothing" (*SL*, 2:290).

In *A Modern Instance*, it is Ben Halleck, not Bartley Hubbard, who is held to a "Caesar or nothing" standard by Atherton; and the ending of the novel centers on the exquisite torments of this more neurotic version of Phelps's Charles Nordhall.[52] Like Phelps's genteel hero, Halleck resists temptation for a while, masochistically befriending the woman he adores but never revealing his love for her. Both men ultimately succumb to their desires, and each tries to justify himself—Ben to Atherton, Charles to Reliance herself—by roman-tically affirming the authenticity of passion over the authority of moral law. Much like Mary Wollstonecraft (and also Bartley Hubbard), Halleck declares to Atherton his intention to "'preach by my life that marriage has no sanctity but what love gives it, and that, when love ceases, marriage ceases, before heaven'" (*MI*, 398)—a notion that the narrator dismisses as the "delusion" of a spiritually exhausted man (*MI*, 399). At the end, when Bartley is dead and Ben's situation more closely resembles Nordhall's, Howells does not permit himself Phelps's bittersweet conclusion, leaving many readers to regret not that the lovers marry, but that they do not.

When asked in an interview in 1899 to "solve the puzzle" as to whether Marcia and Ben were ever joined, Howells replied: "O, I never could see it that way. Such an outcome would have been perfectly right, but Halleck's character, I believe, would have made it impossible for him to marry a woman with whom he had been in love when she was another man's wife" (*INT*, 67). But, in fact, had it seemed "perfectly right" to Howells in 1882? By the turn of the century, his views on marriage and divorce had become more liberal than they were at the time of *A Modern Instance*; and the novel itself suggests that Howells' own character, as much as Halleck's, had made it impossible for him to ignore what Atherton calls the "'indelible stain'" (*MI*, 453) of Ben's having desired another man's wife. Howells could no more condone Halleck's defamation of marriage than he could Hubbard's.

Ben's suffering, like Bartley's, seems excessive, as if Howells were punishing him in the same compensatory way for his dangerous opinions. In fact, Hub-bard is Halleck's *doppelgänger*, as Alfred Habbeger observes: "The reason Ben takes up so much room at the end of *A Modern Instance* is that he is Bartley's double and therefore has to clean up, or at least try to clean up, the mess left by his ungovernable Mr. Hyde. Only a double's irrational *complicity* . . . could explain Ben's compulsive heart-searching."[53]

Beginning with their rhythmically similar surnames (which echo "Howells"), and their identical initials, the affinities between Bartley and Ben are striking. Since their college days, spent together, each has perceived himself to be an outsider, deprived of the success and admiration he thinks he deserves. Both men are strongly attracted to Marcia, whom they envision as a paragon of womanly virtue, capable of "saving" them. Neither possesses an orthodox religious faith or a sure grasp of moral certainty—one reason, perhaps, why they both fail as law students. Ben is literally crippled, but he is also figuratively crippled, like Bartley, by his moral illness: undone by passion, by the power of unconscious impulses, each creates an inner hell for himself. Bartley is literally a drunkard on one occasion at least, and he often tipples Tivoli beer. Ben, who is disgusted by Bartley's inebriation and harrowed by the thought of how it will mortify Marcia, is an emotional sot. One night he keeps a secret vigil at her house and then staggers away in the lamplight, his shadow wavering "across the pavement like the figure of a drunken man" (*MI*, 288). On another occasion Atherton tries to calm his friend "like a man who has attempted to rule a drunkard by thwarting his freak, and then hopes to accomplish his end by humoring it" (*MI*, 366).

The pairing of Bartley and Ben fits the pattern of Howells' earlier novels where, as I have shown, two young men are often pitted in a love rivalry that carries, nonetheless, distinctly homoerotic overtones: Ferris and Don Ippolito, Easton and Gilbert, Ford and Phillips. In *A Modern Instance*, the homoerotic element is mostly displaced into the relationship of Bartley and Henry Bird, whose initials mark him as Hubbard's "invert." When Henry strikes Bartley for having flirted with Hannah Morrison, he seems to be as jealous of Hannah as of Bartley, whom he has served with keen devotion.[54]

Between Ben and Bartley there is ostensibly only hatred. But Halleck loathes Hubbard so passionately (and, at first, so unaccountably) that he appears to be repressing an underlying attraction, the possibility of which registers at least upon Marcia, with her nearly psychic ability to detect any threat to her hold on Bartley. When she first meets Halleck, she is "content" that he should appear so plain and awkward: "She would not have liked even a man who knew Bartley before she did to be very handsome" (*MI*, 215). On two occasions in the last part of the novel, Ben is shown to feel "a perverse sympathy" with Bartley (*MI*, 407). Struck by the opulence of the Athertons' dining room, Ben thinks to himself that "Bartley might never have gone wrong if he had had all that luxury," and he questions the right of Atherton, in his "untempted prosperity," to judge the "guilt of such men as himself and Bartley Hubbard" (*MI*, 407). Later, on the train to Indiana, Halleck is repulsed by

Squire Gaylord's deforming lust for vengeance upon his son-in-law: "'It made me feel a sort of sympathy for that poor dog'" (*MI*, 422).

If Halleck is Bartley's double, he is also Howells' alter ego—as George C. Carrington says, "the civilized half, the surface half, of Howells" in contrast to Hubbard, "the uncivilized, 'natural,' demonic, hidden half of the author." [55] Furthermore, the ending of *A Modern Instance* may be read as a metafiction in which Howells, through Halleck, reflects upon his own breakdown and its causes. In one of the first passages Howells wrote after his recovery, Halleck describes his own obscurely psychological illness in words that seem to apply to the author who had just taken up the job of completing *A Modern Instance* and who was soon to complain of its lack of "texture": "'I'm not strong enough to go on with the line of work I've marked out, and I feel that I'm throwing away the feeble powers I have'" (*MI*, 351). A few pages later, Halleck pours out the guilty anguish he has felt since recognizing his illicit love for Marcia: "'I had been trying not to face the truth, but I had to face it then. I came away in hell, and I have lived in hell ever since. . . . I abhorred it from the beginning as I do now; it has been torment to me; and yet somewhere in my lost soul—the blackest depth, I dare say!—this shame has been so sweet,—it is so sweet,—the one sweetness of life—Ah!'" (*MI*, 368). Ben's guilty suffering for what seems so sweet to him in his blackest depths seems to reflect Howells' own suffering during his breakdown; Ben's loving Marcia seems to be a metaphor of Howells' (and Halleck's) secret sin of having loved Bartley Hubbard not wisely but too well. At one point Ben wishes Bartley dead, an urge that Howells shared and that he gratified by replacing Bartley with Ben in the last quarter of the novel.

This substitution is part of a more general change. As Habegger perceives, "The main characters in *A Modern Instance* fall into two opposed classes, the one consisting of the main actors—the Squire, Marcia, and Bartley—and the other limited to the moral bystanders—Ben and Olive Halleck and Atherton" (p. 97). Howells reversed the figure and ground of the novel after his breakdown by bringing forward the aristocratic and morally fastidious Brahmin characters, who would have felt quite at home in *Friends: A Duet*. Even Marcia, the only main character from the first part of the novel who appears very much in the second, is subtly toned up, made to seem more "tragically" innocent, as if to make her a fitter object for the Hallecks' sympathy.

Shifting his attention toward the more genteel characters was part of Howells' strategy for escaping Bartley Hubbard. By identifying himself with the decent and refined Ben Halleck, he gained psychological distance from his dangerous and unconscious self. But he did not stop with foregrounding his genteel alter ego; he also installed his super-ego. In the earlier part of the novel, Howells' narrator carries most of the moral burden of denouncing

Bartley. But in the later part the narrator is relatively quiet and unintrusive; his function has been taken over by Eustace Atherton, who becomes prominent—and also insufferably self-righteous—only in the scenes written *after* the breakdown.[56]

The role of Atherton in A *Modern Instance* is perhaps the most debated aspect of the novel. The critics tend to line up behind one of two ideas: either that Atherton is clearly Howells' *raisonneur*, or that he clearly is not. One side points to the apparent congruity of Atherton's moral pronouncements with Howells' own opinions; the other points to the apparent undercutting of Atherton, as in the famous scene where he philosophizes about "natural" and "implanted goodness" between sips of "fragrant Souchong, sweetened, and tempered with Jersey cream to perfection" (*MI*, 417).

The complexity of Atherton's function is most nearly captured in Firkins's remark that he acts "as attorney for Mr. Howells" (p. 102). This is true in a double sense that Firkins and other critics have not fully articulated: Atherton is both a prosecutor and, more subtly, a defense lawyer. As the *raisonneur* of Howells' super-ego, Atherton makes the civilized case against Bartley Hubbard and gives voice to the sadistically severe judgments that Howells used to defend himself from this imago of his uncivilized self. But Atherton also defends Howells from Ben Halleck; for as Hubbard's surrogate in the last part of the novel, Halleck comes closer than any other character to expressing the unconscious urges in Howells that still pitted him against his super-ego.[57]

This psychological conflict is dramatized, for example, in the encounter between Halleck and Atherton that Howells wrote just after his recovery, the scene in which Ben all but confesses his lust for Marcia, and Atherton comes to his moral assistance. A terrible tension arises in this scene from the lawyer's reluctance to believe Halleck's protestations of guilt—as if Atherton were refusing to accept his new role in the novel. Howells/Halleck tries to spur Atherton into moral action by divulging his murderous desires against Bartley:

> "Why shouldn't one wish him dead, when his death could do nothing but good?"
>
> "I suppose you don't expect me to answer such a question seriously."
>
> "But suppose I did?"
>
> "Then I should say that no man ever wished any such good as that, except from the worst motive; and the less one has to do with such questions, even as abstractions, the better."
>
> "You're right," said Halleck. "But why do you call it an abstraction?"
>
> "Because, in your case, nothing else is conceivable.". . .
>
> "I wish I could convince somebody of my wickedness. But it seems to be useless to try. . . . I suppose now, that if I took you by the buttonhole and informed you confidentially that I had stopped long enough at

129 Clover street to put a knife into Hubbard in a quiet way, you wouldn't send for a policeman."

"I should send for a doctor," said Atherton.

"Such is the effect of character! And yet, out of the fulness of the heart the mouth speaketh. Out of the heart proceed all those unpleasant things enumerated in Scripture; but if you bottle them up there, and keep your label fresh, it's all that's required of you—by your fellow-beings, at least. What an amusing thing morality would be if it were not—otherwise." (*MI*, 360–61)

Whereas Atherton insists, as he later says, that "'It's our deeds that judge us,'" and that no one is more liable to judgment than a person, like Halleck, who should have conscious control over his deeds (*MI*, 417), Halleck insists that not just our deeds judge us but also our darkest motives. Halleck's text is Matthew, 12.35: "A good man out of the good treasure of the heart bringeth forth good things: and an evil man out of the evil treasure bringeth forth evil things." Atherton's countertext is Matthew, 12.37: "For by thy words thou shalt be justified, and by thy words thou shalt be condemned." Atherton not only refuses at this point to attach guilt to Ben's thoughts (conscious or unconscious), or to believe that his words bespeak an evil heart, but he prefers to evade the whole matter of "worst" motives. Later in the novel, however, acting more vigilantly the part of the super-ego, Atherton comes (inconsistently) to believe in Halleck's unconscious guilt and to judge him mercilessly for it.

The more severe Atherton becomes, the more systematically Howells seems to undercut him: in part by narrative irony, in part by complicity with Halleck in his resistance to moral authority. That is, Howells subverts his commitments of conscience by allowing Halleck to evince his secret brotherhood to Hubbard. On the train to Indiana, for example, in a context that makes them sound absurd, Ben recapitulates Atherton's arguments against divorce to Marcia, telling her, "in bitterness of soul," why she must go to court against Bartley: "'[Y]ou have a *public* duty in the matter. You must keep him bound to you, for fear some other woman, whose husband doesn't care for her, would let *him* go, too, and society be broken up and civilization destroyed. In a matter like this, which seems to concern yourself alone, you are only to regard others'" (*MI*, 430). Standing in for the absent lawyer, the narrator disapproves of Halleck's parody of Atherton, calling it "reckless irony" (*MI*, 431). But the damage to Atherton's credibility is done nonetheless, as Howells unconsciously wished it to be.

It should be clear why A *Modern Instance* is so irreducibly ambiguous. In revising the novel, Howells tried to accomplish an act of moral expiation through an act of artistic renunciation: he got rid of Bartley Hubbard and consciously allied himself with the highest standards of genteel American society. But Howells' repression was imperfect. As in all his earlier novels, the unconscious urges broke through in spite of his intentions, such that Howells was continually questioning the very principles he seemed to be affirming— leading to a climax of ambivalence in Atherton's final but inconclusive words, "'Ah, I don't know! I don't know!'" (*MI*, 453).

VII

Edith Wharton praised Howells as the first writer "to feel the tragic potentialities of life in the drab American small town," but she also regretted that "the incurable moral timidity which again and again checked him on the verge of a masterpiece drew him back even from the logical conclusion of 'A Modern Instance.'"[58] I have tried to demonstrate that Howells' "moral timidity" is more fairly and accurately described as his neurotic fear; and I have argued that the conclusion of the novel, even as it seems to "unwrite" the first thirty-one chapters, obeys both the logic of Howells' conscious commitments and the disruptive counterlogic of his unconscious desires. Howells was to write many books that are more coherent, more composed than *A Modern Instance*, but none more vital for its very discontinuity and discomposure.

Howells regarded *A Modern Instance* as his "strongest book" (*SL*, 4:231), the novel in which he took "the most satisfaction" because he had come "closest to American life" as he knew it (*INT*, 29). What Howells knew from deep within himself were the splits within American life: sexual and moral conflicts, regional and class divisions, these were the warp and woof of the novel. It is important to remember, as Fryckstedt points out, that many of the younger American realists, who benefited from Howells' advocacy and example, "considered *A Modern Instance* the great revolutionary work in American literature" (p. 265). Wharton, Crane, Dreiser, Garland, and others were responding to those undercurrents in the novel that were rising to the surface of their own fiction. Howells' literary "children," in various ways, followed the unconscious impetus of *A Modern Instance* and "completed" its radical design.

Sister Carrie (1900), for example, owes a great deal to *A Modern Instance*. Fryckstedt has remarked some general affinities, including the common focus on "new Americans who rose in society after the Civil War" and the similar pattern of degeneracy in Hubbard and Hurstwood (pp. 267–68). Richard Lehan notes several other parallels: between Bartley's and Carrie's backgrounds and their amoral "desire for success and money"; between the Hubbards' bewildering search for lodgings in Boston and Carrie's struggle to find work in Chicago; between the fated turning points for Hubbard and Hurstwood. "Bartley is driven toward a predestined end by an accident (the stolen wallet) just as Hurstwood is driven toward a predestined end by another accident (the safe slamming shut)."[59]

Such resemblances are striking; but more important—and no less a matter of "influence"—are Dreiser's differences from and his re-visions of Howells. Dreiser seems to have recognized the profound conflicts in *A Modern Instance* and to have resolved them in every case in favor of what Howells had tried to suppress. Free will versus fate: Dreiser takes for granted the psychological and social determinism that Howells feared to acknowledge. "Implanted goodness" versus "natural goodness": Dreiser ignores the upper-class world as if its well-tended seeds of righteousness do not really matter, and he professes a Spencerian faith in evolution toward which Howells was agnostic. Marriage versus divorce: Dreiser obviates Atherton's direst prophecies by showing the moral irrelevance of divorce *and* marriage. Renunciation versus satisfaction of instinct: Carrie thrives as Hurstwood withers because she is more fully a creature of instinct. Marcia as Victorian angel versus Marcia as seductress: Carrie, free of sexual inhibition, remains nonetheless essentially innocent. Disgust versus attraction toward Bartley Hubbard: the wife deserter Hurstwood is treated with unalloyed sympathy, and toward the end of the novel he becomes as central as Hubbard became peripheral after Chapter 31.

Insofar as Howells' novel may be seen as a precursor of Dreiser's, it is not so "curious" as Fryckstedt suggests that "*Sister Carrie* held, in the eyes of the moderns, a position that was in many ways comparable to the place that an earlier generation of writers ascribed to *A Modern Instance*" (p. 267). Of course the filiation of Dreiser to Howells was something that each man in his fashion tried to deny—Howells by his forbidding public silence about *Sister Carrie* at the time Dreiser most needed his paternal blessing, and Dreiser by his subsequent belittling of Howells' work. Since Howells did not fully comprehend until 1911 that he had "drawn Bartley Hubbard, the false scoundrel, from myself" (*SL*, 5:361), it is understandable that he could not, ten years earlier, have recognized what Dreiser had drawn from *A Modern Instance*.[60]

Dreiser, who clearly felt a rivalry with Howells' more favored literary sons (especially Crane), must have felt betrayed; and he did nothing to oppose the ritual slaughter of Howells' reputation during the 1920s, when the supercilious ignorance of Dreiser's own first biographer was so typical. "I suppose Howells was a writer," opined Dorothy Dudley. "I am a reader who will never know. Try as I will, I can't read him, neither his Easy Chair for Harper's Magazine, nor his endless novels. He wrote for the gentry of his times, and must have put to sleep the more restless members." "'Yes, I know his books are pewky and damn-fool enough,'" Dreiser agreed—although he went on to defend to Dudley his admiration for *Their Wedding Journey*.[61]

The climax of such prejudice came in Sinclair Lewis's Nobel Prize address in 1930, when he compared Howells to "a pious old maid whose greatest delight was to have tea at the vicarage" and denounced the "very bad standard" of his literary taste and practice. In the same speech, Lewis embraced Dreiser as he who "more than any other man, marching alone, usually unappreciated, often hated, has cleared the trail from Victorian and Howellsian timidity and gentility in American fiction to honesty and boldness and passion of life." [62] It is supremely ironic that the author of Main Street (1920) and Babbitt (1922), which owed as much to Howells as to Dreiser, should have "forgotten" this literary debt.

Lewis was to be bluntly reminded, however, by Edith Wharton, who herself had drawn from Howells in her greatest novel, The Custom of the Country (1913). Her only quarrel with the Stockholm speech, she told Lewis, was "that you should have made it the occasion of saying anything depreciatory of Howells. In spite of his limitations (which wd probably have been ours, at that date, & in a country reeking with sentimentality & shuddering with prudery) he gave the first honestly realistic picture of the American mediocrity, & 'A Modern Instance,' with Robert Grant's 'Unleavened Bread,' did more than any other two books (though so long before your time that you are probably unconscious of it) to pave the way for 'Main Street.'" Wharton urged Lewis to reread two or three of Howells' best books; that, she was confident, would surely make him want "to unsay what you said of him." [63]

There is no evidence that Lewis took this advice; and Wharton herself was to unsay what she said when, three years later, she revised her opinions for publication. In A Backward Glance, she subordinated A Modern Instance to Unleavened Bread (it had been the other way around in 1931), and she asserted that Howells' "moral timidity" had "left Robert Grant the first in the field which he was eventually to share with Lewis and Dreiser" (p. 148).

Although he was "probably unconscious of it," Lewis had reinscribed A Modern Instance in the ending of Babbitt. Having dallied with Tanis and the bohemian Group, having deviated from the standards of the Good Citizens League, Babbitt realizes, when his wife suddenly takes ill, the error of his ways: "Instantly all the indignations which had been dominating him and the spiritual dramas through which he had struggled became pallid and absurd before the ancient and overwhelming realities, the standard and traditional realities, of sickness and menacing death, the long night, and the thousand steadfast implications of married life." [64] He experiences here the moment of repentance that Bartley never achieves. Babbitt is Hubbard's twin in his rebellion against social proprieties, but unlike Bartley, George ultimately affirms all the conventional codes.

Ostensibly the satiric butt of the novel, Babbitt is also, as many critics have noted, a curiously sympathetic figure. That is, Lewis's ambivalence toward his central character was comparable to Howells'—but with a complete reversal

of psychological polarity. What Lewis imperfectly repressed was not his identification with Babbitt's "criminal element," but his secret sharing of Babbitt's
love for "standard and traditional realities." Forty years after its publication,
A Modern Instance was turned inside out by a self-consciously "iconoclastic"
writer who was unconsciously allied to the same "timidity and gentility" that
he projected upon Howells.[65]

Although *A Modern Instance* came to appear far less "revolutionary" than
Sister Carrie or even *Babbitt*, it is true nevertheless that this novel, precisely
because of the psychic trauma it entailed, was Howells' most prophetic expression of what Joseph Wood Krutch was to call "The Modern Temper." In *A
Modern Instance*, Howells peered into the modernist abyss and foresaw a universe in which, as Krutch says, "the human spirit cannot find a comfortable
home"—where, discomforted and adrift, it clings desperately to the beliefs
"that right and wrong are real, that Love is more than a biological function,
that the human mind is capable of reason rather than merely of rationalization, and that it has the power to will and to choose instead of being compelled merely to react in the fashion predetermined by its conditioning." Be-
reft of these beliefs by science, which has proved that none of them is "more
than a delusion," humankind "will be compelled either to surrender what we
call its humanity by adjusting to the real world or to live some kind of tragic
existence in a universe alien to the deepest needs of its nature."[66]

It was his own vision of such an alien universe that Howells was so desperate to dispel in *A Modern Instance* and throughout his career. It was the "ruin"
that, unlike Bartley Hubbard, he did everything in his power *not* to choose.

CHAPTER SEVEN
MIRACLES OF THE INNER WORLD

Howells' psychic quake in 1881, like that in 1854, was followed by aftershocks. During the composition of *The Rise of Silas Lapham*, he seems to have suffered another collapse—although not one so severe as to have deranged his writing. He told a journalist in 1896 that although his affairs had been prospering and his work "marching as well as heart could wish," still he had been gripped "suddenly, and without apparent cause," by a sense that "the status seemed wholly wrong." "'The bottom dropped out!'" he said.[1] Nothing more is known about this mysterious episode: there is no evidence in either Howells' letters or his autobiographies to corroborate that it even occurred. There are much clearer traces, however, of later upheavals. For the rest of his life, Howells was seldom free from some kind of physical symptoms, any or all of which may be considered to have had a neurotic component.

Wrist pains recurred in December 1886, just after Howells had pondered and then declined Lowell's offer of the Smith Professorship at Harvard (*SL*, 3:174), and again in September 1887, after he had impassionately pleaded the cause of the Chicago anarchists (*SL*, 3:195). With a pun, he related an illness in 1892 to his problems in writing *The World of Chance*: "I have had the grippe on me, but I have not got the grip on my story yet" (*SL*, 4:9).

And there was also vertigo: first in 1891 and then, more persistently, in 1893, when Howells was drafting the initial chapter for what would become *Literary Friends and Acquaintance*.[2] Recalling his youthful pilgrimage to Boston, perhaps because it reanimated his ambivalence toward the Brahmins, was evidently quite stressful. Howells was greatly relieved at Oliver Wendell Holmes's belated but positive reaction to the serial version of "My First Visit to New England": "I had begun to be afraid that I had said something that jarred upon you." Again using a joke that implies a link between his writing and his illness, Howells added that he had been "running a sort of serial headache, for several months past; there seems no dénoûment for it" (*SL*, 4:64). The following year, as he continued his reminiscences, Howells experienced more vertigo; as remedy, riding lessons seemed to be the "best thing."[3]

Gallstone attacks (what Howells called "bilious colic") plagued him in

1895 and 1896. He told Hamlin Garland that he had lost fifteen pounds during one bout with the ailment—"also some brains, if I can judge from my feebleness in work" (*SL*, 4:139). Howells took a water cure at Carlsbad in the summer of 1897, but a year later he was still complaining about "a good deal of back ache" (*SL*, 4:181).

His lecture tour in 1899, undertaken at the urging of Major James B. Pond, produced so much "nervous strain" that Howells limped home and entered the Zander Institute for physical therapy.[4] Nearly every night during the tour, as he told Clemens, he had drugged himself with trional or soaked himself with whiskey in order to achieve "a few hours of blessed stupor." For a whole month he had gone without "one night's natural sleep" (*MT-HL*, 712).

In his last twenty years Howells endured the pains endemic to old age and the natural shocks of mortality as he outlived his wife and most of his friends. As late as 1909, he was still battling his "old gall colic" and his "still older enemy, vertigo" (*SL*, 5:276n). This was more than fifty years after his reeling days in Columbus.

If Howells did not escape its symptoms, he did come to understand his neuroticism and its bearing upon his imagination. For Howells, as for Freud, dreams were to be the royal road to the unconscious—but a road he was long hesitant to take very far.

I

In "Eighty Years and After" (1919), Howells asserted that he had spent "a large part of my life in the [un]conscious cerebration of sleep. There have been nights of mine almost as busy as my days in even more varied experiences, among persons from the other world as well as this; and it is so yet, but I think that I do not dream so much as formerly" (*SL*, 6:166).[5] Formerly he had not only dreamed a great deal but had sometimes noted just what he dreamed. There exists, in fact, a record of well over fifty of Howells' dreams, dating from earliest childhood to his final months—a record far more detailed than that of any other pre-Freudian American writer.[6]

Howells was accustomed throughout his life to retailing his dreams in letters to his family, but he first made them "public" in 1880, in the anonymous "Contributors' Club" column of the *Atlantic*. After describing some of his repeated nightmares, he invited his readers to say whether recurrent dreams were "a common experience, or an idiosyncrasy of mine."[7] His richest treatment of the subject came fifteen years later in a signed article titled, "True, I Talk of Dreams."[8] At this stage of his career, after the death of Winifred in 1889, Howells was turning more and more to what he later called the "miracles of the inner world."[9]

During the decade of Winifred's illness, Howells had become all too familiar with psychiatric theories; but even after she died, he continued to keep
abreast of the literature. "I have liked to read such books of medicine as have
fallen in my way," he wrote in 1895, "and I seldom take up a medical peri-
odical without reading of all the cases it describes, and in fact every article in
it" (*MLP*, 174). Although the full extent of Howells' reading is not known,
he was well enough informed to recognize that William James's *Principles of
Psychology* (1890) was "a most important" book (*LinL*, 2:14), and to write a
knowledgeable review of it.[10]

Howells apparently made an intensive study of dream theory during the
summer of 1890.[11] Again, not all of his sources are known; but in both "I Talk
of Dreams" and *The Shadow of a Dream* (1890), he alluded to Théodule
Armand Ribot's hypothesis that "approaching disease sometimes intimates itself in dreams of the disorder impending, before it is otherwise declared in the
organism" (*I&E*, 119). Ribot, a French psychologist whose staunch positivism
reflected the scientific orthodoxy of the late nineteenth century, contemp-
tuously dismissed "the metaphysics of unconsciousness as conceived by [Eduard
von] Hartmann and others." Ribot proposed instead "to express the unconscious in physiological terms (states of the nervous system), and not in psychological terms (latent ideas, non-felt sensations, etc.)."[12]

It is important to observe that Howells' acquaintance with somatic theories, such as Ribot's, did not lead him to renounce the spiritualistic notions
about dreams that had undoubtedly been impressed upon him in childhood
by his father. William Cooper Howells' immersion in the doctrines of the
New Church made him sensitive to all possible correspondences to the spirit
world. Soon after Winifred's death, he was prompted by a newspaper article
on dreams, which had asserted that "there is nothing supernatural about
them," to write a letter to the editor. "You are certainly right in saying there is
nothing *super*natural about dreams," William Cooper replied. "I would rather
say nothing *un*natural, for I would maintain the theory that this natural life of
ours is made up of a constant mixture of spiritual and material existences, and
that this mixed relation of spirit and matter is *natural* to our whole life in this
world, that we as individuals we [*sic*] are spirits,—clothed in matter <and>
compelled to act through it, and confined to it; while yet the world of mere
spiritual existence is in constant contact and association with us."[13]

Dreams, the elder Howells continued, might be the result of departed spirits' "playing upon our imaginations, and even playing with us *sportively*, not
with much of good or evil intent, but so as to amuse and divert themselves."
Such sportiveness would account for the frivolousness of most dreams. Bad
dreams might be the promptings of "wanton or wicked" spirits who take advantage of the quiescence of reason during sleep; whereas prophetic dreams
might be the work of friendly intelligence from beyond.

Howells may well have read his father's essay before he wrote his own; for at one point in "I Talk of Dreams" he entertained one of William Cooper's ideas—that a dreamer's embodied spirit may consort with the spirits of the disembodied—and then objected: "why should the dreamer's state so much oftener be imbued with evil than with good?" Perhaps wicked spirits are more aggressive than good ones in contacting the living. Or perhaps "the love of the dreamer, which is his life, being mainly evil, invites the wicked spirits oftener." This point Howells preferred to "leave each dreamer to settle for himself," since "nothing seems quite to hold in regard to dreams" (I&E, 113–14).

Howells was as agnostic about spirit contact in dreams as he was about religion in general, but he respected—and perhaps envied—his father's conviction. In December 1890, writing to Howard Pyle, another Swedenborgian believer, Howells professed his uncertainty about the afterlife, which Winifred's death had made so painfully important to him. "I do not always feel sure that I shall live again, but when I wake at night the room seems dense with spirits. Since this dream which I wrote out for my father I have had others about my daughter, fantastic and hideous, as if to punish me for my unbelief" (SL, 3:299).[14]

Howells felt partly responsible for Winifred's death, and the depth of his remorse is revealed by a fantastic and hideous dream he had reported to his father in January 1890. He was about "to be hanged for something" and had a chance to escape; but he reflected, "'No, I am tired of living; and it's only a momentary wrench, and then I shall be with her'" (SL, 3:270). Another time he took her cheeks between his hands and cried over her, saying in the dream, "Have you come back to poor Papa?" Once she appeared in her gray dressing gown in her mother's room. "Elinor said, 'Here's Winny,' and I took her in my arms and held her close and long. When I let her go far enough to speak, she said in a glad way, 'Then you do love me?' and I choked out, 'O love you!'" (SL, 6:179).

Sometimes Winifred visited him in a consoling rather than accusing form. A year after her death, in the dream that Howells told Pyle he had written out for his father, Winifred appeared in the pink of health, as if for family breakfast at some sort of hotel. She assured him that she had overcome her initial loneliness in the hereafter, that she had not "weeped since," and that spirit life was more interesting than it often seemed in spiritists' accounts. Later in the same dream, in fulfillment of his wish that she had recovered instead of died, Howells found himself and Winny climbing a hill, as if to their house in Belmont: "I put my hand on her waist behind, to help her, and said 'I don't suppose you need that now.' 'No,' she said 'I am well,' or something like that; and then the dream ended" (SL, 6:179–80).[15]

In "I Talk of Dreams," referring obliquely to his own experience, Howells suggested that "very few of those who have lost their beloved have failed to receive some sign or message from them in dreams, and often it is of deep and abiding consolation." He conceded that this may be a cruel delusion, merely "our anguish compelling the echo of love out of the darkness where nothing is"; but he was not willing to foreclose the possibility "that there is something there, which answers to our throe with pity and with longing like our own." Pragmatically considered, "Unbelief can be no gain, and belief no loss"; wiser not to refuse "the comfort which belief can give" in a matter "impossible of definite solution" (*I&E*, 123).

In his search for a solution to the riddle of dreams during the summer of 1890, Howells had encountered Carl Du Prel, a philosopher steeped in the German transcendentalism that Ribot rejected. "My reading dream-wards, so far as Du Prol [*sic*] was concerned, ended in an argument for metempsychosis, or paleogenesis! I was deeply disappointed," Howells told Pyle (*SL*, 3:299).

In *The Philosophy of Mysticism* (1889), Du Prel, who anticipated several of Freud's key ideas,[16] argues that the "dream is by no means a mere remnant of the daily consciousness, but a new consciousness qualitatively different from that."[17] Dreaming originates from a "dream organ" independent of the brain; and, along with other subliminal phenomena, such as somnambulism, it provides "confirmation of the fact that our external consciousness has another spiritual background, that the individual intellect has not for its supporter the blind Universal Will of Schopenhauer, that, therefore, with the disappearance of this intellect the conscious personality is by no means abolished, but the transcendental consciousness possessing as a focus its own Ego, and for which the word 'forget' has no application, is released" (2:42).

Since this Kantian "transcendental Subject" is independent of the bodily senses, death cannot affect it; because we belong "essentially to the transcendental order of things," death must bring "to free development those transcendental faculties of which in somnambulism [and also in dreams] we obtain only intimations" (2:157). Set free by death, the transcendental Subject inevitably feels "the impulse to incarnation" (2:205) and seeks renewed earthly life. Thus Du Prel arrives "at the oldest of philosophical conceptions of man, the migration of souls; but this old theory would be revived in a new and incomparably higher form, which could only be described as palingenesis. This would have to be conceived, not as transplacement into another objective space, but rather into a subjectively different world; it would not be change of place, but change of perceptional mode" (2:288–89).

This last conjecture is what Howells criticized to Pyle; and in *The Landlord at Lion's Head* (1897), he attacked Du Prel again by attributing to Jackson Durgin, the credulous spiritist, one of Du Prel's more extreme notions: that the transcendental Subject may put us into contact with higher forms of life elsewhere in the cosmos—as, for instance, on Mars![18] Howells told Pyle that Du Prel had "grievously vexed" as well as disappointed him (*SL*, 3:299). Very likely this vexation was provoked not merely by Du Prel's speculations about transmigration and outer space; far more threatening was his faith in the primacy of the transcendental Subject.

For Du Prel, the direction of evolution itself is "to raise the unconscious into the conscious, to make the possession of the Subject the possession of the Person" (2:293). Although this statement foreshadows Freud's credo for psychoanalysis, Du Prel's unconscious was not exactly Freud's. For Du Prel, the moral imperative "comes ultimately from the transcendental Subject"; therefore "the seat of conscience is in the unconscious" (2:296, 298); and "we thus attain the aim of earthly existence when we subordinate the interests of our person to those of the Subject. . . . [E]very revolt of the person, in its own favour, against the Subject is immoral" (2:294).

Such ideas must have struck Howells as being arrant nonsense. For him, the unconscious was the source of anarchic and immoral passions, which must be controlled by a "critical faculty": the seat of conscience is in consciousness. By dint of these beliefs, Howells was far less optimistic than Du Prel, or even than his own father, about any good's coming from dreams. Rather he stressed their atavistic—what Freud was to call their "regressive"—quality:

> Apparently the greater part of dreams have no more mirth than sense
> in them. This is perhaps because the man is in dreams reduced to
> the brute condition, and is the lawless inferior of the waking man in-
> tellectually, as the lawless in waking are always the inferiors of the
> lawful. Some loose thinkers [such as Du Prel?] suppose that if we give
> the rein to imagination it will do great things, but it will really do little
> things, foolish and worthless things, as we witness in dreams, where
> it is quite unbridled. It must keep close to truth, and it must be under
> the law if it would work strongly and sanely. The man in his dreams
> is really lower than the lunatic in his deliriums. . . . In his wicked
> dreams the man is not only animal, he is devil, so wholly is he let into
> his evils, as the Swedenborgians say. (*I&E*, 110–11)

Or, as Howells says earlier in the essay, the "dream-criminal" and the habitual "deed-criminal" are possibly linked by "the same taint of insanity." Both lack a "soul," defined as "the supernal criticism of the deeds done in the body, which goes perpetually on in the waking mind" but which goes "off duty" in the sleeping mind (*I&E*, 100–101). The active force of this "soul"—what Freud was to call the "censor" and later the "super-ego"—is what makes us lawful and keeps us sane.

Howells considered dreams to be so dangerous because the dreamer, like

Bartley Hubbard in his "ill-advised reveries" (*MI*, 332), is "purely unmoral": "good and bad are the same to his conscience; he has no more to do with right and wrong than the animals; he is reduced to the state of the merely natural man" (*I&E*, 101). Most disturbing of all are those "shameful dreams, whose inculpation projects itself far into the day," as the dreamer "goes about with the dim question whether he is not really that kind of man harassing him, and a sort of remote fear that he may be." Indeed, "but for the supernal criticism, but for his soul, he might be that kind of man in very act and deed" (*I&E*, 104).

In a little-known paper, "Moral Responsibility for the Content of Dreams" (1925), Freud argued that the majority of dreams, "when the distortions of the censorship have been undone," are revealed as "the fulfilments of immoral—egoistic, sadistic, perverse or incestuous—wishful impulses. As in the world of waking life, these masked criminals are far commoner than those with their vizors raised." In sleep, at least, everyone is a "masked criminal." But Freud was prepared to go further than Howells in thinking that one might be "that kind of man" even in waking life, in spite of "the supernal criticism." Whereas Howells wished to discriminate sharply between conscious and unconscious processes, Freud stressed their interpenetration and the power of the latter to encroach upon the former.

Freud was also prepared to embrace a moral corollary that Howells hoped to escape:

> Obviously one must hold oneself responsible for the evil impulses of one's dreams. What else is one to do with them? Unless the content of the dream (rightly understood) is inspired by alien spirits [as William Cooper Howells had argued], it is a part of my own being. If I seek to classify the impulses that are present in me according to social standards into good and bad, I must assume responsibility for both sorts; and if, in defence, I say that what is unknown, unconscious and repressed in me is not my "ego," then I shall not be basing my position upon psycho-analysis, I shall not have accepted its conclusions—and I shall perhaps be taught better by the criticisms of my fellow-men, by the disturbances in my actions and the confusion of my feelings. I shall perhaps learn that what I am disavowing not only "is" in me but sometimes "acts" from out of me as well.[19]

So much guilt and anxiety were attached to Howells' unconscious impulses—so much did he dread *having* to take responsibility for them—that he wished to suppress what he sometimes acknowledged as a "remote fear": that a "masked criminal" was not only in him but sometimes acted from out of him as well.

II

Howells' fear of the unconscious compelled him for most of his career to deny that it played any important role in the artist's imagination. In "I Talk of Dreams," he insisted upon a radical difference between fiction making and dreaming: "In fact there is no analogy, so far as I can make out, between the process of literary invention and the process of dreaming. In the invention, the critical faculty is vividly and constantly alert; in dreams, it seems altogether absent" (*I&E*, 112–13). Furthermore, most dreams resemble romantic novels in their "notoriously stale and hackneyed" plots and in their concern with "incident rather than character," which is the proper focus of the realistic novel (*I&E*, 121, 114). As William C. Fischer suggests, the "nonsymbolic aesthetic" of Howells' realism may be seen as his attempt to evade the "potential moral instability and self-deception" that he attached to reverie and dreams.[20]

In his youth Howells became thoroughly acquainted with the romantic literature of reverie by such writers as Irving, Poe, Hawthorne, De Quincey, and D. G. Mitchell (Ik Marvel), all of whom helped to shape his conception of mental processes. But as much as he was influenced by these predecessors' use of reverie, Howells the realist, says Fischer, gradually reinterpreted "this romantic perspective as a distorted aesthetic point of view." Reverie survived in his work "as the stepchild of a minor literary convention, a device useful for depicting illusions but not for expressing deep subjective truths" (p. 10). Howells' own work, however, often contradicts this moral and aesthetic position: "Although he might consciously believe that the process of literary invention cannot properly function without the presence of a controlling 'critical faculty,' he shows again and again that the kind of temperament most capable of artistic creativity . . . is the kind least capable of disciplining its ordinarily unbridled fancy." Thus, according to Fischer, Howells' "inherent fear of the vigorous workings of the imagination leads him to describe the mental qualities of his moral reprobates (like Bartley Hubbard) as being strikingly similar to those of his more artistically sensitive characters" (pp. 29–30).

Logically, Howells tended to judge his own imagination as reprobate. This was the unconscious implication of his letter to C. D. Warner in 1875: writing a novel *was* like bearing an "unlegalized addition to the census" (*SL*, 2:103): the demon bastard of the "masked criminal" within. Because Howells was in conflict with the vigorous workings of his imagination, he is best understood, as George C. Carrington says, as a neurotic artist: "not as a neurotic only (this is the easy or Lewisohn-Fiedler way of disposing of him), but as a neurotic *artist* . . . a writer harmed but not wholly controlled by defects in his psychic economy."[21]

These defects exist: there is no doubt that the adventurousness of Howells' imagination was often checked by his psychic vulnerability. In a justly famous letter to Samuel Clemens in 1904, Howells himself assessed his limitations with unflinching candor. Speaking of their different approaches to autobiography, Howells said: "You are dramatic and unconscious; you count the thing more than yourself; I am cursed with consciousness to the core, and can't say myself out [as Clemens could in his autobiographical dictations]; I am always saying myself *in*, and setting myself above all that I say, as of more worth." Nevertheless, Howells believed that, for all its enviable veracity, even Clemens' autobiography would not tell "the black truth" that "we all know of ourselves in our hearts," that which underlies the "whity-brown truth of the pericardium, or the nice, whitened truth of the shirtfront" (*SL*, 5:77). Howells' fiction was seldom a matter only of the shirtfront. As in *A Modern Instance*, he sometimes pierced the pericardium and touched the black heart's-truth. Until late in his career, however, he did so in spite of his conscious intentions.

The tragedy of Winifred, which prompted Howells' reading of psychological theory, also impelled him toward an intense self-scrutiny that led in time to a clearer apprehension of his repressed conflicts. And, as Elizabeth Stevens Prioleau has shown, Howells also confronted his neurotic past in the writing of several autobiographical volumes during the 1890s: "With each memoir, as in successful psychotherapy, he came nearer the crux of the difficulty, until he found the tabooed, infantile emotions." During the same years in which Freud was working through his own self-analysis, Howells was painfully exposing "the Oedipal nerve of his neurosis." [22]

In 1893, while struggling with *My Literary Passions*, his second long work of autobiography, Howells complained to his father that he preferred to write fiction because "then I feel quite free, and have no sense of trenching upon my own intimacy." But he was also beginning to admit the play of unconscious forces upon his writing: "The selection [of autobiographical details] is rather puzzling, but I let myself *go*, somewhat, and trust to what comes first" (*SL*, 4:38). This letting go, which resembled free association, became more possible for Howells as a result of his deepening self-awareness and growing sophistication about psychology. Eventually he learned to apply the lessons of writing autobiography to writing fiction. "No man, unless he puts on the mask of fiction, can show his real face or the will behind it," he wrote near the end of his life. "For this reason the only real biographies are the novels, and every novel if it is honest will be the autobiography of the author and biography of the reader" (*YMY*, 110).

Many critics have noted the inwardness of Howells' later fiction, starting with *The Shadow of a Dream* (1890) and continuing through *The Leatherwood God* (1916). [23] Howells himself felt swept up by a new literary movement, what he called in 1901 "A Psychological Counter-Current": "Quite as surely

as romanticism lurked at the heart of realism, something that we may call
'psychologism' has been present in the romanticism of the last four or five
years, and has now begun to evolve itself." [24] A year later he asserted that "it is
probable that the psychological novel will be the most enduring as it has been
the most constant phase of fiction. Every other kind of novel lives or dies by
so much or so little psychology as it has in it." [25]

Like his earlier commitment to realism, Howells' later engagement with
psychologism reflected his personal needs. As his self-analysis made him more
aware of the functioning of his psychological juggle, he began to make it into
a conscious principle of composition by daring to experiment with the dramatic method in a frankly therapeutic way. He went so far as to write the kind
of reveries he had earlier believed were the stuff of romantic illusion—as in
some of the nearly 100 fictional sketches that Howells did for *Harper's* "Editor's Easy Chair" between 1900 and his death in 1920. As Carrington remarks
of a group of Christmas "Easy Chairs," Howells used the allegorical form of
them "to project uncertainties, anxieties, guilt, and other painful feelings
into fiction while concealing, *when he wished*, the fact that he was doing any
such thing" (my emphasis). [26] In his earlier fiction, such projection had not
often been subject to Howells' wishes; he had not been aware of the process.
Now he knew exactly what he was doing.

When he collected some of the "Easy Chairs" into *Imaginary Interviews*
(1910), he added a revealing paragraph to the first in the series, in which he
personified the Easy Chair as his own imagination:

> There in Franklin Square, still dreaming, it [the Easy Chair] was set up
> in the rear of the magazine, where it has become not only the place,
> but the stuff of dreams such as men are made of. From month to month,
> ever since, its reveries, its illusions, which some may call deliverances,
> have gone on with more and more a disposition to dramatize them-
> selves. It has seemed to the occupant of the Easy Chair, at times, as if
> he had suffered with it some sort of land-change from a sole entity to a
> multiple personality in which his several selves conversed with one
> another, and came and went unbidden. . . . [H]e became satisfied from
> their multitude and nature that they were the subdivisions of his own
> ego, and as such he has more and more frankly treated them. (*ImI*, 12)

Having learned to recognize his subliminal selves as "subdivisions of his own
ego," Howells no longer needed to treat his fears "as if they were alien." [27] The
masked criminals of the unconscious, who had once threatened to possess
him, became "those convertible familiars of the Easy Chair, who 'Change and
pass and come again'" (*ImI*, 22). The dramatic method, used formerly to say
himself in and set himself above his characters, now was used to say himself
out, to give voice to those repressed "recurrent selves" who appeared to

Howells "with every effect of exterior identities" (*ImI*, 127). "Illusion" itself served the purpose of psychological "deliverance."

By the end of his career, Howells' higher tolerance of the unconscious enabled him to reformulate a belief in the human capacity for moral choice. In *The Son of Royal Langbrith*, Dr. Justin Anther has an acute awareness of unconscious impulses in himself and others. Such "cognitions which refuse anything more positive than intimation" do not come to those who deal "conventionally" with their own consciousness. "It was because Anther was not one of these that he was a nature of exceptional type; and because he could accept the logic of his self-knowledge that he was a character of rare strength" (*SRL*, 227–28). Like Freud in his self-analysis, Dr. Anther is a physician who has healed himself. He represents the deep self-knowledge that Howells had achieved in his autumnal years.

The narrator of *The Son of Royal Langbrith*, a Hawthornean tale of inherited guilt, intrudes at one point to remark: "Up to a certain moment in every evil predicament, men are the victims of it, and after that if they continue in it they are its agents, though as little its masters as before. They are exceptionally happy men if they realize this early enough in life to make choice of their better selves against their worse, and in that choice finally prevail over their evil predicament" (*SRL*, 251). The "certain moment," Howells implies, is the instant of self-consciousness. Those who have discovered their unconscious springs of motivation are henceforth responsible for their actions. Those who remain passive in self-knowledge of their "natural evil" become its agents.

This is a more sophisticated version of Atherton's position in *A Modern Instance*: it is still our deeds that judge us, but only those "deeds," conscious *or* unconscious, that we come to recognize as our own. The only moral response is to resist destructive psychological impulses, to choose the better self. Through this melioristic faith in free will, which was derived in part from William James,[28] Howells tempered his own earlier pessimism and moved toward Freud's hope (at least in his early work) in the moral efficacy of self-knowledge.

Such insight might be characterized, by turning Howells' own phrase, as "self-implanted goodness." Free will, once deemed by Howells to be the privilege of the civilized, was finally seen by him to be the burden of the analyzed.

NOTES

PREFACE

1. See, for example, Edwin H. Cady's summary of the "many elements of greatness" in the novel: "a potent illusion of personalities, settings, and action, achieved by fine artistry in the handling of symbols, tone, atmosphere, dialog, and the textures of description and style. There is expert penetration to the abstract significance of social custom, moral condition, moral choice, and their effects on fate and character, and to the sense of a profound movement of cultural change revealed in the lives of people who bear it in their minds and bodies." *The Road to Realism: The Early Years 1837– 1885 of William Dean Howells* (Syracuse, N.Y.: Syracuse University Press, 1956), pp. 208–9.

2. *The Achievement of William Dean Howells: A Reinterpretation* (Princeton, N.J.: Princeton University Press, 1968), p. 4.

3. *Stuff of Sleep and Dreams: Experiments in Literary Psychology* (New York: Harper & Row, 1982).

4. "William Faulkner: Construction and Reconstruction in Biography and Psycho-analysis," *Psychoanalytic Inquiry* 3 (1983): 337, 298, 328.

CHAPTER ONE

1. Even about the peach blossoms Howells confessed a doubt. In a canceled passage he called the memory an "impression, (for I cannot be sure that it is a memory and not an illusion, the shadow of a dream)" (*BT*, TS, 181/2). Unless otherwise noted, all quotations from unpublished Howells material are taken from documents in the Houghton Library and are used by permission of the Houghton Library, Harvard University, Cambridge, Mass., and of William White Howells for the heirs of the Howells Estate. No republication is authorized without the same permissions.

2. In light of this canceled passage, an earlier deletion has associative importance. Immediately after recounting the memory of the peach blossoms, Howells went on to write: "<The first impressions of consciousness> < ↑ Early associations ↓ are so strong and so quaintly persistent that> When <I> he first saw London, and <inhaled a> breath ↑ ed ↓ <of> its bituminous air, <I> he was instantly spirited back to the remotest years of my life, and in the capital of the world I went about <teased> ↑ haunted ↓ with a sense of Martinsville" (*BT*, TS, 18). As my transcription indicates, the earliest draft of A Boy's Town was written in the first person; only later did Howells employ the device of referring to himself in the third person as "my boy." Although he intended "my boy" (perhaps like the character of Nikolenka in Tolstoy's *Childhood*) to represent "a boy in general, as well as a boy in particular" (*BT*, 2), Howells also told H. H. Boyesen that the book "is in all essentials autobiographical. . . . The environment of my early life was exactly as there described" (*INT*, 25).

On *A Boy's Town* as autobiography, see Tom H. Towers, "Savagery and Civilization: The Moral Dimensions of Howells's *A Boy's Town*," *American Literature* 40 (January 1969): 499–509; Thomas Cooley, *Educated Lives: The Rise of Modern Autobiography in America* (Columbus: Ohio State University Press, 1976), pp. 73–99; Marcia Jacobson, William Dean Howells's (Auto)biography: A Reading of *A Boy's Town*," *American Literary Realism* 16 (Spring 1983): 92–101.

3. Richard J. Hinton, "The Howells Family," ed. Clara M. and Rudolf Kirk, *Journal of the Rutgers University Library* 14 (December 1950): 22. Hinton's essay originally appeared in the New York *Voice*, 15 July 1897.

4. Ibid., p. 21.

5. Ibid., p. 16. Lida R. McCabe, a friend of Howells in his Columbus years, describes William Cooper Howells as "a man of cultivation and fine literary taste, but dreamy and impractical"; and she relates an anecdote she may well have heard from his son. William Cooper was once sent out for butter by his wife; distracted by a book he bought along the way, he disappeared for hours, later to be discovered reading in a back room of the house. He had completely forgotten about the butter. "Literary and Social Recollections of W. D. Howells," *Lippincott's Monthly* 40 (October 1887): 547–48.

6. Waldon Fawcett, "Mr. Howells and His Brother," *Critic*, o.s. 35 (November 1899): 1028.

7. "The Contributors' Club," *Atlantic Monthly* 45 (June 1880): 860. Howells noted that the airy nothing had been perfectly described in "an account of an almost precisely similar vision of horror" experienced by Alexander Kinglake. In *Eothen, or Traces of Travel Brought Home from the East* (Auburn and Geneva, N.Y.: J. C. Derby & G. H. Derby, 1845), Kinglake compares the effect of his first sight of the ancient pyramids to the effect of a dreadful fantasy from his early childhood: "When I was very young (between the ages, I believe, of three and five years old), being then of delicate health, I was often in time of night the victim of a strange kind of mental oppression; I lay in my bed perfectly conscious, and with open eyes, but without power to speak, or to move, and all the while my brain was oppressed to distraction by the presence of a single and abstract idea,—the idea of solid Immensity. It seemed to me in my agonies, that the horror of this visitation arose from its coming upon me without form or shape—that the close presence of the direst monster ever bred in Hell would have been a thousand times more tolerable than that simple idea of solid size; my aching mind was fixed, and riveted down upon the mere quality of vastness, vastness, vastness; and was not permitted to invest with it any particular object. If I could have done so, the torment would have ceased. When at last I was roused from this state of suffering, I could not of course in those days (knowing no verbal metaphysics, and no metaphysics at all, except by the dreadful experience of an abstract idea), I could not of course find words to describe the nature of my sensations, and even now I cannot explain why it is that the forced contemplation of a mere quality, distinct from matter, should be so terrible" (pp. 176–77).

Howells misremembered the context of this passage when he related it to the "delirium of a fever" suffered by Kinglake. In fact, the delirium incident appears elsewhere in *Eothen*, where Kinglake is recounting his hypochondriacal dread of plague, which he feared having contracted in Egypt. Kinglake's fear of death and his development of symptoms he mistook for plague closely parallel Howells' fears and symptoms during his 1854 breakdown (see Chapter 2). In confounding the hypochondriacal episode with Kinglake's childhood dread, Howells made an unconscious connection (expressed by a "lapse" of memory) that suggests a relationship between his own "airy nothing" fantasy and his 1854 breakdown.

8. "The Contributors' Club," pp. 859–60.

9. Howells combined the "Arms Poe" dream and the floating clown dream, as well as some others, into the fictive nightmare attributed to the title character of *The Flight of Pony Baker: A Boy's Town Story* (New York: Harper, 1902).

10. Fawcett, p. 1027.

11. Calvin Dill Wilson and David Bruce Fitzgerald, "A Day in Howells's 'Boy's Town,'" *New England Magazine* 36 (May 1907): 294.

12. Fawcett, p. 1027.

13. George T. Earhart, quoted in Wilson and Fitzgerald, p. 293.

14. Ibid., p. 291. George T. Earhart's explicit identification of Rorick is confirmed by the typescript of *A Boy's Town*, in which Howells canceled Rorick's name. Almost none of the characters in the published book is named, including, of course, Howells himself and the members of his family.

15. In a 1905 letter to his sister Aurelia, Howells recalled: "What a rich nature she had, and what a great heart for her children. We were all alike to her; she was the home in which we were all equal and dear" (*SL*, 5:134). Similarly, in 1910, he asked Joe: "How *did* she ever get through all the work she did, and yet make us each feel that she was peculiarly and most devotedly his or her mother?" (*LinL*, 2:282). Kenneth S. Lynn questions whether Mary Dean Howells had really been so impartial as her son remembered (p. 31).

16. In a magazine story about Howells in 1893, H. H. Boyesen reported that William Cooper was "no exacting disciplinarian": "When their mother, provoked at some piece of mischief of which they had been guilty, complained at his laxity, and demanded sterner measures, he would call them up to him and say solemnly: 'Boys, consider yourselves thrashed.'" "Mr. Howells at Close Range," *Ladies' Home Journal* 10 (November 1893): 7. A similar anecdote appears in *BT*, 13.

17. Howells made fictional use of this directional "obsession" in "Captain Dunlevy's Last Trip," a narrative poem first published in *The Daughter of the Storage* (New York: Harper, 1916). The narrator of the poem, a passenger on a riverboat, has been talking to others at breakfast about "some psychological subtleties . . . [t]ouching that weird experience every one knows when the senses / Juggle the points of the compass out of true orientation, / Changing the North to the South, and the East to the West" (pp. 68–69). Later he listens to Captain Davis spin a yarn about the famous Captain Dunlevy, whose nearly fatal loss of bearings on one occasion induced him to quit piloting for good. Davis's tale is made doubly mysterious by its apparently telepathic connection to the narrator's breakfast conversation. Davis tells this particular yarn as if by chance, after being distracted from another tale by one of the passengers.

18. *The Interpretation of Dreams* (1900); *SE*, 4:162. Although Freud stresses the difficulty, or impossibility, of interpreting a dream unless the dreamer "is prepared to communicate to us the unconscious thoughts that lie behind its content" (*SE*, 4:241), he also asserts that "our interpretative activity is in one instance independent

of these associations—if, namely, the dreamer has employed *symbolic* elements in the content of the dream" (*SE*, 4:241n). In practice, Freud recommends "a combined technique, which on the one hand rests on the dreamer's associations and on the other hand fills the gaps from the interpreter's knowledge of symbols" (*SE*, 5:353). Freud also implies that "some knowledge of the dreamer's personal relations" may serve as a substitute for his or her free associations, thereby allowing us "to interpret certain pieces" of a dream independently of the dreamer (*SE*, 5:342). We do have a few associations about some of Howells' dreams included in his accounts of them. These clues, plus a knowledge of his "personal relations" and of dream symbolism, permit some reasonably informed conjectures to be made—although posthumous dream interpretation is inevitably a slippery business.

19. Freud himself had a similar obsession with the Commendatore. See Marie Balmary, *Psychoanalyzing Psychoanalysis*, trans. Ned Lukacher (Baltimore: Johns Hopkins University Press, 1982), pp. 30–34.

20. Although Howells may well have witnessed some such event at the age of three, his recollection was probably a "screen memory," an authentic childhood memory upon which later conflicts were embroidered. As Freud realized in his analytic work, "One is . . . forced by various considerations to suspect that in the so-called earliest childhood memories we possess not the genuine memory-trace but a later revision of it, a revision which may have been subjected to the influences of a variety of later psychical forces." *The Psychopathology of Everyday Life* (1901); *SE*, 6:47–48. That Howells remembered "nothing else of the incident, nothing whatever after the man went down in the water"—a fact that Howells uses to support the idea that this was "truly a memory" (*BT*, 9)—implies just the opposite: that a selective amnesia masked repressed material from a later period of childhood.

21. In Freudian terms, the ladies' cabin may be seen as a symbol of the mother's uterus (*SE*, 5:354), and the little men as symbols of the boy's penis: "Children in dreams often stand for the genitals; and, indeed, both men and women are in the habit of referring to their genitals affectionately as their 'little ones'" (*SE*, 5:357). Furthermore, "If one of the ordinary symbols for a penis occurs in a dream doubled or multiplied, it is to be regarded as a warding-off of castration" (*SE*, 5:357). The one-legged man represents the fulfillment of the boy's wish to castrate his father-rival, just as his fear of being castrated by him is protected against by the multiplication of the little men. Castration anxiety has been neutralized in the fantasy by its opposite, Oedipal aggression; similarly, the boy's guilt for fantasies of Oedipal murder has been neutralized by his sense of justifiable homicide: he *had* to act peremptorily to protect himself. The cross-canceling of affects accounts for the eerie numbness of the memory, its emotional neutrality.

22. Dating this episode is problematical. Howells said in 1893 that it had occurred either "in the early spring after our first winter in the log-cabin [i.e., early 1851], or in the early part of the second winter [i.e., late 1851], which found us still there" (*MYLC*, 50). But in 1916, he said it had occurred "in the early part of the second winter" (*YMY*, 53). The earlier date seems more likely. On the general problem of chronology in Howells' Eureka year, see *YMY*, 267.

23. William Cooper Howells, *Recollections of Life in Ohio, from 1813 to 1840*, ed. W. D. Howells (Cincinnati: Robert Clarke, 1895), p. vi.

24. A *Compendium of the Theological Writings of Emanuel Swedenborg*, ed. Samuel M. Warren (1875; reprint, New York: Swedenborg Foundation, 1974), pp. 202, 205.

25. Howells did not name the woman in *Years of My Youth*, but he did in letters to his brother concerning *New Leaf Mills*: see *SL*, 5:344, 356. The Stepmeyer incident and several others of this period were fictionalized in this intriguing late novel.

26. In 1869, when Harriet Beecher Stowe exposed Byron's incestuous relations with his half sister in her notorious article in the *Atlantic*, "The True Story of Lady Byron's Life," Howells was standing in as editor for James T. Fields. Although Stowe was roundly abused for her decision to publish the essay, Howells defended her, at least in private. He wrote to his father: "The world needed to know just how base, filthy and mean Byron was, in order that all glamour should be forever removed from his literature, and the taint of it should be communicated only to those who love sensual things" (*SL*, 1:340).

CHAPTER TWO

1. There is a discrepancy between Howells' biographers as to the year of this collapse: Cady asserts that it occurred in 1856, Lynn in 1854. For my argument in favor of 1854, see "Dating Howells' Adolescent Breakdown," *The Old Northwest* 8 (Spring 1982): 13–22.

2. W. D. Howells' conclusion to W. C. Howells, *Recollections of Life in Ohio*, p. 202.

3. Fawcett, "Mr. Howells and His Brother," pp. 1027–28. Howells himself mentioned that he had been bitten by a dog sometime after the Bowers incident (*YMY*, 79), but he did not say exactly when. Cady believes it was during the Hamilton years (p. 24).

4. "Diary and Spanish Exercises," p. 13. MS in the Houghton Library. Other quotations are documented in the text.

5. "The Real Diary of a Boy," p. 7. MS in the Houghton Library. A short section of this essay was published in *Years of My Youth*. Encountering the word "hydraphobia" in his own boyish hand must have sent a shock through Howells, who claimed that it was years after his breakdown before he could endure the sight of the word: "I shut the book or threw from me the paper where I found it in print; and even now, after sixty years, I cannot bring myself to write it or speak it without some such shutting of the heart as I knew at the sight or sound of it in that dreadful time" (*YMY*, 81).

6. "How I Lost a Wife. An Episode in the Life of a Bachelor," *Ashtabula Sentinel* 23 (18 May 1854). The story appeared anonymously; for attribution to Howells, see Edwin H. Cady, "William Dean Howells and the *Ashtabula Sentinel*," *Ohio Archaeological and Historical Quarterly* 53 (January–March 1944): 39–51.

7. In *My Literary Passions*, Howells remembered that he had very early "tried to write in the style of Edgar A. Poe, as I knew it from his *Tales of the Grotesque and Arabesque*" (*MLP*, 15–16). He may have been imitating Poe in "How I Lost a Wife" by creating a "mad" narrator. If so, Howells was demonstrating, in his fourth published work of fiction, a precocious grasp of narrative technique. Even if we take the narrator to be designedly unreliable, however, we can still assume that a correspondence may well exist between the form of his "madness" and the unconscious life of his creator at a moment of mental crisis.

8. Such aggression is detectable in the incident of the rose throwing itself. In using it as an example of his father's aggressive "humor," Howells implies that he resented his father's treatment of his mother. He also resented his father's having put him up to a prank that was no comfort either to the boy or his mother—a prank, on the contrary, that temporarily severed the bond between them. The Oedipal theme is plainly figured here, both in its aspect of rivalry between father and son for the mother's love and in its aspect of mutual aggression. This conclusion receives added weight from Howells' allusion, just after recounting the rose-throwing incident, to his fictional use of the same material in *The Flight of Pony Baker*, where its Oedipal significance is transparent. See Elizabeth Stevens Prioleau, *The Circle of Eros: Sexuality in the Work of William Dean Howells* (Durham, N.C.: Duke University Press, 1983), pp. 139–41.

9. On little Hans, see "Analysis of a Phobia in a Five-Year-Old-Boy" (1909); SE, 10:3–149. On the "wolf man," see "From the History of an Infantile Neurosis" (1918); SE, 17:3–122.

10. *Inhibitions, Symptoms and Anxiety* (1926); SE, 20:106. Prioleau points out that dogs were "symbols of lust" to Swedenborg (p. 189n).

11. Jim Williams, who was later killed by a sniper in the Civil War, apparently was one model for Jim Millon, the army comrade of Silas Lapham, who died in the same way, leaving his wife and infant daughter on Lapham's hands. Jim Williams and Harvey Green were identified only by their initials in *Years of My Youth*; see YMY, 272, 274.

12. Goodrich was not named in *My Literary Passions*, but he was identified by Mildred Howells in *Life in Letters*, 1:121–22.

13. Feminist scholars have shown that passionate (but not genital) relationships between women were unexceptionable in Victorian society. What was called "romantic friendship" or "the love of kindred spirits" or "Boston marriage" was recognized "as a socially viable form of human contact—and, as such, acceptable throughout a woman's life." Carroll Smith-Rosenberg, "The Female World of Love and Ritual: Relations Between Women in Nineteenth-Century America" (1975), reprinted in *A Heritage of Her Own: Toward a New Social History of American Women*, ed. Nancy F. Cott and Elizabeth H. Pleck (New York: Simon and Schuster, 1979), p. 331. Although the range of such "homosocial" attachments among men has not received much attention as yet, Lillian Faderman suggests that male "romantic friendships" were also commonplace: "Thoreau was speaking for his time when he observed in his mid-nineteenth-century essay, *Friendship*, that intimacy was much more possible 'between two of the same sex' than 'between the sexes.'" *Surpassing the Love of Men: Romantic Friendship and Love Between Women from the Renaissance to the Present* (New York: William Morrow, 1981), p. 159.

Howells was capable all his life of establishing warm male friendships, including some with men he must have known to be homosexuals (Charles Warren Stoddard, for example). More important, as I will show in Chapter 5, there are submerged homoerotic fantasies in Howells' fiction, played out through a series of androgynous male characters. See also George M. Spangler, "*The Shadow of a Dream*: Howells' Homosexual Tragedy," *American Quarterly* 23 (Spring 1971): 110–19.

14. *Gender, Fantasy, and Realism in American Literature* (New York: Columbia University Press, 1982), pp. 62–63, 233.

15. "The infantile phobias are not only the prototype of the later ones which we

class as 'anxiety hysteria' but are actually their precondition and the prelude to them. Every hysterical phobia goes back to an infantile anxiety and is a continuation of it, even if it has a different content and must thus be given another name." *Introductory Lectures on Psycho-analysis* (1917); *SE*, 16:409.

16. Aurelia Howells recalled that her brother's premonition had come in a dream and that both their parents had been well aware of his dread before his sixteenth birthday: "The day before you had asked mother the exact time (to the hour,) of your birth, *and*, its [sic] my impression that it was about four o'clock in the morning. AND, that father suspecting that you would consult the clock, *had turned it on ahead!* Therefore when you, poor little soul, looked, it was *past the hour* as mother was able to assure you!—" Quoted in Crowley, "Dating Howells' Adolescent Breakdown," p. 17. It is especially interesting that Howells should have mentioned only his father's part in this incident. When he transformed it into fiction, in *New Leaf Mills*, Howells attributed the presentiment of death to the miller Overdale, who is released from his fears, as Howells had supposedly been, by logical "magic." Powell, modeled closely on William Cooper Howells, tells Overdale that he has unknowingly lived beyond the fatal deadline.

17. *The Interpretation of Dreams*; *SE*, 5:581; "Obsessive Actions and Religious Practices" (1907); *SE*, 9:124.

18. It is suggestive that Howells should have turned to his father for relief from psychic burdens that were attributable to ambivalence toward him. Howells was seeking William Cooper's help and love but also, unconsciously, seeking his judgment. Since the death fantasy represented, in part, Will's repressed Oedipal anger, he was confessing to those feelings when, "with shame," he was confessing to the fantasy; he was inviting his father to punish him. Psychologically, the situation resembled that on the day when Howells had wished his father dead and had fearfully awaited his wrath. In both instances, however, the father expressed love rather than rage. The breakdown produced another situation in which the son could cast himself upon his father's mercy, a situation that deepened the intimacy between father and son that Howells had wanted all along. One basis for this intimacy was their mutual experience of neurotic fears. As Howells said, he had been greatly helped by William Cooper's "recurrence, as often as I chose, to his own youthful suffering from hypochondria" (*YMY*, 80–81). The elder Howells had apparently broken down in 1835; see *Recollections of Life in Ohio*, p. 189.

19. Freud discussed similar cases of "self-destruction with an unconscious intention" in *The Psychopathology of Everyday Life*; *SE*, 6:180–86. It seems to be no coincidence that the number of the fatal year (when Howells was between sixteen and seventeen) equals the sum of the age at which Howells had his presentiment (nine or ten, he said) plus the incubation period of hydrophobia (seven years, he believed). It is probable that he had heard about the "seven years" of incubation—no matter whether it was true or not—well before 1854, perhaps at the time of his dog bite (also when the presentiment probably appeared), or at the time of the Bowers case in 1841.

20. Howells may have been briefly smitten by Dune Dean herself, who spent the summer of 1857 in Jefferson. In March 1859, he wrote to his friend and fellow poet J. J. Piatt: "I do not understand what story [of mine] you refer to as being a decided case of falling in love. I have seen a very charming sonnet of yours to certain beautiful-eyed

Indiana cousins. *Hab' acht!* Cousins are very dangerous. I've tried it" (*SL*, 1:26). Another early flame, Kate Jones, was identified by her initials as Howells' "first love" in his Venetian diary (*SL*, 1:15n). That she had once sent him a "very precious" Valentine he still remembered fondly in 1897 (*SL*, 4:144).

21. Noah Webster, *An American Dictionary of the English Language*, rev. ed. (New York: Harper, 1846), p. 475.

22. The novel ran in the *Ashtabula Sentinel* from 23 November 1854 through 18 January 1855. Howells erroneously recalled that he had forced the novel to "a tragic close without mercy for the heroine, hurried to an untimely death as the only means of getting her out of the way" (*YMY*, 83–84). In fact, there is no clear heroine in "The Independent Candidate." The closest is Merla Cuffins, whose name was changed halfway through the novel, without explanation, to Merla Carman; and she is very much alive at the end.

23. Howells himself, after insisting how poorly the novel had turned out, defended it: "and yet I do not think it was badly conceived, or attempted upon lines that were mistaken. If it were not for what happened in the past I might like some time to write a story on the same lines in the future" (*MLP*, 67).

24. In a sad example of life's imitating art, the specter of hereditary insanity became real for Howells in the fate of his youngest brother Henry. Having sustained a head injury at about the age of four (ca. 1856)—sources differ on the exact cause of the injury and its date—Henry ceased to develop mentally and grew up to be, as Cady says, "the walking tragedy which many a nineteenth-century rural family knew: a household idiot" (p. 44). Much too late for corrective surgery, it was discovered by x-ray that Henry's condition had been caused by a bone spur growing into his brain. But until this discovery, all the Howellses lived in the shadow of a possible hereditary taint.

25. *Young Man Luther: A Study in Psychoanalysis and History* (1958; reprint, New York: Norton, 1962), p. 14. Other quotations are documented in the text.

26. As it turned out, Howells' career made him both a rich man and a frequent guest, if not a resident, in the White House. Beginning with Abraham Lincoln, of whom he wrote a campaign biography and from whom he received his appointment to Venice, Howells was associated with most of the Republican presidents during his lifetime, especially his cousin by marriage Rutherford B. Hayes, and his fellow Ohioan James A. Garfield.

27. *The Man of Letters in New England and the South: Essays on the History of the Literary Vocation in America* (Baton Rouge: Louisiana State University Press, 1973), pp. 91–92, 8.

28. "The Theology of Realism" is the title of Henry Nash Smith's chapter on Howells in *Democracy and the Novel: Popular Resistance to Classic American Writers* (New York: Oxford University Press, 1978).

29. The decision must have exacerbated the sibling tensions between Will and Joe. As Howells wrote to Aurelia in 1915: "I remember it once came to my wanting to go to Austenburg Institute and it was decided (mainly by dear old Joe, who grieved over it to me late in life) that they could not spare me from the office or the money for the academy's fees. I dare say I should not have gone, or if I did would have been too homesick to stay" (*SL*, 6:82).

CHAPTER THREE

1. For Vic, there was to be no place outside the village home, and after a few weeks she "went back to those bounds where her duty lay" (*YMY*, 108). Although she had literary ambitions of her own, Vic, unlike her brother and her sister Annie, never managed to fulfill any of them. She also suffered personal tragedies. She was engaged in 1864 to a surgeon in the Ohio regiment who subsequently died of a fever contracted in the hospitals. Thereafter she committed herself to the care of her brain-damaged brother Henry; and in 1883, when she agreed to marry John Mulholland of Toronto, it was on the condition that she was to continue to live at home. After two years, taking a page from Bartley Hubbard, Mulholland left his wife on the pretext of making a business trip and never returned. A year later Vic died of malarial typhoid at the age of forty-eight.

2. In the first chapter of *Afraja*, John Marstrand, a Danish man of the world, is aboard the ship of a Norman trader named Helgestad. Marstrand is depressed by the rugged fiords through which they are winding, but Helgestad assures him that the landscape is not so bleak as it seems. As they come within sight of the Lofodden Islands, the sun suddenly breaks through the clouds: "The Westfiord opened before the astonished vision of the Dane, and exhibited land and sea in all their glory and splendor. Upon one side lay the coast of Norway, with its snowy summits. Salten [Mountain] loomed up behind, with its needle-like peaks, stretching with their inaccessible ice-covered declivities into the heavens, and its ravines and abysses half concealed in gloom. Upon the other side, six miles to the seaward of the Westfiord, extended a chain of dark islands far into the bosom of the ocean—a granite wall against which the ocean, in its most savage fury, for thousands of years had dashed its billows. Innumerable perpendicular pinnacles rose from this insular labyrinth—black, weatherbeaten, and torn to their base by the tempests." Marstrand is "ravished by the wonderful grandeur and wildness of the scene." *Afraja, a Norwegian and Lapland Tale; or, Life and Love in Norway*, trans. Edward Joy Morris (Philadelphia: Lindsay & Blakiston, 1854), pp. 21–22.

3. McCabe, "Literary and Social Recollections of W. D. Howells," pp. 550–51.

4. Letter of 24 August 1859; Houghton Library.

5. Sam, who was three years younger than Will, was the family ne'er-do-well. Twice married, sometimes unemployed, usually penniless, Sam was a constant aggravation to his brother and also a drain upon his income—even after Sam finally settled into a job at the government printing office. After grumbling about him for years, Will was surprised to discover in their old age that he actually liked Sam. As for Joe, until the death of their mother in 1868 brought them together in grief (see *SL*, 1:306), the brothers maintained a guarded relationship. They became more friendly in time. In *Years of My Youth*, Howells claimed that they had forgiven each other "long ago, long before our youth was passed"; and he protested that the "years since were years of such mutual affection as I could not exaggerate the sense of in tenderness and constancy, and the exchange of trust and honor" (*YMY*, 85). Nevertheless, as Kenneth S. Lynn points out, "it is significant that the family relationships Howells later delineated in such brilliant variety in his novels do not include a single portrayal of a warm and understanding friendship between brothers" (p. 73).

6. "En Passant," *Ohio State Journal* (24 July 1860); reprinted in "The Road to Boston: 1860 Travel Correspondence of William Dean Howells," ed. Robert Price, *Ohio History* 80 (Spring 1971): 113.

7. "Niagara, First and Last," in *The Niagara Book* (Buffalo: Underhill & Nichols, 1893), pp. 12–13.

8. Howells wrote a brief notice of "The Professor's Story" (the serial title of *Elsie Venner*) when it was appearing in the *Atlantic* during 1860; see *SL*, 1:65n.

9. Quotations from "Geoffrey Winter" are taken from the manuscript in the Houghton Library, Harvard University, and are documented in the text. Throughout the novel Howells uses the term "unconscious" in a way that anticipates its psychoanalytic meaning. For example, when Walters decides to fall "'a little in love'" with Jane, the narrator interjects: "On the stage they are obliged to present such ideas as soliloquy, with an awkward advance to the footlights; but in a subjective story like this, every one understands that this bit of reasoning was one of the unconscious operations of the brain" (p. 170).

10. "Mourning and Melancholia" (1917); *SE*, 14:244. Other quotations are documented in the text.

11. See Ginette de B. Merrill, "The Meeting of Elinor Gertrude Mead and Will Howells and Their Courtship," *The Old Northwest* 8 (Spring 1982): 23–47.

12. In a draft of *Years of My Youth*, Howells gave another version of his nonenlistment: "But with varying accesses of irresolution I still thought of volunteering, and one night, as Price and I sat waiting for the latest despatches, I was in question so extreme that I said to my fellow-editor, 'Price, if you will volunteer, *I* will.' 'Well,' he answered, 'I *won't*,' and that, for such reason as it was, seemed to close the question. If in all this I seem to be accusing myself, it is only partially an appearance; I am also excusing the innumerable majority of my contemporaries who also failed to volunteer" (*YMY*, 404). This passage was deleted by Howells before publication.

13. *The Unwritten War: American Writers and the Civil War* (New York: Knopf, 1973), p. 122.

14. See my article, "Howells's Obscure Hurt," *Journal of American Studies* 9 (August 1975): 199–211.

15. Hinton, "The Howells Family," p. 22.

16. Letter of 5 November 1861; Massachusetts Historical Society, Boston.

17. Howells reported the same dream in a letter to his mother in 1862 and years later in "I Talk of Dreams," where he said it had recurred for a period of eight to ten months: "I dreamed that I had gone home to America, and that people met me and said, 'Why, you have given up your place!' and I always answered: 'Certainly not; I haven't done at all what I mean to do there, yet. I am only here on my ten days' leave.' . . . Then, suddenly, I was not consul at Venice, and had not been, but consul at Delhi in India; and the distress I felt would all end in a splendid Oriental phantasmagory of elephants and native princes, with their retinues in procession, which I suppose was mostly out of my reading of De Quincey" (*I&E*, 126).

18. Letter of 3 August 1862; Houghton Library.

19. Letter of 4 March 1863; Houghton Library.

20. "The Turning Point of My Life," *Harper's Bazar* 44 (March 1910): 165.

21. See, for example, the long and complex dream that Howells reported to his

father on 2 May 1869 (*SL*, 1:325). As late as 1910, he told a woman who had written to him about Mary Dean Howells that "I still dream of her among the living who visit me in sleep, and I dream of her often" (*SL*, 5:313).

CHAPTER FOUR

1. *The Novels and Tales of Henry James*, New York Edition (New York: Scribner, 1907–17), 14:597.

2. *Italian Journeys* (New York: Hurd & Houghton, 1867), pp. 83, 220.

3. *Venetian Life*, 2d ed. (New York: Hurd & Houghton, 1867), pp. 38, 383.

4. *In Quest of America: A Study of Howells' Early Development as a Novelist* (Cambridge, Mass.: Harvard University Press, 1958), p. 155.

5. "Howells," *Literary World* 10 (2 August 1879); reprinted in *Howells: A Century of Criticism*, ed. Kenneth E. Eble (Dallas: Southern Methodist University Press, 1962), p. 15.

6. "James's *Hawthorne*," *Atlantic Monthly* 45 (February 1880); reprinted in *W. D. Howells as Critic*, ed. Edwin H. Cady (London and Boston: Routledge & Kegan Paul, 1973), p. 54.

7. The year after this interview, in "The Man of Letters as a Man of Business" (1893), Howells wrote that the writer of realistic fiction "needs experience and observation, not so much of others as of himself, for ultimately his characters will all come out of himself, and he will need to know motive and character with such thoroughness and accuracy as he can acquire only through his own heart. A man remains in a measure strange to himself as long as he lives, and the very sources of novelty in his work will be within himself; he can continue to give it freshness in no other way than by knowing himself better and better." *Literature and Life*, Library Edition (New York: Harper, 1911), pp. 29–30.

8. See my essay, "'A Completer Verity': The Ending of W. D. Howells' *A Foregone Conclusion*," *English Language Notes* 14 (March 1977): 192–97.

9. "*Their Wedding Journey*: A Review," *North American Review* 114 (April 1872); reprinted in Eble, ed., *Howells: A Century of Criticism*, pp. 11–12.

10. "The Dark Side of *Their Wedding Journey*," *American Literature* 40 (January 1969): 474.

11. "Uneasiness at Niagara: Howells' *Their Wedding Journey*," *Studies in American Fiction* 4 (Spring 1976): 18, 23–24.

12. "'A Reality That Can't Be Quite Definitely Spoken': Sexuality in *Their Wedding Journey*," *Studies in the Novel* 9 (Spring 1977): 18. Other quotations are documented in the text.

13. Price, ed., "The Road to Boston," p. 105.

14. "The Limited Realism of Howells' *Their Wedding Journey*," *PMLA*, 77 (December 1962): 624–25. Before serial publication, Howells first added and then deleted from the manuscript an entire scene, in which these prostitutes encounter Basil and another man; and between serial and book publication, he removed all hints that the burlesque actress was sizing up Basil and Colonel Ellison as potential clients. "The total effect of the changes in the hotel scene," says Reeves, "is to remove even the

slight suggestiveness, which might have caused Victorian cheeks to blush" (p. 625). On the lewdness of burlesque actresses, see also "Some Lessons from the School of Morals" (1869), added to the enlarged edition of *Suburban Sketches* (Boston: James R. Osgood, 1872), pp. 220–40. In this review of the theatrical season in Boston, Howells shuddered at the indecent exposure and lascivious gestures that were everywhere to be witnessed on the stage; it was "a shocking thing" to behold the "burlesque sisters" with their "horrible prettiness, their archness in which was no charm, their grace which put to shame" (p. 240).

15. In the same month *Their Wedding Journey* was completing its serial run, and in the same letter in which he worried about the possible coarseness of the hotel scene, Howells congratulated his father on his editorial about "Mrs. [Victoria] Woodhull and Her Set": "I think your article on the Women's Rights trollops is very good. What an abomination they are!" (*SL*, 1:386). On Howells and the Woman's Movement, see Gail Thain Parker, "William Dean Howells: Realism and Feminism," in *Uses of Literature*, ed. Monroe Engel, Harvard English Studies, no. 4 (Cambridge, Mass.: Harvard University Press, 1973), pp. 133–61; John W. Crowley, "W. D. Howells: The Ever-Womanly," in *American Novelists Revisited: Essays in Feminist Criticism*, ed. Fritz Fleischmann (Boston: G. K. Hall, 1982), pp. 171–88.

16. See also Fryckstedt, *In Quest of America*, p. 268. Dreiser is quoted by Dorothy Dudley in *Dreiser and the Land of the Free* (New York: Beechhurst Press, 1946), p. 143.

17. Review of *A Foregone Conclusion*, *North American Review* 120 (January 1875): 212.

18. *The New England Girl: Cultural Ideals in Hawthorne, Stowe, Howells and James* (Athens: University of Georgia Press, 1976), p. 12.

19. "William Dean Howells: The Indelible Stain," *New England Quarterly* 32 (December 1959): 491. Other quotations are documented in the text.

20. In "The Problem of Ego Identity," Erikson defines "negative identity" as "an identity perversely based on all those identifications and roles which, at critical stages of development, had been presented to the individual as most undesirable or dangerous, and yet also as most real." *Identity and the Life Cycle: Selected Papers by Erik H. Erikson*, Psychological Issues, vol. 1, no. 1 (New York: International Universities Press, 1959), p. 131.

21. The idea of the super-ego was a late, and somewhat confusing, development in Freud's work. The term itself was not coined until *The Ego and the Id* (1923), although Freud had written a decade earlier of the "ego-ideal," referring to the internalized model of perfection by which the ego judges itself. In practice Freud sometimes used "super-ego" and "ego-ideal" interchangeably, but other times he implied distinctions between these and related terms, such as "conscience"—distinctions that arose from his perception that the super-ego could be influenced by the id, that is, could be partially unconscious. The "unconscious" part of the super-ego embodies the archaic and often sadistic remnants of the child's magnified view of parental and social authority. Some followers of Freud have tried to clarify matters by postulating a conscious-unconscious continuum within the super-ego and by using "super-ego" to refer to the more unconscious and regressive part and "ego-ideal" to refer to the more conscious and adaptable one. Thus "ego-ideal" would correspond roughly to Howells' idea of "implanted goodness," while "super-ego" would correspond to "implanted goodness"

tainted by what I am calling "natural evil"—or what might be called "implanted evil." For a clear exposition of psychoanalytic thinking on this subject, see J. C. Flugel, *Man, Morals and Society: A Psycho-analytical Study* (1945; reprint, New York: Viking, 1961).

22. In "William Dean Howells: Perception and Ambivalence," Clayton L. Eichelberger also recognizes Kitty's doubleness and relates it to her perception of the Ursuline nuns. For Eichelberger, the duality of Kitty's character is defined less in psychological than in aesthetic terms; her responses are seen to be "alternately and somewhat ambiguously motivated by 'fancy' and, more perceptively, by 'heart,' reflecting what in a general sense may be labeled as romantic and realistic tendencies. In this fluctuating duality of Kitty's portrayal one glimpses Howells the critic pondering the fusion of the romantic and the real in both literature and life." *The Chief Glory of Every People: Essays on Classic American Writers*, ed. Matthew J. Bruccoli (Carbondale and Edwardsville: Southern Illinois University Press, 1973), p. 135.

23. In fact, the Brahmins were delighted with *A Chance Acquaintance*. Howells wrote to Vic in January 1874 about his attending a men's dinner at the home of Joseph Randolph Coolidge: "The people there were Dr. [Oliver Wendell] Holmes, Messrs. [Benjamin R.] Curtis, [Thomas C.] Amory and [Horace] Gray, all distinguished lawyers, and Mr. Coolidge's son-in-law, and son. The party represented one of the most exclusive Boston circles, but I found them very charming people, and what amused me most of all was that they had every one read A Chance Acquaintance, and were delighted with the way Boston was hit off in it. They evidently wanted me to talk about it; but I concluded I would let the record stand, and so fought shy of the subject" (*SL*, 2:50).

24. Howells reported to James that he had received some forty letters "from people unknown to me—begging for a sequel" (*SL*, 2:35). A letter from James Parton to Howells, 18 May 1873, nicely captures the disappointment caused by the ending of *A Chance Acquaintance*: "You aggravating wretch! Just as I had forgiven Boston, just as you had got him where he could do himself most good—humbled, on his knees—and in a fair way to become, at last, not wholly unworthy of the Princess of Erie Creek [*sic*]—then you up and stop. Too bad! No: too *good*—too *true*—just the very way it would have been, and ought to be. But you must fight it out with the hardened novel-reader. Your little book does honor to your genius, but more to your courage, your faith, your truth, your loyalty" (quoted in *CA*, xvii).

25. "Archetypes of American Innocence: Lydia Blood and Daisy Miller," *American Quarterly* 5 (Spring 1953): 31–32.

26. *The House of the Seven Gables*, Centenary Edition (Columbus: Ohio State University Press, 1965), p. 76.

27. *Poems of Tennyson*, ed. Jerome Hamilton Buckley (Boston: Houghton Mifflin, 1958), pp. 109–10.

28. William McMurray asserts: "Unconsciously, Lydia responds to the unstable Hicks, sensing in him perhaps a lawlessness that complements her own conventional morality." *The Literary Realism of William Dean Howells* (Carbondale and Edwardsville: Southern Illinois University Press, 1967), p. 23.

29. Edward Wagenknecht, *Cavalcade of the American Novel: From the Birth of the Nation to the Middle of the Twentieth Century* (New York: Holt, 1952), p. 141.

30. *Hawthorne* (1879); reprinted in *The Shock of Recognition: The Development of Literature in the United States Recorded by the Men Who Made It*, ed. Edmund Wilson (New York: Modern Library, n.d.), p. 520.

31. *Henry James Letters: Volume II, 1875–1883*, ed. Leon Edel (Cambridge, Mass.: Harvard University Press, 1975), pp. 226–27.

CHAPTER FIVE

1. Howells gradually shifted his emphasis from the mother to the father as controlling parent. Both Kitty Ellison and Lydia Blood are orphans; Florida Vervain and Grace Breen (*Doctor Breen's Practice*), having lost their fathers, are mother-dominated. Constance Wyatt, Egeria Boynton, Marcia Gaylord, and Helen Harkness (*A Woman's Reason*) are all father-dominated. Also, as we shall see, the parent figure became more and more prominent in Howells' novels, such that the triangle of suitor-American Girl-parent became at least as important as the triangle of suitor-American Girl-male rival.

2. Olov W. Fryckstedt argues convincingly that, starting with *A Foregone Conclusion*, Howells was experimenting with the technique of Turgenev in such novels as *Rudin*: "The reader was forced to try to understand Rudin's personality on the basis of what he learned about him—from his speech and actions and from the words of others. The reader was as apt to misjudge Rudin as were the characters in the novel. He had to revise his opinions and judgments just as he did about people he met in real life. 'We are taught a merciful distrust of our own judgments,' Howells observed [in a review of Turgenev]. And in the end he found it hard to say whether we really fully understood Rudin." *In Quest of America*, p. 173.

3. Like all of Howells' suitors of the American Girl, Ferris tends, like some of Freud's male patients, to express his "psychical impotence" in a disunion between the "affectionate" and the "sensual" currents of erotic feeling: "The whole sphere of love in such people remains divided in the two directions personified in art as sacred and profane (or animal) love. Where they love they do not desire and where they desire they cannot love." Freud came to the same "gloomy" conclusion that is implicit in Howells' early novels about the tainted American Girl: "the idea that it is quite impossible to adjust the claims of the sexual instinct to the demands of civilization." "A Special Type of Choice of Object Made by Men" (1910); *SE*, 11:183. "On the Universal Tendency to Debasement in the Sphere of Love" (1912); *SE*, 11:190.

4. "It marks the point [in Howells' career] at which he decided that as American women were the most numerous readers of fiction, he would have in some way to compromise with them by giving them what they wanted in the way of pictures of themselves." Van Doren quoted in George N. Bennett, *William Dean Howells: The Development of a Novelist* (Norman: University of Oklahoma Press, 1959), p. 44.

5. This is the opinion of Bennett, pp. 44–46. For confirmatory evidence, see Howells' letters to Aldrich (3 March 1876; quoted in Bennett, p. 45) and to Boyesen (21 November 1878; *SL*, 2:213).

6. At least one other triangle lies outside of my diagram: the one consisting of Belle, Rachel, and Rachel's brother Ben, whom Belle allures late in the novel.

7. Howells is alluding to 2 Sam. 1:26: "I am distressed for thee, my brother Jonathan: very pleasant hast thou been unto me: thy love to me was wonderful, passing the love of women."

8. "Splitting" is regarded by Melanie Klein as the most primitive defense mechanism, by which the infant reduces the anxiety of ambivalence toward the mother by splitting her into "good" and "bad" imagos. The "bad" mother, like Belle Farrell, is often perceived as a wicked witch. For a summary of Klein's views, see the "Explanatory Notes" to *Envy and Gratitude and Other Works, 1946–1963*, ed. R. E. Money-Kyrle (New York: Delta, 1977), p. 324.

9. In the confession of forgery that Wyatt has extracted from the cad, and which he shows to Constance, there is nothing at all about the fact that "'a woman was living who had the just and perhaps the legal claim of a wife upon him'" (CP, 36). The cad's sexual felony is obviously more outrageous to Wyatt than his forgery, but genteel propriety dictates his covering it up to his virginal child. This conscious concealment, however, points to the repression of Wyatt's own bond to Constance in her Electra complex: what is so threatening about the cad's adultery is that it resonates with Wyatt's own illicit desire, which is as unspeakable to him as the cad's offense is unsayable to Constance. The term, "Electra complex," referring to the feminine Oedipus complex, was coined by C. G. Jung in 1913.

10. For the text of this third act and for a thorough discussion of Howells' composition of the play, see Walter J. Meserve, ed., *The Complete Plays of W. D. Howells* (New York: New York University Press, 1960). Howells regarded this play, as well as *Out of the Question* (1877), as experiments in "a middle form between narrative and drama, which may be developed into something very pleasant to the reader, and convenient to the fictionist" (SL, 2:158). It is not certain what Howells meant by "a middle form," but it seems to have been a logical step in his use of the dramatic method, as if Howells wondered what would happen if he were to subtract from his early novels everything but the dialogue. In the plays the characters' speeches are, in fact, more often novelistic than dramatic—the sort that read better on the page than they would play on the stage—and Howells asserts his novelistic presence in long passages of narrative scene setting and stage direction.

11. *William Dean Howells: A Study* (Cambridge, Mass.: Harvard University Press, 1924), pp. 236–37.

12. Letter of 24 June 1880; quoted in Bennett, p. 98.

13. On the relevance of Robert Dale Owen to *The Undiscovered Country*, see Howard Kerr, *Mediums, and Spirit-Rappers, and Roaring Radicals: Spiritualism in American Literature, 1850–1900* (Urbana: University of Illinois Press, 1972), pp. 121–54.

14. Howells' use of Hawthorne in *The Undiscovered Country* has been noticed by several critics. For a good discussion, see Robert Emmet Long, *The Great Succession: Henry James and the Legacy of Hawthorne* (Pittsburgh: University of Pittsburgh Press, 1979), pp. 139–46.

15. Letter of 22 September 1879; quoted in Bennett, p. 84. Howells wrote the first draft of *The Undiscovered Country* in late 1877 and then asked his friend Thomas Sergeant Perry to read it and offer suggestions. Other projects intervened, and Howells did not complete his revisions of the novel until 1879–80.

16. Vanderbilt, *The Achievement of William Dean Howells*, p. 18.

17. *The Writings of Oliver Wendell Holmes*, Riverside Edition (Boston: Houghton Mifflin, 1891), 8 : 284–85. Other quotations are documented in the text.

18. What survives is the manuscript (Houghton Library) that was used to set galleys for the *Atlantic* serial. As was his custom, Howells regarded such galleys as the equivalent (in an age before typewriters) of a typed draft, and he did not hesitate to revise them extensively. What I quote below and later in this chapter are passages that were deleted at galley stage, that is, passages that appear in the manuscript but not in the published serial. I am quoting from the draft emendations list (as yet unpaginated) for the text of *The Undiscovered Country* forthcoming in the Howells Edition. This list, which David J. Nordloh has generously supplied to me, does not include any cancellations made in the manuscript before galleys were set. For some of these see Vanderbilt's chapter in *The Achievement of William Dean Howells*.

19. In general Howells' revisions had the effect of diminishing Phillips's role in the novel. A good deal of verbal byplay between him and Ford was cut, as well as a long comic scene involving Phillips's gourmandish delight in a Shaker breakfast.

20. Nevertheless, only Kenneth S. Lynn has mentioned "the undertone of homosexuality in Phillips's way of talking and behaving" (p. 246). Robert Emmet Long notes that his friendship with Ford is "incongruous," and he sees in Phillips's character an anticipation of "James's somewhat effeminized young Bostonian men like Burrage and Gracie" (p. 144).

21. See *The Achievement of William Dean Howells*, pp. 24–40.

22. Both Vanderbilt and Lynn erroneously state that Boynton's wife died in childbirth; whereas the novel states that she died "during the infancy" of Egeria (*UC*, 179). In a sense, however, these critics are correct because in the manuscript, which both of them studied, Howells *did* write that Egeria's mother died "in giving birth" to her. This phrase was changed in galleys. What matters, after all, is that Egeria's life is associated by Boynton with his wife's death.

23. *In Quest of America*, p. 185.

24. As Ford and Egeria rapturously embrace, Sister Frances, "who had not ceased to watch them, threw her apron over her head" (*UC*, 411)—a compromise reminiscent of Mark Twain's watching a bawdy performance of the can-can, in *The Innocents Abroad*, with his hands covering his face, but with his fingers spread apart.

25. Quoted in Vanderbilt, p. 37.

26. Vanderbilt shows that Howells was invoking the legend of Egeria and Numa, in which a Roman king (Numa) "consorted spiritually with Egeria after his own wife's death." Egeria was a water nymph who possessed "beyond the gift of prophecy, the power of healing" (p. 28). As Long points out, Egeria was also the goddess of childbirth (*The Great Succession*, p. 145). By having Phillips refer to Egeria as the "Pythoness," Howells associates her as well with Apollo's Delphian priestess, who had the spirit of divination.

27. Although it is obvious in the novel that the woman, with a "thick, hard [cosmetic] bloom on her somewhat sunken cheeks" and her "wild black eyes," is a whore (*UC*, 148), the manuscript is even clearer, adding the detail of her "foolish painted face."

28. The dream resembles a "primal scene" in that Egeria is a shocked spectator/ voyeur of sexual acts that seem inexplicably and dreadfully violent. As Vanderbilt ob-

serves, the dream itself was toned down in Howells' revisions: "Especially significant among his deletions in the rough-draft rendering of Egeria's nightmare orgy is the phrase, 'and the walls were dripping with snakes,' which recalls the phallic suggestion of her earlier fear of fish" (p. 33). Vanderbilt also recognizes the trappings of an orgy in the earlier séance, "where spiritual ecstasy merges with the sexual." Howells is hinting, says Vanderbilt, "that this obsession to commune with the spirit world carries overtones of sexual repression, not only among the customers of Mrs. LeRoy but also in Boynton" (pp. 25–26)—and, one might add, in Egeria.

29. Howells became friendly with Fiske as early as 1869. While the two men lived near each other in Cambridge, there were frequent opportunities for socializing and informal exchanging of ideas. With Howells' encouragement, Fiske wrote up some of their discussions for a series of articles in the *Atlantic*, later published as *Myths and Myth-Makers* (1872). The book was dedicated to Howells, who reviewed it anonymously. During the years of Howells' editorship, Fiske continued to be a regular contributor to the *Atlantic*, and Howells was thoroughly familiar with his ideas. In *A Modern Instance*, he alluded to Fiske's lectures on cosmic philosophy (*MI*, 414).

30. *The Beginnings of Critical Realism in America, 1860–1920* (1930; reprint, New York: Harcourt, Brace and World, 1958), p. 209.

31. Fiske quoted in Warner Berthoff, *The Ferment of Realism: American Literature, 1884–1919* (New York: Free Press, 1965), p. 178.

32. *The American Mind: An Interpretation of American Thought and Character Since the 1880's* (New Haven: Yale University Press, 1950), pp. 86–87.

33. *Beyond the Pleasure Principle* (1920); *SE*, 18:42.

34. For a full discussion of the pastoral elements in *The Undiscovered Country*, see Vanderbilt.

35. *Beyond the Pleasure Principle*; *SE*, 18:42.

36. In his review of *Mechanism in Thought and Morals*, Howells expressed relief that "it is no part of our business to pronounce upon the correctness" of Holmes's ideas. Howells put particular stress on Holmes's discussion of unconscious mental phenomena and on his moral arguments. "Recent Literature," *Atlantic Monthly* 27 (May 1871): 653–54.

CHAPTER SIX

1. *Letters of Charles Eliot Norton*, ed. Sara Norton and M. A. DeWolfe Howe (Boston: Houghton Mifflin, 1913), 2:36.

2. Letters to William Cooper Howells, 15 January and 1 May 1870; Houghton Library.

3. Letter to Elinor Mead Howells, 7 June 1871; Houghton Library.

4. Letter of 25 June 1871; Houghton Library. Howells' sore wrist also returned soon after this trip: "I change the style of my handwriting, and my manner of holding the pen, half a dozen times a day; but it all amounts to the same thing at last: the muscles of the wrist seem to be quite worn out" (letter to William Cooper Howells, 30 July 1871; Houghton Library).

5. Letters to William Cooper Howells, 9 and 23 July 1876; Houghton Library.

Howells, who became quite stout during the 1870s, had also collapsed from heat prostration in New York in the summer of 1870; he later fictionalized the incident in *Their Wedding Journey* (see *TWJ*, xxiii–xxiv).

6. *Suburban Sketches* (New York: Hurd & Houghton, 1871), p. 96.

7. "'The Fashionable Diseases': Women's Complaints and Their Treatment in Nineteenth-Century America," *Journal of Interdisciplinary History* 4 (Summer 1973): 27.

8. The evidence for Elinor's miscarriage in 1865 consists of Howells' playful allusion, in one of his letters, to a child ("Llewellyn") who was never born (*SL*, 1:235). The evidence is stronger for the 1867 miscarriage; see the entries for 3 March and 7 April in Elinor's "Pocket Diary"; Houghton Library.

9. See Ginette de B. Merrill, "Redtop and the Belmont Years of W. D. Howells and His Family," *Harvard Library Bulletin* 28 (January 1980): 33–57.

10. Sidney H. Bremer estimates that about "one-fourth of the married or widowed women who figure importantly in Howells's fictions are literally physical invalids." These include: Mrs. Vervain (*A Foregone Conclusion*); Mrs. Gilbert ("Private Theatricals"); Mrs. Maynard (*Doctor Breen's Practice*); Mrs. Mavering (*April Hopes*); Mrs. Dryfoos (*A Hazard of New Fortunes*); Mrs. Faulkner (*The Shadow of a Dream*); Mrs. Meredith (*An Imperative Duty*); Mrs. Denton (*The World of Chance*); Mrs. Lander (*Ragged Lady*); Mrs. Bentley ("A Pair of Patient Lovers"). "Invalids and Actresses: Howells's Duplex Imagery for American Women," *American Literature* 47 (January 1976): 601. Bremer's list does *not* include either the never-married invalids in Howells' work or the characters (both female and male) who suffer psychological breakdowns.

11. Letter to Charles Eliot Norton, 4 January 1880; letter to William Cooper Howells, 1 February 1880; Houghton Library.

12. Quoted in Howells' privately printed memoir, *Winifred Howells* (1891), p. 20; Houghton Library.

13. "Winifred Howells and the Economy of Pain," *The Old Northwest* 10 (Spring 1984): 41–75.

14. Letter to William Cooper Howells, 11 July 1880; Houghton Library.

15. "Magnolia," *Youth's Companion* 14 (October 1880); quoted in *Winifred Howells*, p. 22.

16. Letter in Rutherford B. Hayes Presidential Center, Fremont, Ohio.

17. Letter to William Cooper Howells, 28 November 1880; Houghton Library.

18. "'The Fashionable Diseases,'" pp. 31–32.

19. Letter to William Cooper Howells, 17 November 1881; Houghton Library.

20. Elinor Mead Howells to William Cooper Howells, 20 November 1881; Houghton Library.

21. Letter to William Cooper Howells, 12 December 1881; Houghton Library.

22. I am adapting to my own purposes the phrase that the Reverend Mr. Sewell offers to Silas and Persis Lapham as a moral clarification of the tangled romantic affairs of their daughters and Tom Corey: "'One suffer instead of three, if none is to blame? . . . That's sense, and that's justice. It's the economy of pain which naturally suggests itself'" (*RSL*, 241).

23. As psychologists have shown in recent years, families ordinarily seek an emotionally dynamic steady state. When a family contains one or more neurotics, achieving this "homeostasis" may involve a trading of intensity in symptoms, such that at

any given time one member is unconsciously designated the "scapegoat" or "symptom bearer" for the others. See Don D. Jackson and John H. Weakland, "Conjoint Family Therapy: Some Considerations on Theory, Technique, and Results," in *Changing Families: A Family Therapy Reader*, ed. Jay Haley (New York and London: Grune and Stratton, 1971).

24. Mildred was forty at the time of her breakdown, which occurred in late 1912 and persisted into 1913. Details are lacking because she apparently destroyed most of her own correspondence from this period, and because Howells' allusions to her case are cryptic.

25. *Studies on Hysteria* (1895); SE, 2:174–75. "Fragment of an Analysis of a Case of Hysteria" (1905); SE, 7:40.

26. Letter of 20 December 1881; Houghton Library. In the *New York Tribune* (27 November 1881), there was a report that Howells had been "seriously ill with rheumatism—an alarming trouble, for he felt it about the heart." Quoted in *John Hay— Howells Letters: The Correspondence of John Milton Hay and William Dean Howells, 1861–1905*, ed. George Monteiro and Brenda Murphy (Boston: Twayne, 1980), p. 54n.

27. Warner to Howells, 20 December 1881; Houghton Library.

28. In July 1881, in a letter to James R. Osgood, Howells alluded to an announcement in *Youth's Companion* of a forthcoming item he had promised to write but had no time to do (*SL*, 2:291). This was probably "Year in a Log-Cabin: A Bit of Autobiography," which was finished in 1885, and which finally appeared in the magazine in 1887.

29. "Garfield," *Atlantic Monthly* 48 (November 1881): 708.

30. *The Achievement of William Dean Howells*, pp. 85–86. Quotations are documented in the text.

31. "Moral Anxiety in *A Modern Instance*," *New England Quarterly* 46 (June 1973): 238. Other quotations are documented in the text.

32. *In Quest of America*, p. 245. For the anonymous review, see Eble, ed., *Howells: A Century of Criticism*, pp. 19–33.

33. Edwin H. Cady's estimate that the composition broke down "somewhere between the middle of Chapter XXXI and the beginning of XXXII" (p. 210) seems to be confirmed by the available evidence.

34. *Democracy and the Novel*, p. 87. Other quotations are documented in the text.

35. *William Dean Howells*, p. 103. Other quotations are documented in the text.

36. See Vanderbilt, pp. 64–75; William Wasserstrom, *Heiress of All the Ages: Sex and Sentiment in the Genteel Tradition* (Minneapolis: University of Minnesota Press, 1959), pp. 84–87. The bond between Ben Halleck and his sister Olive also has strongly incestuous overtones.

37. See Allen F. Stein, "A New Look at Howells's *A Fearful Responsibility*," *Modern Language Quarterly* 39 (June 1978): 121–31.

38. The term "unconscious cerebration" was invented in 1853 by the English physician W. B. Carpenter, whose *Principles of Mental Physiology* (1874) Howells may well have read. "Unconscious cerebration" was defined as "'an unconscious reflex action of the brain,' or 'process of Modification' of the brain, only the terminal results of which enter awareness." Carpenter quoted in Lancelot Law Whyte, *The Unconscious Before Freud* (1960; reprint, New York: Anchor, 1962), p. 147. Howells first used the term,

apparently, in his anonymous essay on dreams in the "Contributors' Club," *Atlantic Monthly* 45 (June 1880): 859, where he referred to "'unconscious cerebration,' which I believe is the scientific term for dreaming."

39. *Howells and Italy* (Durham, N.C.: Duke University Press, 1952), pp. 169–70.

40. The novel reflects the Howellses' rotating invalidism in this period, what I have called the familial "economy of pain." Elmore collapses at one point from the strain of Lily's affairs; his wife too is subject to nervous attacks,. which seem to have been modeled on Elinor's: "What these attacks were I find myself unable to specify, but as every lady has an old attack of some kind, I may safely leave their precise nature to conjecture. It is enough that they were of a nervous character, that they were accompanied with headache, and that they prostrated her for several days" (*FR*, 19).

41. *Expression in America* (New York: Harper, 1932), p. 249. Other quotations are documented in the text.

42. *The New England Girl*, p. 117.

43. As Anthony Channell Hilfer points out, Howells never enters Marcia's mind as deeply as he does Bartley's: "We find out no more about Marcia than she shows through the external language of gesture. . . . Howells can hint at a pathology in Marcia but her consciousness, unlike Bartley's, is too deeply irrational for convincing ethical structuring—which is why Howells shies away from it." *The Ethics of Intensity in American Fiction* (Austin: University of Texas Press, 1981), p. 69.

44. In age, Tom and Bella March correspond roughly to John and Mildred Howells in 1882. Because Basil and Isabel married much later than the Howellses did, the Marches could not have had a child equivalent in age to Winifred, whose closest fictional counterpart was to be Ellen Kenton in *The Kentons* (1902).

45. In *The Rise of Silas Lapham*, after a quarrel between Silas and Persis, the narrator remarks: "The silken texture of the marriage tie bears a daily strain of wrong and insult to which no other human relation can be subjected without lesion; and sometimes the strength that knits society together might appear to the eye of faltering faith the curse of those immediately bound by it. Two people by no means reckless of each other's rights and feelings, but even tender of them for the most part, may tear each other's heart-strings in this sacred bond with perfect impunity; though if they were any other two they would not speak or look at each other again after the outrages they exchange. It is certainly a curious spectacle, and doubtless it ought to convince an observer of the divinity of the institution" (*RSL*, 49). Régis Michaud calls this passage "a *reductio ad absurdum* argument in favor of matrimony," one reflective of "the monstrous paradoxes to which Puritan rigorism led Howells." *The American Novel To-Day: A Social and Psychological Study* (Boston: Little, Brown, 1928), pp. 69–70.

46. In the "Topics of the Time" column published in the same issue as the final installment of *A Modern Instance*, the editors of the *Century* compared the novel to *Uncle Tom's Cabin* in its "moral bearing" and its "power to affect public sentiment." While admitting that *A Modern Instance* was a "many-sided, and artistic work," the editors also believed that Howells was making a "timely" and "deliberately intended point" that was "worth reprinting . . . in every journal in the United States"—the gist of which is contained in the passage I quote below: Atherton's diatribe against divorce. *Century* 24 (October 1882): 106–7. For Scudder's (anonymous) review, see *Atlantic Monthly* 50 (November 1882): 709–13.

47. "Recent Literature," *Atlantic Monthly* 44 (July 1879): 124–25.

48. "The Demystification of Style: Metaphoric and Metonymic Language in *A Modern Instance*," *Nineteenth-Century Fiction* 28 (March 1974): 386, 388. Other quotations are documented in the text.

49. *Civilization and Its Discontents* (1930); *SE*, 21:97, 115.

50. "Realism and the Dangers of Parody in W. D. Howells' Fiction," *The Old Northwest* 8 (Spring 1982): 73.

51. Letter of 10 March 1880; Houghton Library.

52. In the novel Howells, like Bartley, seems to resent that a woman who "gives more of her heart than the man gives of his" is held to be so "pitiable" a spectacle that "we are apt to attribute a kind of merit to her, as if it were a voluntary self-sacrifice for her to love more than her share." Not only men but women look upon this spectacle with "canonizing compassion": "for women have a lively power of imagining themselves in the place of any sister who suffers in matters of sentiment, and are eager to espouse the common cause in commiserating her" (*MI*, 60). Women, that is, are the chief enforcers of a double standard by which a woman is sainted by her love, however irrational and excessive it may be, and a man who arouses such "self-sacrifice," however unwittingly, is deemed a scoundrel. That the same judgments do not obtain in reverse is shown by what happens to Ben Halleck, who is damned for his irrational love of Marcia; she, however, is never blamed for having inspired it. Thus Howells himself upholds the genteel code his narrator seems to question.

53. *Gender, Fantasy, and Realism in American Literature*, p. 96. Other quotations are documented in the text.

54. Among the revisions Howells made after his breakdown was changing the name of Bartley's assistant from Richard Wray to Henry Bird. He also canceled in the manuscript a passage that had made more explicit Bird's homoerotic attachment to Hubbard: "He [Bartley] was apt to put his arm across the boy's shoulder when he approached him, in and at all times he instinctively recognized in him a feminine quality which appealed for caresses and protection. Bird repaid his favor with an anxious divination of all his moods" (*MI*, 535).

55. *The Immense Complex Drama: The World and Art of the Howells Novel* (Columbus: Ohio State University Press, 1966), p. 74. Habegger suggests that "Ben and Bartley represent the two opposed gender ideals that divided Howells. . . . Ben was the better half of Howells, decent, prudish, and feminine. But Bartley was the man, and had the lion's share" (p. 96).

56. In the early part of the novel, Atherton appears in only one major scene, in which he seems quite reasonable and tolerant. His sanctimoniousness, and Howells' undercutting of it, are confined to scenes written after the breakdown.

57. Aside from Halleck, only the fatuous Clara Kingsbury Atherton offers much resistance to Atherton's opinions. She sometimes serves with wifely tact as a check on the lawyer's Calvinistic severity.

58. *A Backward Glance* (New York: Appleton-Century, 1934), pp. 147–48. Other quotations are documented in the text.

59. *Theodore Dreiser: His World and His Novels* (Carbondale and Edwardsville: Southern Illinois University Press, 1969), pp. 241–42.

60. Just a year before the publication of *Sister Carrie*, Howells read his brother

Joseph's account of the scandalous elopement of an Ohioan girl—the very sort of situation that Dreiser was to use. "Your story is a whole novel," Howells remarked, "a novel I should like to write, and of course must not; but I could not write it better than you have done it" (*SL*, 4:209). Dreiser could probably have borne Howells' public silence more easily had he received such a letter. Instead, as Dreiser reported to Dorothy Dudley, Howells once "passed him hurriedly with the words, 'You know, I don't like *Sister Carrie.*'" Dudley, *Dreiser and the Land of the Free*, p. 197.

61. Ibid., pp. 115, 143. As I have noted in Chapter 4, it is plausible that Dreiser meant to praise *A Modern Instance* when he singled out *Their Wedding Journey* as Howells' "one fine piece of work." If so, his misremembering the title is possibly symptomatic of a wish to repress his indebtedness to Howells. At best it was a backhanded compliment for Dreiser to favor Howells' first novel over his later and finer ones. Even if he really meant *Their Wedding Journey*, however, it seems likely that Dreiser had also read *A Modern Instance*—although there is no proof that he did.

62. "The American Fear of Literature," in *The Man from Main Street: A Sinclair Lewis Reader*, ed. Harry E. Maule and Melville H. Cane (New York: Random House, 1953), pp. 15, 7.

63. Letter of 9 February 1931; quoted in Ellen Phillips DuPree, "Wharton, Lewis and the Nobel Prize Address," *American Literature* 56 (May 1984): 265.

64. *Babbitt* (New York: Harcourt, Brace, 1922), p. 383.

65. According to Mark Schorer, Lewis once met Howells—in St. Augustine, Florida, in 1916—and presented him with a copy of *The Trail of the Hawk*; and Howells later thanked him in a cordial letter. "The occasion is interesting not only because less than fifteen years later the famous Sinclair Lewis was to treat Howells rather unfairly . . . but more particularly because in fact Howells's middle-class liberal optimism was so much like Lewis's own, his social criticism, again like Lewis's, deeply tempered by it. Both, steering a clear line between a surly proletariat and a stuffed plutocracy, wished to assure the middle class that the promise of American life lay in its best values. Savage and boisterous as Lewis's writing was sometimes to be, his reticence about sex and the turmoil of the subjective life were Howells's too. Yet one cannot assume that the meeting in 1916 involved a shock of recognition." *Sinclair Lewis: An American Life* (New York: McGraw-Hill, 1961), pp. 230–31.

66. *The Modern Temper: A Study and a Confession* (1929; reprint, New York: Harcourt, Brace and World, 1956), p. xi.

CHAPTER SEVEN

1. Marrion Wilcox, "Works of William Dean Howells—(1860–96)," *Harper's Weekly* 40 (4 July 1896); reprinted in *Critical Essays on W. D. Howells, 1866–1920*, ed. Edwin H. and Norma W. Cady (Boston: G. K. Hall, 1983), p. 182. For a discussion of this incident, see Cady, pp. 243–45; Lynn, pp. 280–82; Vanderbilt, *The Achievement of William Dean Howells*, pp. 96–143; Prioleau, *The Circle of Eros*, pp. 70–87.

2. "My vertigo still continues, but I am being actively treated for it; and I hope that I shall get rid of it before very long. I am trying electricity. It does not stop me from working, but I feel that I work with greater effort on account of it. Heretofore, I have

not much minded it, but this attack, while it is not severe, is very persistent. I do not know what brought it on." Letter to William Cooper Howells, 20 August 1893; Houghton Library. Howells added, however, that he had recently finished "My First Visit to New England." The spells of vertigo lasted at least until November.

3. Letter to Aurelia Howells, 13 January 1895; Houghton Library.

4. Ibid., 14 January 1900. Howells endorsed the "curious Swedish treatment" at the Zander Institute: "they put a flat leather covered disk over the top of my heart, and by means of machinery give it a good wobbling for five minutes. . . . I take a good many other exercises, which are all passive as far [as] I'm concerned. Different machines shake my legs, gripping them in half a dozen places, and pound them up and down, all over with soft rubber fists. . . . Other machines take my feet and twist my legs. I am strapped into a chair, and made to twist from side to side, so as to exercise the muscles of the waist and back. There is a broad stirrupless saddle, called the camel, which when you mount it gives you the motion of the camel's walk. . . . At the end I am as fresh as when I began, for I have had to make no exertion, and the effect is delightful."

5. "Conscious cerebration" in undoubtedly a slip of the pen, which has slipped un-corrected from the serial text of the essay into the Howells Edition text. Howells must have meant "unconscious cerebration"; see chap. 6, n. 38.

6. The only dream record that is even comparable, though far less abundant than Howells', is that of Hawthorne. See Rita K. Gollin, *Nathaniel Hawthorne and the Truth of Dreams* (Baton Rouge: Louisiana State University Press, 1979).

7. *Atlantic Monthly* 45 (June 1880): 860.

8. *Harper's Monthly* 90 (May 1895): 836–45; collected, under the title "I Talk of Dreams," in *Impressions and Experiences* (New York: Harper, 1896). Not coincidentally, perhaps, Howells began this essay just after the death of his father on 28 August 1894.

9. "Editor's Easy Chair," *Harper's Monthly* 124 (March 1912): 636. See also G. Ferris Cronkhite, "Howells Turns to the Inner Life," *New England Quarterly* 30 (December 1957): 474–85.

10. "Editor's Study," *Harper's Monthly* 83 (July 1891): 314–16.

11. See the letter of Howard Pyle to Howells, 21 December 1890: "I wish I knew what has been the result of your last summer's reading upon the subjects of dreams. I myself mistrust all such philosophical speculations most heartily" (*SL*, 3:299n).

12. Ribot, *Diseases of Memory* (New York: Appleton, 1882), p. 32; *The Diseases of Personality* (1894), 4th ed. rev. (Chicago: Open Court, 1906), p. 5. For Ribot's ac-count of diagnostic dreams, see *The Diseases of Personality*, p. 24.

13. "Dreams. To the Editor of the Chronicle Telegraph," incomplete manuscript in the Howells/Fréchette Papers, Herrick Memorial Library, Alfred University, Alfred, N.Y. Quoted by permission of Dr. Van Derck Fréchette and of William White Howells. The article to which William Cooper was responding—although he may never have sent his reply—appeared on 7 March 1889, just five days after Winifred's death. An earlier essay on dreams by William Cooper—"Dreams and one of them" (dated 1 May 1876)—may also be found in the Howells/Fréchette Papers.

14. Howells showed Pyle the same dream report that he had sent to his father on 30 March 1890 (see *SL*, 6:178–80) and that William Cooper had copied and then re-turned (see *SL*, 3:278). After "True, I Talk of Dreams" appeared in 1895, Pyle was quick to congratulate Howells, whose answer indicates how seriously he regarded this

essay: "You mustn't call my dream paper 'clever.' I can't stand it! If it isn't something more than clever, a thing of that sort must be indefinitely less" (*LinL*, 2:62).

15. For a fuller analysis of these dreams and of Howells' relationship to his daughter, see my essay, "Winifred Howells and the Economy of Pain."

16. Freud apparently did not read Du Prel until after the first publication of *The Interpretation of Dreams*. In 1914, however, Freud gave him due credit, adding in a footnote: "That brilliant mystic Du Prel, one of the few authors for whose neglect in earlier editions of this book I should wish to express my regret, declares that the gateway to metaphysics, so far as men are concerned, lies not in waking life but in the dream" (*SE*, 4:63n).

17. *The Philosophy of Mysticism*, trans. C. C. Massey, 2 vols. (London: George Red-way, 1889), 1:32. Other quotations are documented in the text.

18. Compare *The Philosophy of Mysticism*, 2:273–74, with *The Landlord at Lion's Head* (New York: Harper, 1897), pp. 192–93.

19. "Some Additional Notes on Dream-Interpretation as a Whole" (1925); *SE*, 19:132–33. See also Freud's discussion of "The Moral Sense in Dreams" (*SE*, 4:66–74). In summarizing the position of F. W. Hildebrandt—that "'we can hardly escape the conviction that a sin committed in a dream bears with it at least an obscure minimum of guilt'" (*SE*, 4:70)—Freud might have been describing Howells' own views: "The line of thought adopted by Hildebrandt and others who share his fundamental position inevitably leads to the view that immoral impulses possess a certain degree of power even in waking life, though it is an inhibited power, unable to force its way into action, and that in sleep something is put out of action which acts like an inhibition in the daytime and has prevented us from being aware of the existence of such impulses. Thus dreams would reveal the true nature of man, though not his *whole* nature, and they would constitute one means of rendering the hidden interior of the mind accessible to our knowledge" (*SE*, 4:72).

20. "William Dean Howells: Reverie and the Nonsymbolic Aesthetic," *Nineteenth-Century Fiction* 25 (June 1970): 5. Other quotations are documented in the text.

21. *The Immense Complex Drama*, p. 227.

22. *The Circle of Eros*, p. 14.

23. See Prioleau, passim; Edwin H. Cady, "The Howells Nobody Knows," in *The Light of Common Day: Realism in American Fiction* (Bloomington: Indiana University Press, 1971), pp. 138–60. My own studies of Howells' psychological fiction include "The Length of Howells' *Shadow of a Dream*," *Nineteenth-Century Fiction* 27 (September 1972): 182–96; "The Oedipal Theme in Howells's *Fennel and Rue*," *Studies in the Novel* 5 (Spring 1973): 104–9; "Howells' *Questionable Shapes*: From Psychologism to Psychic Romance," *ESQ: A Journal of the American Renaissance* 21 (3d quarter 1975): 169–78; "Howells' Minister in a Maze: 'A Difficult Case,'" *Colby Library Quarterly* 13 (December 1977): 278–83; "Howells and the Sins of the Father: *The Son of Royal Langbrith*," *The Old Northwest* 7 (Summer 1981): 79–94; (with Charles L. Crow) "Psychology and the Psychic in W. D. Howells's 'A Sleep and a Forgetting,'" in *The Haunted Dusk: American Supernatural Fiction, 1820–1920*, ed. Howard Kerr, John W. Crowley, and Charles L. Crow (Athens: University of Georgia Press, 1983), pp. 151–68.

24. "A Psychological Counter-Current in Recent Fiction," *North American Review* 173 (December 1901): 872–73.

25. "Will the Novel Disappear?," *North American Review* 175 (September 1902): 293.

26. "Howells' Christmas Sketches: The Uses of Allegory," *American Literary Realism* 10 (Summer 1977): 252. See also Carrington, "Howells: The Aging Artist in the Easy Chair," *The Old Northwest* 8 (Summer 1982): 157–88.

27. Howells' understanding of the "subdivisions of his own ego" was probably influenced by William James's summaries of the work of Pierre Janet on cases of hysteria and "multiple personality." See *The Principles of Psychology* (1890; reprint, New York: Dover, 1950), 1:384–88; "The Hidden Self" (1890), reprinted in *A William James Reader*, ed. Gay Wilson Allen (Boston: Houghton Mifflin, 1971), pp. 90–108. The latter, written for a popular audience, appeared in *Scribner's Magazine* just at the time Howells was beginning his intensive study of dreams. It is likely that Howells was also familiar with the theory of "subliminal selves" developed by the psychical researcher F. W. H. Myers. See *Human Personality and Its Survival of Bodily Death* (New York, London, and Bombay: Longmans Green, 1903).

28. In his review of *The Principles of Psychology*, Howells paraphrased James's conception of free will: "In fact the will of the weak man is *not* free; but the will of the strong man, the man who has *got the habit* of preferring sense to nonsense and 'virtue' to 'vice,' is a *freed* will, which one might very well spend all one's energies in achieving." *Harper's Monthly* 83 (July 1891): 315.

INDEX